Person-Centred Counselling for Trans and Gender Diverse People

of related interest

Counselling Skills for Working with Gender Diversity and Identity
Michael Beattie and Penny Lenihan with Robin Dundas
ISBN 978 1 78592 741 6
eISBN 978 1 78450 481 6
Part of the Essential Skills for Counselling *series*

Counseling Transgender and Non-Binary Youth
The Essential Guide
Irwin Krieger
ISBN 978 1 78592 743 0
eISBN 978 1 78450 482 3

Supporting Young Transgender Men
A Guide for Professionals
Matthew Waites
ISBN 978 1 78592 294 7
eISBN 978 1 78450 601 8

A Reflective Guide to Gender Identity Counselling
Madison-Amy Webb, (MBACP) Acc
ISBN 978 1 78592 383 8
eISBN 978 1 78450 733 6

Theorizing Transgender Identity for Clinical Practice
A New Model for Understanding Gender
S.J. Langer
ISBN 978 1 78592 765 2
eISBN 978 1 78450 642 1

PERSON-CENTRED COUNSELLING for TRANS and GENDER DIVERSE PEOPLE

A Practical Guide

SAM HOPE

Jessica Kingsley *Publishers*
London and Philadelphia

First published in 2019
by Jessica Kingsley Publishers
73 Collier Street
London N1 9BE, UK
and
400 Market Street, Suite 400
Philadelphia, PA 19106, USA

www.jkp.com

Library of Congress Cataloging in Publication Data
A CIP catalog record for this book is available from the Library of Congress

British Library Cataloguing in Publication Data
A CIP catalogue record for this book is available from the British Library

ISBN 978 1 78592 542 9
eISBN 978 1 78450 937 8

Printed and bound by CPI Group (UK) Ltd, Croydon, CR0 4YY

Contents

Acknowledgements

An astonishing number of trans and gender divergent people have been my teachers, too numerous to name, but I first want to express my profound thanks to all of them, and to a vast and diverse community, historical and current, that never stops wrestling with difficult questions or being afraid to question the status quo and challenge orthodoxies. I am lucky to count so many trans people among my friends, colleagues and fellow organisers. I am forever grateful to be surrounded by a vibrant community full of the very best people. Without them, this book could not have been written.

In particular I would like to thank Ben Vincent, Ruth Pearce and CN Lester for the conversations and learning that their recent published works have generated, as well as the more informal conversations we have had. Thank you to Nat Titman for expanding my brain on the subject of neurodiversity. I also wish to thank Ibtisam Ahmed, Uditi Sen, Onni Gust and Maryam Din for all they have collectively taught me about queer intersectionality, and Laurie May for resources and grounding in the Person-Centred Approach.

Thanks also to the team at Jessica Kingsley Publishers for their efficient, smooth and timely help and encouragement, in particular Andrew James, who saw potential and believed in me, and has continued to support and encourage me through what turned out to be a year of unexpected challenges.

Without the help of Beck Thom of Body Curious, Pippa Hennessey and Rachel Phillips for their proofreading, inspiration and input on particular chapters, I would have been doomed. You all are amazing.

My clinical supervisor, Lisa Anthony, kept me going at the times I was almost on my knees in 2018. What can I say? Excellent supervision is beyond price.

And thank you to Briar Dunn for so patiently teaching me some important lessons about disability activism as well as for, over the course of the year this book was written, becoming family. You are a wise soul and I hope you realise how much I appreciate everything you are.

Most of all I would like to thank my partner Robin Edwards, for encouraging my writing, for being patient with my messy process, for proofreading and encouragement even whilst going through his own spectacularly trying year, and in general not just putting up with me but apparently believing in me – you're astonishing and I love you.

Preface

This is a precarious time in the story of trans civil rights. In the USA, rights have dramatically reversed under the Trump/Pence administration. Trans people have been disqualified from serving in the US Army, can be denied any healthcare by people who object to them on religious grounds, and can now be discriminated against at work and school and in state legislature with impunity (National Centre for Transgender Equality 2018).

Here in the UK, things may look rosier to some, but government plans to reform the Gender Recognition Act (2004) have sparked an unprecedented backlash from the media and anti-trans campaigners, with major steps back in how trans issues are reported. The organisation Trans Media Watch even raised concerns about troubling and misleading information about trans children from the BBC (Trans Media Watch 2017).

An organisation campaigning against transgender recognition has sent professional-looking booklets full of misinformation to UK schools advising them not to support trans students and encouraging what amounts to conversion therapy, i.e. therapy to 'cure' people of their gender identity or sexual orientation (Whittaker 2018a). This is a delicate time, as we have only just reached agreement from all the major UK psychological organisations and the NHS that conversion therapy for trans people is unacceptable. In 2017, they updated their updated Memorandum of Understanding against conversion therapy to include trans and asexual people (COSRT 2017). Meanwhile, 41 per cent of trans people experienced hate crime in 2017, according to the LGBT+ charity Stonewall (2017a). Trans people are a community under pressure.

If we only read the papers, peruse social media, or watch mainstream documentaries, we might be forgiven for thinking that trans people are a new phenomenon and their existence is still very much up for debate. I liken this to reporting on climate change: a consensus has been reached and over a hundred years of study have proved both climate change and trans people are real, and yet here we are still acting like there is a debate to be had.

In 2016, a crucial study published in the *Lancet* (Robles *et al.*) put to rest the idea that trans people are inherently mentally ill and paved the way in 2018 for the World Health Organisation (WHO) to remove gender dysphoria from the International Classification of Diseases ICD-11 section on mental health. Pflum *et al.* (2015) back up the fact that environmental and social factors are responsible for poor mental health in trans people, rather than being trans itself. In other words, it is not mad to think you are trans.

Closer to home, in my own county of Nottinghamshire, UK, a survey showed that 60 per cent of trans respondents had self-harmed and 48 per cent had attempted suicide (Nottinghamshire Healthcare NHS Foundation Trust 2017). Sadly, similar results are replicated in other studies from the UK and other countries (PACE 2015; Veale *et al.* 2017; Virupaksha, Muralidhar and Ramakrishna 2016). As someone who does a considerable amount of voluntary work and community organising with trans people in Nottinghamshire, I am sorry to say these results do not come as a surprise.

Some people find it hard to reconcile the crisis in trans mental health with the removal of gender dysphoria from the ICD-11, but what research tells us is that trans people's environment is the disabling factor. The social model of disability suggests that people are disabled by their environment as much if not more than by their individual medical situation (Oliver 2013); we can now confidently take a social model approach to trans mental health. For example, Bauer *et al.* (2015) found in their research that among other things, suicidal ideation was 66 per cent lower in trans subjects who had experienced relatively little transprejudice. This is not to say medical healthcare is not important for trans people; Bauer *et al.* (2015) also found that suicide risk lowered alongside the ability to access both social and medical transition options, a finding echoed by a systematic literature review performed at Cornell University (2017). Being recognised as legitimate, and having access to appropriate healthcare, is a positive thing for trans mental health.

Hence, responsible practitioners take a trans-affirmative approach to trans lives, an approach that echoes that of Davies for LGB people (Davies 1996). This does not mean telling people they are trans or diagnosing them, or privileging trans over other possible identities. It means *believing* them when they say who they are and what they need, and supporting them to figure that out without introducing negativity or erasure in relation to trans people, transition, non-binary identities or any other aspect of being trans. Other practitioners have called this a trans-positive approach (Riley, Wong and Sitharthan 2011, p.397).

A person-centred approach is rooted in the social model, inherently believing in the potential of all people given the right conditions. The approach seeks to remove barriers to our relating warmly and congruently, and on an equal footing, with the people we are supporting. It seeks to destabilise professionals' ideas of 'knowing better' than the client and judging the client. It aims for relationship and connection, and believes psychological wellbeing comes through this connection.

Humans thrive through being supported within the human pack. Trans people's distress is rooted in the inability of the pack to accommodate them. This is particularly true for non-binary trans people, who lack even the civil rights trans men and women have gained, at least in the UK and most of the US.

Trans clients are frequently doubted, misunderstood, infantilised and judged by professionals, and this creates a strong barrier to that person-centred relationship. The client's reality is lost through a fog of bias and lack of experience. Professionals can be so immersed in misinformation about trans people and gender itself that they do not even realise the barriers are there. This can leave trans people withdrawing from services and becoming profoundly isolated and unsupported.

This book is as much about unlearning as it is about learning. It is about aiming to bring into our awareness the stories we create around gender and sex. Once we understand that our grasp of gender is subjective and fallible, we are much more able to accept the way trans people rewrite this story to better include them. It is impossible to offer a client the core conditions of empathy, congruence and unconditional positive regard, the foundations of a person-centred approach (Rogers 1957), unless the narratives we have introjected as truth, what some people call *unconscious bias*, have been explored. For example, how can we not judge a client if we are making assumptions without realising?

How can we offer empathy if we have been taught to mistrust trans stories?

The issue is that we do not know what is outside of our own awareness. Learning to move away from a defensive 'I'm not prejudiced' and towards a more open-minded 'I've almost certainly got prejudices I'm not aware of' is a good place to start. Throughout the book, I invite readers to use the closing sections of each chapter for reflective writing. This is a chance to look back and see if any themes are emerging, and if this points at issues to take to supervision, therapy or personal exploration.

Another theme of the book is power imbalance, an issue that is central to Rogers' theories, but often gets forgotten (Rogers 1961). Society is a web of invisible hierarchies. A person-centred approach seeks to address the hierarchy of counsellor above client and centre the client as the expert on their own life. However, unaddressed social hierarchies can affect how much we are able to trust our clients to be self-aware and make the right decisions. This is particularly true for trans people, who are frequently infantilised by society and services. Again, if our socially influenced attitudes are outside of our awareness, this might affect our sense of trust in the autonomy of the client. In the words of Tina Clark:

> It feels to be time that society changed its opinion about gender diversity being disordered, and acknowledged trans-identified people as equal human beings who can be trusted with their own life decisions as much as anyone else. I believe the person-centered approach holds the key to opening that relational door. (quoted in Livingstone 2011, p.143)

The book is written by a non-binary author and takes an unashamed non-binary view of gender. This is not to say that men and women, whether trans or not, do not exist, but that gender and sex demonstrably are not simplistic, binary, either/ors. There are many casualties of the artificial enforcement of a gender binary, from intersex people to indigenous cultures all over the world, as well as women and trans people, and the book explores ways we can move away from this binary and unlearn the stories it has told us.

A NOTE ABOUT TERMINOLOGY

There is no perfect umbrella term for the huge diversity of people who we sometimes call trans. I use *trans* for simplicity, to mean anyone who feels incongruence with the gender they were assigned into. When I use trans I mean anyone who could fall under the widest reaches of the trans umbrella, and I appreciate this word is a modern and imperfect invention for genders that have been included and celebrated in other cultures and times with different language. I also appreciate that not all non-binary people identify with the word trans, but nevertheless my definition of trans does fully include non-binary people. At times, I will also use the term 'gender divergent' for people whom it would be disrespectful or inappropriate to use the term trans for.

The word *cis* means someone who does not experience incongruence with the gender they were assigned into. Or put more simply, it means 'not trans'. Cis/trans comes from Latin meaning 'same side'/'opposite side', and naturally, it does not accurately work for something that is not a binary, but it is a useful word to describe people who are not trans in a neutral way.

I use the word *transprejudice* throughout rather than the word transphobia, proposed by Burnes *et al.* (2010, p.138) as 'a more helpful term to use when describing the actual discrimination that transgender people experience'. There has been a certain amount of protest over the use 'phobia' as an inaccurate and individualised way of describing a systemic problem.

I personally use they/them/their/themself pronouns and would like to reassure readers that singular they is grammatically acceptable and wholly to be encouraged in your speaking and writing. It is very useful for a client who is just figuring themself out, as well as for non-binary clients. Please note also that 'themself' rather than 'themselves' is the correct form, no matter how much autocorrect dislikes it.

A full glossary of terms can be found at the rear of the book.

Chapter 1

THE STORY OF GENDER AND SEX

We live in an age of facts, whether real or 'alternative', where we like to think that out there somewhere is an objective, knowable truth that is unequivocal. Our increasing need for certainty leads us to try and fix everything down with firmness and precision. Even when things are uncertain, we are praised for confidence rather than tentativeness, for taking a sure stance rather than changing our minds. For anyone favouring a person-centred approach, this is the strong current we are often trying to swim against. As we try to build a relationship with the unique human in front of us, we attempt to put aside our certainties, our assumptions, our foregone conclusions, and meet people where they are, which is often in a state of complexity, contradiction, incongruity and difference.

The most familiar foundations of Rogers' person-centred approach are empathy, congruence and unconditional positive regard (1961). These conditions have become a cornerstone for many types of therapy. We strive to fully meet our clients and put aside things that may get in the way. Our preconceptions and prior knowledge or assumptions are barriers. As person-centred practitioners, we are urged to set aside what we think we know.

Many counsellors have a warm and fluffy idea in their hearts that they can just turn the core conditions on and clear these barriers away with a sweep. But people in a majority or socially supported position, no matter how well-meaning, are often so protected in their assumptions about the world that they do not even know they are making assumptions.

I will give an example. A person walks into a counselling room. The counsellor looks at them, and before they speak, the counsellor has almost certainly made the judgement we are trained from birth to make: 'Do I label them male or female? Do I call them he or she when I write up my notes?' Behind that assumption are many other assumptions that go with the labels. Even the most feminist of us cannot fully escape the enormous web of ideas and stories that go with assigning a gender to a person.

The person tells the counsellor, 'I'm K. I'm non-binary.'

Is it possible for us, schooled as we are in the habit of assigning gender, to take this comment at face value? As someone who works and socialises with a lot of non-binary people, and is non-binary themself, I would say the answer is no. No matter how hard I try to 'unsee' what I assume is this person's original gender assignment, I cannot. Despite someone's fundamental experience of who they are, the result of a lifetime of self-knowledge, my casual appraisal of superficial clues in the structure of their face or sound of their voice will trump this. How the person looks at a glance will dominate how I experience them, will dictate what pronoun comes readily to my mind and my pen when writing notes, no matter how hard I work at using 'they' or 'xe'. I cannot escape the fact I am making the most fundamental assumptions about this person based on how they superficially appear to me. I have been trained from birth to judge them.

How do we overcome these assumptions, this story that has been laid down in our brains and is constantly reinforced? Hard work! This is work trans clients have been forced into taking on, because for us cultural ideas about gender and sex cannot be taken for granted. That is not to say we are always able to see the wood for the trees; the landscape of gender is complicated terrain. Sometimes we are trapped in those cultural stories and they feel inescapable. I will use this chapter to take a step back from some of these stories of gender and sex and take a hard look at them.

ASSIGNING SEX

The most prevalent idea we have is that sex is a biological fact. There are people with penises and we call them men. There are people with vaginas and we call them women. These are scientific facts, and that's the end of it. A great many people believe this.

Feminism popularised the idea of 'gender' being separate to this – gender had originally been used in linguistics to describe, for instance, French 'le' and 'la'. Feminists used it to mean the social ideas and structures that we built on top of biological sex. The idea of people having a socially constructed gender separate from sex was originated by John Money (Money, Hampson and Hampson 1955), founder of the John Hopkins Gender Identity Clinic (Vincent 2018).

Simone de Beauvoir (1949, p.267) said, 'On ne naît pas femme: on le devient', translated as: 'One is not born, but rather becomes, a woman', describing the way society channels women down certain paths that are not related to nature at all, but are culturally prescribed, or at least heavily influenced. Fine (2010, 2017), in two prominent books, lays out just how much our ideas about natural gender differences turn out to be down to socialisation, although room is left for *some* biological influences.

A simple example of this is how much little girls today seem to love pink, when 150 years ago pink was a boy's colour. There is nothing inherent in either little girls or the colour pink that puts them together, but currently there is a strong cultural influence that pink is 'girly' and both cis and trans girls who want to enact or display 'girliness' are attracted to pink, possibly without awareness of the cultural messages they are re-enacting. Wearing pink does not make you a girl, but if you identify as a girl, social messages will influence you into favouring pink.

Some people have faith in a simple concrete reality that sex is biological, gender is socially constructed, and that's that. Naturally, it turns out to be much more complicated. In the 1960s, it was believed that gender was so entirely separate from the facts of biology that you could raise a boy as a girl and there would be no adverse consequences (Money *et al.* 1955). The case of David Reimer, famously assigned female after losing his penis in a botched circumcision, threw some doubt onto this belief. David strongly identified as male despite attempts to turn him into a girl (Money and Ehrhardt 1972; Diamond and Sigmundson 1997).

In the 1990s, during a backlash both against feminism and the ideas of gender being socially constructed, a raft of junk science books appeared claiming men and women were fundamentally different in more than just their genitals. Most of these ideas have also been debunked – women and men are not from Venus and Mars after all, but from Earth, and are not so very different from each other (Fine 2010).

But these books did serve a purpose in halting the emerging questions about the social implications of biological sex.

So confident are we of the essential differences of biological sex, that we turn people's biological sex into a legal status. Our birth certificates record whether we are male or female, as do our passports and marriage and medical records. We also socially encode gender by using pronouns for people, and greetings like sir or madam, ladies or gentlemen. This ensures that we must decide what people's 'biological sex' is whenever we interact with them.

It should by now be apparent that we have crossed over a line that seemed to be neatly drawn: If there are all these legal and social implications of 'biological sex', is it not becoming a little more like 'gender', i.e. the social stuff we build around sex?

This is why the trans community use the term 'sex/gender assigned at birth' and talk about trans men being 'assigned female at birth' rather than calling them 'natal females' or 'biologically females' or worse, 'born women'. We are born babies and we are assigned into boxes called male or female, man or woman, and because this is a social process it is not biology at all, but rather a process of socially enforcing and legislating gender. Because intersex people are not always assigned into a sex, or rather a binary gender, at birth due to genital ambiguity, I personally tend to talk about people being 'assigned male/female' rather than 'assigned female/male at birth'.

THE EXISTENCE OF INTERSEX PEOPLE

I am always surprised when I train that so few people have heard of intersex people. Estimates vary depending on what is included, but according to Fausto-Sterling (2000) two per cent of people have a condition that *could* be described as intersex. This is as common as redheads, and certainly as common as trans people, who may not be socially accepted, but have at least been heard of by most people.

There are a variety of 'differences of sexual development' (another term for intersex). These are differences in hormones, chromosomes or reproductive organs. Some of these differences are discovered at birth, some in puberty, and some by chance later in life. People who think men have XY and women XX chromosomes are surprised to learn that some XY people are assigned female at birth, and some XX people are assigned male. There are also many other chromosome combinations such as XO, XXX, XXY and chimerism, where a person has both XX and XY chromosomes (Intersex Society of North America 2018).

Genitals come in a range of shapes and structures. Sadly, many intersex children born with irregular genitalia are given non-consensual and medically unnecessary surgery to make their genitals conform to typical ideas of maleness and femaleness. This happens in the UK and elsewhere to this day (Kirkland 2017). Malta is the only country that has outlawed medically unnecessary surgery of intersex infants to normalise genitalia to the social binary (Koch and Wisdom 2017). A child with too long a clitoris may have it shortened, despite how this may impair sexual enjoyment later in life (Minto *et al.* 2003), and a child who doctors deem 'should' have a vagina may have one constructed at a very young age – a painful and invasive process seemingly based on the idea of the necessity of a particular, heteronormative kind of sex (Guarino *et al.* 2013; Papisova and Kheraj 2017). XY children with an underdeveloped penis have had healthy testicles removed and been raised as girls. Often decisions about what surgery to perform are based not on chromosomes but on what is surgically possible or easier (Kirkland 2017).

This practice stems from the belief that gender is *entirely* socially created, and that we can mould a child successfully into any gender we impose on them. Intersex kids, just like David Reimer, were expected to grow up healthily and happily in whatever gender doctors and parents decided they would be given.

Unsurprisingly, perhaps, it turns out not to be that simple. Although there is a wealth of evidence that many of our ideas around gender are socially created (Fine 2010, 2017), assigning gender onto intersex kids fails a lot more than expected. Not all intersex kids grow up to want to reassign their gender, but many more do than in the general population (Reiner 2005).

GENDER IDENTITY

There has been mounting evidence of a third strand, separate from either socially constructed 'gender' or the physical but complex set of characteristics (hormones, chromosomes, genitalia, secondary sexual characteristics) called 'biological sex'. The most established term for this phenomenon is 'gender identity', but other terms that have been played with are 'subconscious sex' (Serano 2007, pp.77–93) or 'brain gender/sex'. The idea that 'sex is between the legs, gender is between the ears' was once a popular cliché, but the idea that there is a male or female brain has been debunked by many studies (Fine 2010). Our biological sex influences our entire body, including our brain, but in more complex ways than to suggest there are two types of brain. Joel (2012) states that all brains are 'intersex', i.e. a mosaic of characteristics associated with maleness and femaleness, rather than being as 'highly dimorphic' as what she calls '3G sex', i.e. 'genetic-gonadal-genital sex'. Fine (2017) expands on this, with her thorough analysis of the weak scientific evidence that testosterone causes profound behavioural differences in the domains of, for instance, risk-taking and sexuality in men. Meanwhile, trans people's divergent experiences are often embodied, and do not just reside in the brain, although they may be affected by the ways in which our brains map onto our bodies.

My own preferred way of thinking about this is as a *gender instinct* or a *gender orientation.* In simple terms, I think of it as the instinct to either follow the social cues of those of our own assigned gender or the other, or neither, or a mix of the two. Deeper still, it appears to be a powerful and often embodied sense of who we are that is so strong it can contradict both our physical bodies and our legally assigned social categories.

Roughgarden (2004, p.224) asks 'whom will a baby emulate and whom will he or she merely notice?' when talking about the formation of gender identity, which she believes, and studies of intersex people also suggest, can happen in the third trimester of pregnancy, and is related to hormonal influences *after* the formation of genitalia (Reiner 2005). Roughgarden talks of gender identity as a 'lens' through which a baby sees the world, leading them to focus on men and women as 'tutors' to greater or lesser degrees (2004, p.224).

I am acutely aware of how the words we use around this tell a story about trans and intersex people, and men and women too, that will be forever incomplete. There is something a bit insubstantial about the term 'gender identity' that can make it seem weak in relation to a person's apparent biology and the social gender legally enforced onto them. And yet this experience is so strong it trumps the attempts at socially programming us to be what we are told to be and, more importantly, to not be trans. Young trans girls (that is, kids assigned male who identify as girls) often find it hard work to learn how to be boys, and pick up ways of being 'girly' with ease, as if the messages meant for girls are meant for them. And this process happens very young for many trans people, seemingly an instinctive rather than conscious thing.

Gender identity, for want of a better term, is a proven phenomenon. The idea of 'male and female brains' is a more complex area of study, and awash with sexism. For now, we can just accept that what it is to be a man or woman does vary across time and culture, and that we are profoundly influenced by the stories we tell ourselves and each other about gender. The concept of gender is layered and multi-faceted, rooted in tradition, oppression, history, science, social convenience and much more.

THE BUILDING BLOCKS OF GENDER

There are no proven definitions of what gender is, nor of where sex ends and gender begins, nor of how much gender is constructed and how much it is biology. We are just beginning to discover the complexity of these issues. Aspects of gender are oppressive and, for some, aspects of gender are valuable and meaningful. There is an endless nature/nurture debate over gender, and yet scientists are now beginning to understand the 'sheer exhilarating tangle of a continuous interaction among genes, brain and environment' (Fine 2010, p.177).

We have a tendency as humans to create models for phenomena we experience in the world. Culturally, we have developed tendencies in our thinking. There are two tendencies I am going to encourage us to challenge during the course of this book – the tendency to think in a linear way about causation, and the tendency to think in terms of binary opposites.

The interminable 'nature vs. nurture' argument is an example of linear thinking. We know enough to understand that in most cases it is a bit of both. Clinicians and researchers increasingly subscribe to a *biopsychosocial* model. Much is yet to be settled, and we are rightly sceptical of the motives of scientists devoting their time to 'proving' (often in deeply biased studies) the differences between men and women.

Gender is multi-determined, much like other complicated things – plants grow to strength due to a variety of conditions, relationships rarely stand or fail on a single issue, and buildings need more than just bricks to hold them up. Sometimes, we allow what is within our circle of care to be complex, multi-determined and plural, while fitting the 'other' into a more narrow and linear narrative. Noting ourselves creating a causal narrative about a person in our mind is a good way to spot that we are holding them at distance, and out of relationship.

Examples of linear ideas about trans people include 'I think their relationship with their mother made them that way' or 'the way they are dressed is based on stereotypes'. We are less likely to see the dress of our very feminine cisgender auntie as 'based on stereotypes' or wonder if our own deeply held identity is caused by a single early relationship.

The other simplistic approximation we make is to place things in binary opposites. Men and women are not opposites, they are humans with a great deal more in common than they have differences. Those differences they have exist on continuums – tallness, strength, hairiness, hormonal profile, fertility, genital shape and size. While it is true that human reproductive sex is dyadic, this is one tiny aspect of our complex lives. Not all humans are fertile, not all humans are interested in heterosexual sex, and of those, even fewer are thinking about parenting for all but a fraction of their lives, if at all. Fine (2017, pp.46–79) demonstrates how human sexuality separated itself from reproduction a long time ago, showing that male and female sexuality is not fundamentally different, is varied and is more about pleasure and bonding than reproduction. In what sense, exactly, are assigned male and assigned female people opposite? Trans feminist writer Julia Serano calls this tendency to place men and women in opposing positions *oppositional sexism* (Serano 2007, p.104).

Assigned male people cannot currently give birth, it is true, although with the introduction of uterus transplants this might change. Reproductive rights matter and are specific to a certain group of people. But not all assigned female people can give birth – does this make them opposite to the ones who can? Do people change their legal/social identity when they enter puberty, and again when they go through menopause, and if the ability to give birth is so fundamental to identity, then why not?

The 'Guevedoce' boys of the Dominican Republic do not grow a penis until they enter puberty, due to a rare genetic intersex condition that happens to be concentrated (one in 90) in this population. Interestingly, even children diagnosed with the condition are raised as girls until their penis grows, and then transition to live as boys. For this society, the possession of a penis is integral to being a boy, and a child without a penis is a girl even though they will grow up to have a penis, even though they can never give birth to children but can one day make someone else pregnant, and even though many (but not all) of these children being raised as girls have a clearly male gender identity (Wilder 2015).

The case of Guevedoce boys may seem obtuse in its arbitrariness, but it is no more arbitrary than our own gender system, it is just unfamiliar. In our system too, we assign gender based on genital shape (and size) and anti-trans campaigners loudly insist that 'penis=male'. XY children with testicles but an underdeveloped penis are often surgically altered and raised as girls in our culture because a penis is seen as so integral to being a man (Papisova and Kheraj 2017). And yet I am certain that if an adult man loses his penis in an accident, he does not instantly become a woman, or stop being a man. Penis or no penis, fertile or infertile, even without the complexities of intersex people, our social attachments to reproductive sex start to reveal themselves as stories rather than facts.

Our literature and history is full of dichotomies that we create and project onto maleness and femaleness: anima/animus, sun/moon, mind/body, reason/emotion, dominance/submission, strength/weakness. Few of these things are truly opposite and none have a clear relationship with maleness and femaleness, we are just used to thinking of them in that context. The sun is a massive nuclear fusion reactor at the centre of our solar system and the moon is a big lump of rock, but it is convenient for some to think of the man being the powerful, shining thing and the woman being there to reflect his light. Mind and reason are now understood to be deeply interconnected with body and emotion, but there has been a long history of portraying women as emotional (see the origins of the word 'hysterical') and men as rational, in many ways to the detriment of both.

Trans people are not immune to these stories and stereotypes, but due to those gendered instincts I mentioned earlier, they experience the impact very differently to their peers. Trans people do not stand outside gender and are no more objective to it than anyone else. It is impossible for any human to find an objective place to see this all from, or to untangle the complex web we are caught within. But what is true for trans people, and many intersex people, is that the prescribed ways to navigate this web simply do not work.

When I train, I sometimes tell people that my intention is to make them leave more confused than when they begin. 'Are trans people confused about gender?' I ask. 'In many ways, yes. Because if you're *not* confused about gender, you haven't been paying attention.'

Trans people are not more objective, but in general we have been forced to consider gender, read about gender and think about gender a lot more than most people. Few trans people are unable to give a 101 lecture at will on gender issues that most people have not even considered. Sadly, though in other times and cultures trans people would have been perceived as wise and spiritual, in Western culture this knowledge resource is rarely drawn upon.

GENDER THROUGH HISTORY AND ACROSS THE WORLD

Our western ideas of gender are often rooted in the story of Adam and Eve. It is a story we tell ourselves that binary sex and heterosexual relating is the foundation of all things. What is interesting to me is that ancient Judaism in fact had up to eight genders recorded within the Talmud (Falk 2015), and although ancient Judaism does also have texts that reinforce the gender/sex binary and male supremacy we can see in this culture, and in fact most cultures across history, an understanding of the complexity of gendered experiences.

> Our earliest ancestors do not appear to have been biological determinists. There are societies all over the world that allowed for more than two sexes, as well as respecting the rights of individuals to reassign their sex. And transsexuality, transgender, intersexuality, and bigender appear as themes in creation stories, legends, parables, and oral history. (Feinberg 1996, p.43)

What went wrong? The story of the Americas is one illustration. When the indigenous peoples were encountered by settlers, their embracing of many genders, same-sex marriage and other more liberated practices were perceived by European colonists as 'perverse' and used to reinforce the conqueror's belief in their own superiority and right to dominion (Morgensen 2012). This is somewhat ironic, when we examine how anti-LGBT+ sentiments in some countries (often former British colonies) are now used once again to evidence white European superiority.

In what is now India, Pakistan and Bangladesh, there is another example where colonialism changed attitudes towards the Hijras – a group of assigned male people who were, prior to British rule, given a spiritual role in Indian society. The term Hijra does not accurately map onto our own terms but constitutes a spectrum of what we might call queer, intersex and trans identities (Gannon 2009, p.4). 'The hijra are distinct from the more modern, Western understanding of transsexual women. Their identities and status, changeable across time, have a considerably longer heritage, which is grounded in religious practice and spiritual belief' (Gust 2014). The British stigmatised Hijras and criminalised them 10 years into their rule: 'early European travellers showed that they were repulsed by the sight of Hijras and could not comprehend why they were given so much respect in the royal courts and other institutions' (Michelraj 2015, p.18). Gust (2014) describes colonisers referring to Hijras as 'the vilest and most polluted beings'.

It is only now that Hijras are beginning to regain their rights, with changes in the law in India, Pakistan and Bangladesh allowing them recognition as 'third sex/gender', a position that has historical significance in South Asian culture (Michelraj 2015, p.18). India, Pakistan and Bangladesh therefore now legally recognise genders 'outside of the binary', while the UK Gender Recognition Act 2004 only legally recognises trans people who fully identify as men or women.

This raises interesting challenges when working with British people of South Asian descent who identify as trans, because 'Hijra' is currently still a stigmatised identity, on the edge of society and often engaged in marginalised work such as sex work, and it does not accurately map onto 'trans woman' (Gust 2014). Some people will want to embrace the term and claim it, but others might distance themselves from it. Clumsy attempts by white counsellors (and I own that I have been guilty of this myself) to raise the Hijra history with their British South Asian clients to locate them within an important cultural history can easily go awry. Equally, though, white counsellors must examine our understanding of the difficulties our clients face within some communities. If we do not locate those difficulties correctly as part of the legacy of racism and colonialism, we might rest ourselves on the lie that our white society is somehow more 'progressive'.

A lot of work has been done in the last 10 years to uncover the way much of the troubling attitudes to LGBT+ people internationally correlate with the legacy of colonialism (Ahmed 2017). This is not to have some starry-eyed view that indigenous cultures were all perfect, but to acknowledge that colonialism stripped the world of much cultural diversity and exchanges of ideas that could have enriched our understanding of human nature (and nurture).

The Victorians instituted registry of births, and it appears legal gender was an accidental or intentional offshoot of this. Prior to this, it had been much easier for people to live and marry as the opposite sex, and they would have to be physically 'found out' for their marriage to be annulled. They also legislated against male homosexuality and introduced indecency laws about crossdressing. In the 18th century, a social class of people called 'hermaphrodites'[1] – an unclear category that at different times seemed to include what we now call gay, trans and intersex people – were known about, but an emerging science of sexual dimorphism meant that the idea of intersexuality was slowly erased (Vincent 2018; Welz Geselowitz 2016).

We also see, throughout history, evidence of people modifying their bodies and people living as the opposite sex (Morgan 2018). One of the difficulties is imposing our modern words onto these practices. Were some of the people who history recorded as 'eunuchs' what we would call trans? We cannot really say, but what we can say is that sometimes eunuchs were allowed into women's spaces and occupied a cultural position that has some echoes with transness as we now understand it.

There are also clues to the existence of trans men in history. We hear stories constantly of 'women passing themselves off as men', often to enter an exclusively male domain. These familiar stories range from Mulan to Joan of Arc. But even when these people consistently and full-time live as and identify themselves as men, they are often recorded retrospectively as women. The doctor James Barry is one such character. Presented to us as a woman who lived as a man in order to be a doctor, the evidence suggests that he actually lived both publicly and privately as a man and may well have identified as one. There was no word for 'trans' in Barry's day, and thus it is easy to erase the transness of his story (Ottoman 2015).

We cannot assume that an absence of words or information means trans people were not there, or trans people were persecuted more than they now are. We do, however, have one very significant incident of violent trans erasure, and that was in Nazi Germany.

1 Hermaphrodite is now understood as a scientifically correct term for creatures such as snails and a highly offensive and incorrect term that is still sometimes used for intersex people.

I only discovered relatively recently that male homosexuality was ruled to be decriminalised in Germany in 1927 (Marhoefer 2008, p.ii). This is a surprising fact to those whose understanding of gay liberation is that it started in the 1960s. As now, trans rights seemed to go hand in hand with gay rights, and there was an upsurge in understanding of trans people, and even an institute, the Institut für Sexualwissenschaft, that sought to study and work with trans people in a non-pathologising way, alongside other study of human gender and sexual diversity (Vincent 2018, pp.48–49).

Magnus Hirschfield, the openly gay leader of this institute, performed the first trans surgery on Dora Richter in 1930, and shortly after performed surgery on the intersex person Lili Elbe, the protagonist of the film *The Danish Girl*. There are a number of interesting things that say a good deal about our current perspective on these historic events. One is the conservativeness of the film by comparison to the life of Lili Elbe. Lili's partner, Gerda Wegener, was in fact a bisexual artist who used LGBT+ people as the subjects of her art. She was much more accepting of Lili than the film portrayed. The film says much more about 2015 attitudes to trans people than it does about 1930s ones (Karin 2009; Russell 2015; Vincent 2018).

But the main historic omission in our understanding of the events of the late 1920s and early 1930s in Germany is what came after. Most of us have seen those iconic photos of Nazis burning books, but few of us know that the photos are from their sacking of Hirschfield's institute. These were not just any books, these were books about sexology, studies of trans and LGB people and gender and sexual diversity, the world's largest queer repository, and not only was it destroyed, but history has been complicit with the Nazis in failing to mention just *what* was destroyed (Vincent 2018).

We also recount the Holocaust while frequently omitting the fact that LGBT+ people were among those who died in the concentration camps. Unlike other liberated prisoners, 'homosexuals' continued to be criminalised, many serving more jail time or being registered as sex offenders. At the time of the Nazis, there was no clear distinction between gay men and trans women, and both were persecuted, either for sexual acts as 'homosexuals' or in the broader category 'asocial', which was the group that earned the black triangle now associated with lesbian persecution, but in fact was earned by many people seen as socially deviant. The term asocial was so broadly used, in fact, that it makes it impossible to know how many LGBT+ people died under the Nazis (Garkawe 1997; Transgender Foundation of America 2008).

CONCLUSION

My intention throughout this book is to move us away from certainty and simplistic models to a more curious and creative way of lightly holding diverse ideas and theories around gender. I hope to strengthen our ability to fully meet our client's own unique relationship with the biopsychosocial complexity of gender and sex.

I hope that this chapter raises many questions. I hope too that it creates certain awareness shifts. The most fundamental of the unconscious errors we replicate around gender is that 'assigned sex' is the same as 'biological sex'. This is one of the most frustrating things about many anti-trans activists, that they seem to believe that pronouns, and birth certificates, and all the paraphernalia we build up around what we assume about a baby's reproductive status, are 'biological'. They also tend to see intersex people, rather than being a natural part of human diversity, as a 'mistake' that needs correcting and erasing.

This is the 'gender binary', a tool that is used to ensure a certainty about other human beings that does not exist. As trans health researcher Ruth Pearce says, it is an '*idea with power* shaping *how* the world works' (2018, p.7). When we look at a baby we can say 'congratulations, your child has a vagina' and that would be factual. But 'your child has a vagina and is therefore a girl and must be assigned into the legal and social position of girl/woman and use she/her pronouns for life' is a social construction. With this comes social programming to recognise what pronouns and salutations a person requires, based on the look of their face or the sound of their voice, alongside all the introjected rules and unconscious biases about roles, clothes and appropriate behaviour that we have developed.

We do not know anything about the child other than the external appearance of their genitalia. We do not know about their chromosomes, or their ability to reproduce. We do not know how they will instinctively see themselves in relation to gender as they grow, or who they will be socially drawn to and how and if they will form sexual and romantic bonds when they are older.

It is more than likely that whatever the current social conventions are for gender, a child will instinctively align with them. But this is far from certain, and for a significant minority the relationship with assigned gender is much more complicated and fraught.

Assigning gender in a way that has such profound legal and social implications elevates gender above other human differences. We do not legally register people based on race, disability, sexual orientation or other natural diversity. If we did so, people would quite probably be alarmed. We can still protect those differences in law. Gay people are protected against prejudice by equality law, for instance. Nor do we encode those differences in our social interactions, as we do in English and many other languages with gendered pronouns and salutations.

This social importance placed on gender is accepted as normal and natural, to the extent that we might struggle to understand how a culture that has no pronouns, like Bengali, functions. We might be confused by societies that create a greater number of gender categories, like Indigenous Americans.

The number of countries that are allowing a legal option outside of male and female is increasing. In Germany, intersex children can be registered as third gender. This change met with mixed reactions from intersex people – if we do not change society to accommodate third gender people, how will these 'othered' children fare in school, for instance? As stated before, India, Pakistan and Bangladesh recognise a legal third gender, as does Thailand. In Australia, citizens are allowed an X on their passports. In the UK a 2016 parliamentary inquiry recommended allowing a third option on passports, and even some US states have allowed this.

This could be the beginning of a hopeful revolution, but we need to be cautious. There will always be some trans people who fully align with the 'opposite' sex, just as there will always be trans people who are non-binary. It is important that the full continuum of identities is recognised and counted equally. 'Third gender' cannot be a stigmatised and segregated category that all trans and intersex people are pushed into against their will.

The stark contrast between attitudes to medical treatment of trans and intersex kids reflects the importance placed on the gender binary. For the past few years, British newspapers, and not just the tabloids, have been full of alarmist headlines about medical interventions for trans children, even though the only treatments available to trans children are reversible and non-invasive: counselling, social transition and puberty blockers that press 'pause' on puberty. Meanwhile, the non-consensual surgery performed on intersex infants is barely mentioned. This hyper-visibility of trans people and erasure of intersex people is to the detriment of both communities.

I know from my work of cases where social workers have claimed leaving intersex children medically untreated is 'child abuse'; at the same time allowing trans children simply to express their identified gender and have access to supportive therapy can also be regarded by social workers as 'child abuse'. The take-home message is it is okay to treat children with surgery and hormones only if it reinforces the importance of assigning a binary gender. Even transgressions of clothing, names and pronouns are cast as fundamental and problematic in such a rigid system.

It is imperative that we as counsellors and other person-centred workers question this and put the welfare and self-actualisation of all humans before the need to replicate a social convention for its own sake.

PERSONAL REFLECTION

After each chapter, I would like to give the reader a chance to collect their thoughts. I strongly recommend journalling answers, feelings, ponderings and questions that arise in this chapter.

Do not worry if not all these questions speak to you, or if this chapter takes your mind in other directions. I encourage you to explore.

1. What things have informed your own ideas about gender and sex growing up? What were the messages from your immediate family? Your school? Your friends? Your community? In what ways did you conform to these ideas and in what ways did you diverge from them?

2. What do you believe now? Where do you stand on the nature/nurture debate? What has informed your current ideas about gender and sex? Where are the gaps in your understanding? What are you curious about?

3. Do you have a picture in your head of the way gender and sex, male and female, interrelate? Can you draw a diagram, graph or scale representing your ideas? Feel free to doodle some pictorial representations of your idea of how men, women and everyone else fit together.

4. Most of us have, consciously or unconsciously, some ideas of a model for gender. We might, for instance, put gay and trans on the same linear axis, where trans is no more than a form of 'extreme gay'. We might think of men and women as separate, boundaried things with no overlap, or we might see maleness and femaleness on a linear spectrum. We might believe everyone is a combination of 'maleness and femaleness' but not consider the possibility of anything outside of that.

   Ask the following questions of your model: Does my model imply that some men are 'less men' and some women are 'less women'? Does it idealise or prioritise a particular kind of person? Is there space in my model for people to be outside of male and female, or are those people perched on a vanishingly small line? Does my model allow for trans people to exist? What about intersex people? Does my model allow for the differences between someone who identifies as bigender or polygender (having more than one gender), third gender (a gender outside of male and female) and agender (having no gender)? Does my model cast men and women as 'opposites', and if so, why? Do masculinity, maleness and manliness all mean the same thing in my model, or each mean something different?

5. One of the better models that exist is the Gender Unicorn (Trans Student Educational Resources 2014), The best thing about this model is that it separates out the different strands of experience, rather than making them either oppose or align with each other. So, you can be, like Eddie Izzard, 'all boy' with an 'extra girl bit' (Farndale 2006) – in other words, having a female aspect to your identity does not necessarily negate or dilute your maleness or legitimacy as a man (though it might for some!). You can be a feminine man, too, without your femininity undermining your manliness, or meaning you in any way identify as a woman. Likewise, you can be a masculine or 'butch' woman and still 100 per cent be a woman.

6. Have a go at completing the Gender Unicorn for yourself by marking an X on each line of the diagram.[2] Does this model

2 See www.transstudent.org/gender

feel complete enough to you? For many it is still imperfect, particularly in the way it conflates biology and DNA with sex assigned at birth – let us not forget all the intersex people who were assigned female but later discovered they have XY chromosomes, and vice versa!

Chapter 2

WHO ARE THE TRANS COMMUNITY?

Sadly, if we watch a mainstream documentary or read an article about trans people, we will often hear the same story over and over, and this can lead, somewhat understandably, to people believing there is just one type of trans person. Phrases like 'trapped in the wrong body' and 'sex change', plus an obsession with before and after photos, transformation and surgery, place a very clear emphasis on the idea that trans = transformation. Inaccurate terms that imply a process, such as 'transing' and 'transgendered', 'transgenderism' or 'transgendering' contribute to this myth.

One thing to be very clear about is that trans is not something people *do*, it is something people *are*. The obsession with portraying trans as a process anyone can go through is at the heart of one of the biggest misunderstandings of trans lives.

There is an emerging, although complex, picture of a 'durable biological element underlying gender identity' (Endocrine Society 2017). As I said in the previous chapter, though, trans people do not have to be a biologically proven phenomenon to exist, when the whole of assigned sex and gender is a complex biopsychosocial web. Suffice it to say that there is probably something biological going on for some if not all trans people, but that it is also true that things that are not remotely biological, but are purely socially constructed, such as money, can have a profound and material impact on our lives and wellbeing.

What we do know is that most trans people have some sense of divergence from typically cisgender experiences early on in their lives, and that many if not most trans people have a fixed sense of their gender identity by the age of eight. Olson, Key and Eaton (2015) demonstrated that trans identities are every bit as stable as cis identities. But that does not mean that 'trans' is just one thing or that all trans people (or all cis people) have similar experiences in relation to gender. Multiple factors influence our relationship with our assigned gender, so our identities are pluralistic, in fact quite possibly infinitely variable.

Once we realise this, it starts to be possible to embrace the richness and diversity of language that describe people's trans or transish experiences. People may quite playfully or even disrespectfully play around with words and categories, just like I did in the last sentence by using the made-up word 'transish'. We end up with a multitude of words to describe experiences, and they are still not always enough – demiboy/girl, neutrois, androgyne, trans dyke, genderqueer, transfem, genderfuck, gender anarchist, gender capitalist...

It is best not to get too bogged down with a sense of needing to learn and understand all these words. What is important is what the person using them is trying to communicate, and if we take a person-centred approach, all we need do is ask 'what does that word mean to you?', because we may each use these words to express something slightly different. A little time afterwards spent online researching the word a client uses never hurts, but they might be using the word differently than the internet describes. Our efforts to describe our gender will always be inaccurate, variable and subjective *and that is okay*. The words man, woman, he, she are also inaccurate, variable and subjective. They have merely acquired a dominance that makes them seem more authoritative than they are.

What matters is allowing people a rich language to describe their experience. Asking people to paint with only two colours is limiting; telling them those two colours never mix is more limiting still. Saying even that pink is one colour and the words rose, magenta, fuschia, etc. are unnecessary is far too restrictive. The deeply interesting and complex world of gender and sex is stifled by our attempts to rigidly categorise and legalise it.

WHY 'ALL THESE LABELS'?

It is important when we listen to our clients' words, words that may well be new to us, to notice our own processes. How open are we to this new language? What are the points of resistance? When I train,

I frequently encounter certain responses. I will share these over the next few sections, and hopefully we can use them to examine our own resistances. Naturally, I will not be covering all possible resistances, only some that I have encountered.

The most common resistance I come up against, and this happens particularly from person-centred practitioners, is 'Why do people need to label themselves?' Part of this comes from a principle I was taught as a trainee person-centred counsellor – it is disrespectful to diagnose and label our clients because this can create a barrier to their own self-experience. I still absolutely agree that this is true, but it is important to be aware of drawing a distinction between a useful descriptive term somebody can use to describe themself, and a 'label'.

For example, if I experience a client as 'angry' I might offer the word and not consider that this is a 'diagnosis' or a 'label', even though my experience and concept of anger might differ from my client's. In fact, what seems to me to be clearly anger might be seen quite differently by the client. 'Anger' is a pathological and scary label for some, much to be avoided, and for others, myself included, it is a healthy and necessary emotion. So, I might be quite tentative about offering the 'A' word to a client, aware of its controversial position, and yet at the same time I would personally see it as a useful, descriptive word to describe the natural human emotion that comes up when a boundary is transgressed, or something is lost. In other words, whether we embrace a term as a useful part of language or a pathologising label to be avoided depends on our relationship with it.

For many if not most trans people, the gender they were assigned into at birth is akin to a medical diagnosis by doctors, and an unwanted and incorrect one. So 'boy', 'girl', 'man', 'woman', 'he' and 'she' become the uncomfortable and restrictive labels put onto us unwantedly by others. This is the disrespectful, non-person-centred labelling that is against the client's will and wishes. Unfortunately, because we are so seamlessly schooled that this process is 'natural' and fitting in with this process is 'normal', it is hard to see it as an imposition or see these words as 'labels'.

I often find that people have a clear divide in their minds between words like man, woman, he, she, gay, straight, heterosexual, which they see as useful, correct, descriptive words and asexual, non-binary, bisexual, trans, cis, genderqueer, pansexual, etc. which they see as 'unnecessary labels'. Of course, 30 years ago the words gay, straight, and heterosexual would have also been seen as 'unnecessary labels' that people would have rejected in favour of saying, 'I'm just normal/they are abnormal'.

Beneath the resistance to certain words there can be a sense of hierarchy – what is 'normal and okay' and what is 'something we don't need to talk about'. Not talking about things is a way to ensure those experiences are suppressed, and those stories go untold. This, naturally, perpetuates the fragility of those stories.

For example, I did not hear the words 'non-binary' and 'genderqueer' until I was over 40, and up until that point I had made do with other much less accurate words to describe myself – 'tomboy' or 'lesbian' – both of which inherently positioned me under the category woman/girl, in the understanding that this was non-negotiable.

It is important that we as counsellors interrogate our lexicon – which words do we see as fundamental, unequivocal, vital words needed to describe human experience? Which words do we see as frivolous, pathological, unnecessary, uncomfortable, diagnostic? A bit of self-reflection can chase down our own discomfort or problematic relationship with these words and reflect on the story we are telling ourselves about gender and sex.

Where these words do become diagnostic is when we impose them on other people, and this is a difficult dance. Sometimes, offering a word to a client that they have never heard before to describe their experience can be liberating, but at other times it can be an imposition. Just like offering the word 'anger' to a client, with all its associated baggage, can be an imposition, or a relief.

I would never want anyone to 'diagnose' another person as being trans, and although the idea that children or adults are being diagnosed by outside forces as trans is largely a myth, we have to be very careful not to get in the way of, or attempt to mould, our clients' emerging identities.

In a society that is so erasing of or warping of trans identity, making space for possibilities through our language is vital, however. When I counsel a black client, who is being treated unfavourably, it is important as a white counsellor I mention the possibility of racism, or it may remain invisible and unspoken. I cannot say for certainty that discriminatory treatment is down to racism, but I can acknowledge the possibility, and signal that it is okay for my client to speak about racism. With my trans clients I will try to signal in the broadest possible way that trans people exist and are very welcome in my therapy room. And the more familiar I am, and comfortable I am, with language around trans issues, the easier it is to do that.

FEAR OF 'GETTING IT WRONG'

Another point of resistance I find in trainees around the language of being trans is anxiety about getting things wrong/saying the wrong things. Unfortunately, this anxiety can strongly root a person in their own experience, and lead to a withdrawal away from the trans person they are supposed to be in a relationship with. That fear of 'getting it wrong' is often connected to our own shame around competence and knowledge, and we are often more worried about being told we've made a mistake than about how that mistake might impact on our client.

There is a lot to unpick in this phenomenon. The first and overriding message we need to battle through is the idea that *we already know* enough about gender. If the client's words do not fit our knowledge, it is easy to belittle them or be dismissive of our need to learn about them. We may even experience resistance to learning because we must unlearn concepts we previously took as read.

From there, it can be easy to pathologise the importance the client puts on these unfamiliar ideas and terms. Surely, from our knowing perspective, these things are trivial and unimportant – why do they seem so important to our client? Without realising it, we may have created a hierarchy where we are aggrandising our own understanding and infantilising the trans person's, or at least elevating conformist and dominant views and values and applying a judgement to views and values that do not match this.

This means that at least some of our outrage and upset about being corrected by or instructed by trans people needs to be understood in the context of disturbed social hierarchy. As counsellors who believe in a relationship of equality and non-judgement with our clients, it can be very difficult to bring these hidden hierarchies into our awareness, as it goes against our self-concept of being a fair person who is committed to equality.

But the social hierarchy that places trans identities as lesser than cis identities is deeply entrenched in our understanding of society, so deep it is often invisible to us. Counsellors would hopefully not consciously think of trans clients as lesser, but almost certainly do unconsciously.

And naturally, because we do not exist outside of society, trans people internalise these hierarchies too; we may also think of ourselves as lesser, trivialise our own needs and experiences, or maintain existing hierarchies consciously or unconsciously.

It is crucial that we realise that every time a different pronoun comes to our mind or lips than the one the client uses, every time we struggle with their language or their concept of self, we are without realising it elevating our understanding of gender above that of the client's. The word for this is *cissexism*. Just like sexism elevates qualities associated with men over those of women, so cissexism elevates qualities of cis people over those of trans people. Cissexism says that it is better to be described as 'he' and 'a man' if you were born with a penis. Cissexism says we can guess the gender of people by a casual glance, or from the sound of their voice. Cissexism says our external appraisal of people's gender is more real than their lifelong self-experience.

Cissexism is the cumulative effect of being taught one very simplistic and binary story about gender and sex our whole lives, and it is crucial that we understand we will never fully unlearn that story. All we can do is continually bring into our own awareness the ways that story influences us, and repeatedly challenge this narrative with ideas and ways of thinking that provide alternatives.

The cis/trans hierarchy is at its most obvious when a cis person makes a mistake. While someone low in a social hierarchy is liable to be apologetic for a mistake, someone higher in the hierarchy is likely to feel more entitled to anger or justification. When we are low in the hierarchy, we are forced to empathise with others, when we are higher, there is less need to do the emotional work and we often fail to empathise. So, when we feel entitled not to be challenged we might say things like 'this is really hard for me', or 'I'm trying' – appealing to the trans person to empathise with *us* rather than the other way around. Or we might simply get annoyed and claim that we have done quite enough work on their behalf, and the labour they are requiring is too much – 'you are hurting your cause', 'you expect too much', 'other trans people don't have these same expectations', 'I have trans friends who are fine with this', 'I know plenty about trans issues, thank you very much'.

For me, the crucial element to being person-centred is equalising such power differentials, but sometimes we can be oblivious to their existence. If we do not know they are there, we will never be able to address them and equalise them in the therapy room. Unequal dynamics tend to be instrumental rather than relational – how can we make psychological contact if we cannot clear away these barriers?

This might be a good time for you to check in with yourself. Do you believe me when I say there is a hidden cis/trans hierarchy? If you do, are you committed to dismantling it or do you think it should stay just where it is? That might be a bold question, but currently most people, including most trans people, including this writer, are likely to be influenced by the idea that it's better to be cis than trans. And we need to be honest about that and understand why that hierarchy exists.

ANXIETY AROUND DIFFERENCE

Anxiety around difference is another thing that gets in the way of us fully hearing a client's language and unique self-expression. At times humans can be quite fearful and desperate for a homogenous and conformist approach to being a human. An example of how this manifests is that 200 years ago, left-handedness was a highly stigmatised identity. Even a hundred years ago, my left-handed grandmother was forced to write with her right hand. My mother was allowed, but with much reluctance, to write with her left. Now, the traces of this stigma have almost disappeared, remaining only in words like *sinister.*

At the same time as being socially conformist and very quick to adapt to whatever current social norms hold sway, humans are also creative, novelty-seeking, curious and embracing of diversity. I do not believe we can say that it is in our nature to be rejecting of difference, but there are certainly times when difference seems to make us insecure or anxious. Clearly *which* differences make us anxious can change enormously over time.

There is a social narrative that exists that states we should not call attention to our differences, otherwise they will divide us. This can play out in the counselling world as much as anywhere, and our desire not to label can veer into wanting to see people as 'all the same' and being averse to looking at the way our experiences can be so thoroughly divergent from one another.

This also ties in with hierarchy. Not only can we see some experiences as superior to others, we can start to see some experiences as more authentic than others. For example, a cis woman may at one and the same time see her own jewellery and lipstick as self-expression, and see her expressed identity as authentic, but regard a trans woman's jewellery and lipstick as 'performance' or 'copying female stereotypes'. All humans perform, and all humans copy, and there is no reason to believe a cis woman's self-expression is any less performed or copied than a trans woman's. Neither of them is the first person to wear lipstick or jewellery, both are communicating something about themselves in doing so.

When anxiety around difference comes up, some people are expected to leave their differences outside the door. In my experience, the more stressed people are, the more anxious they become about difference, and the less permitted to express their differences minorities become. Sometimes this stress just happens, and sometimes it is incited. Post the 2016 Brexit referendum, hate crime is on the rise, including towards the trans community. LGBT+ hate crime alone rose by 147 per cent in the months after the Brexit vote (Townsend 2016). These kinds of social stresses are replicated in other countries as well, and we also see these tensions play out within very stressed or marginalised communities. For example, some of the deprived ex-mining communities close to where I live are places where hate crime towards trans women is much more frequent. I do not think this phenomenon is a natural occurrence, but stirred up in a top-down way from media, academia and politics.

As counsellors, we have a responsibility to be aware of these wider events, and to examine our own anxieties around difference. It is not enough to say things like 'we're all one race, the human race', or say 'I don't see colour/gender/disability' etc. It is not helpful to think that talking about the specific issues affecting minority groups sows divisions. They divide us if we let them. It is our job, when we are in the more socially advantaged position, to reach out with empathy and acceptance to experiences that diverge from our own. Being trans has the potential to be as unremarkable as being left-handed or red-headed, at which point we will feel comfortable, rather than panicked, to notice it.

As pack animals, one of our deepest anxieties is being rejected from the security of the pack – in our wild state, that would have threatened our very survival. Perhaps the anxiety some carry when they see others standing out is a projection of their own fear of not 'fitting in', but it can be deeply rejecting and othering of trans people. Trans people are human, and part of society, whatever they wear, however they look, whatever they do or do not do to their bodies.

THE PLURALITY OF TRANS EXPERIENCE

I have no intention of listing all the different kinds of trans person, like some sort of spotters' guide. Even two trans people who seem very similar can have two significantly diverging narratives. But I do want to try and give an insight into the diversity of trans experience that might not be gained from a documentary made by cis people, which is often the most readily available source of 'information' about trans people.

The traditional trans narrative is a very medicalised one. Not so long ago, this was the only valid narrative available for a trans person to survive in a hostile world. It is a narrative that has been somewhat imposed on the trans community by the medical profession. In this narrative a person is transformed from one thing to another by a medical process and tends to call themself a transsexual – a word that is no longer acceptable to many in the trans community. There is also a tendency to pathologise transness, to see it as a mental disorder, even though this has now been debunked.

We might want to intellectually argue with this way of seeing things, but if this is the only available narrative to help a person understand themself, then it is important for us as counsellors to have respect for the way our client tells their story, even if we might have a slightly broader understanding of trans identity.

This traditional narrative sees 'trans' as a state somebody is in whilst transitioning, rather than something somebody *is*. People following this narrative are also much less likely to see themselves as trans once they have transitioned and are likely to refer to themselves as a person with a trans history, but primarily they will see themselves as a complete woman or man, just like any other. Crucially, the medical process is what made them a woman or a man. While this is the dominant narrative we see on screen, it does not echo many people's experiences.

A more current view is to think of trans as something a person *is* rather than a process they go through. Given most trans people's lifelong experiences of difference, it is more accurate. A trans woman, recognising that on the inside her identity has been static since her earliest memories, is more likely these days to say that she was always a woman. Lana Wachowski, director of film *The Matrix*, explains transition not as going from being a man to a woman, but going from invisible to visible (Human Rights Campaign 2012).

Some trans people feel their gender has been stable throughout their lives, and that transition merely brought it into the open. They may feel they were 'born this way'. Others experience their gender as changing over time, and being fluid, changeable over the years or even from day to day. These experiences are as authentic as each other, but we are likely to feel more supportive of some identities than others. If we show bias towards 'nurture' arguments we may support change and fluidity more than the idea of a fixed gender identity, for instance.

There is no evidence to suggest that some experiences are more genuine than others, but rather that there is a continuum of experiences in relation to biological, psychological and social aspects of gender and sex.

The word 'transgender' emerged in the 1970s but was popularised in the 1990s by Leslie Feinberg, someone we might now call 'non-binary' (1996). Transgender was conceived as an umbrella term. It encompasses a wide variety of experiences that are somehow at odds with assigned gender, including drag, crossdressing and non-binary identities as well as the more familiar experiences of binary-aligned medical transitioners. Over the years, 'trans' has become a more accepted umbrella word, as it can be short for transgender, transsexual or transvestite. For a while, 'trans*' was popular, but it quickly fell out of favour due to many and ambiguous interpretations. Different people might use different words, or the same words differently. They may use the words inclusively, or less so. Some attempt to draw clear lines between different groups, others, like myself, see a continuum of different experiences with no clear borders between them.

For example, some might say the lines between trans women, crossdresser/transvestite and drag are very clear, but I believe it is much more complicated than that. Drag culture is historically seen as being part of the trans community; in the 60s and 70s, drag queens like Stonewall riots veterans Sylvia Riviera and Marsha P. Johnson, were in fact living full time in 'drag' and mostly using female pronouns. Retrospectively, they are seen more akin to trans women who did not medically transition (Equality Archive 2015).

The drag community as it is today is more about performance than identity. However, it has always held within it trans people – both people who are transitioning, and non-binary people like Courtney Act who identify themselves outside of the gender binary but do not want to transition. For some, drag is a way to explore identity, find empowerment or pay for transition.

Other drag performers are much more likely to see drag entirely as a performance and might consider themselves to be cisgender. Often drag performers, like Paul O'Grady or RuPaul, identify as gay men. Inevitably, there are tensions between these different groups within drag. Some cis drag performers are dismissive of trans-identified people as 'taking it too far', failing to understand that not everyone has the same relationship with gender as they do themselves. Trans people are sometimes accused of conforming to more typical rules about gender expression. However perhaps the greatest transgression is to refuse to identify as the gender we were assigned into. Cis drag performers like RuPaul, Lily Savage and Hinge and Bracket have always been entitled to be visible and accepted in society in a way that trans women have not.

Changing clothes is not as transgressive as changing our gender marker, pronouns or permanent social identity, even though there is stigma attached to crossdressing offstage. Drag performance has provided an important and socially acceptable outlet for people exploring their gender, although this is not true for all people doing drag, and not all trans people want anything to do with drag. Many trans people worry about the confusion in the public mind between drag performance and trans identity. Not everyone understands the difference between a cis drag queen like RuPaul and a trans woman like Paris Lees, and there is a profound difference between their experiences and identities.

In America, the word transvestite is no longer acceptable, but it is still used by some in the UK, alongside the word crossdresser. Again, there will be some that try to create a binary of 'crossdressing men' and trans women, as if there is a hard boundary between them. The crossdressing community is made up of a huge diversity of people, and there is a continuum of experience. Some crossdressers privately identify as trans women, but do not feel ready to come out. Sometimes this is to do with safety, career, relationships or parents, and often it is related to the way trans people are treated in society. For a lot of us, there is a right time and wrong time for transition, and for many being out as trans is still not a safe option.

Some trans women may have a rich hidden life living as 'Susie' at home or in groups and on the internet, whilst going to work as 'Steve'. Society may see her as crossdressing when she presents as Susie, but Steve is the real disguise. During transition, presenting in two different ways is very common, and this can go on for a long time. There are people who go to work as their more authentic self but hide in their private life, or vice versa. Some trans women will dress congruently 100 per cent of the time from the second they come out, and others I know have been entirely through medical transition but still have not fully transitioned socially. All manner of considerations will play a part in this.

Other crossdressers may not identify as women, and this may or may not change in the future. Sometimes crossdressing can be a pathway to acknowledging a trans identity, and sometimes it is just a pastime. A lot of crossdressers are openly transgender and could be described as non-binary, like Eddie Izzard. I know many crossdressers who feel their female and male identities are both authentic, an experience that can be described as bigender.

But what of assigned female trans people? The narrative is very different for us, at least in the west, because there is not such a strong taboo of women 'crossdressing', perhaps thanks to a century of feminist campaigning, as well as changing work, wartime roles and other social change. It is still not fully acceptable for someone perceived to be a woman to wear a suit and tie to a formal event, or men's clothes in a professional role, but the boundaries are looser, and they would certainly be censured less than a man wearing a dress.

Sexism plays a big part in this discrepancy. If women are perceived as inferior, then a man dressing as a woman is seen as more degrading, a woman dressing as a man more aspirational. Misogyny plays a huge part in negative social attitudes specifically aimed at trans women.

This has meant that assigned female people, particularly within the lesbian community, could crossdress publicly. There is still stigma attached to this, and employment barriers, and a lot of historic violence, but someone perceived as a woman wearing 'men's' clothing is not sexualised or degraded in the way society tends to see assigned male crossdressing.

Iggy Pop has an insightful comment on this double standard: 'I'm not ashamed to dress "like a woman" because I don't think it's shameful to be a woman' (Yaeger 2015). The word for the way misogyny and transprejudice combine to undermine trans women is called *transmisogyny*.

Trans men tend to be invisibilised in society for several reasons. The acceptability of masculine expression in women leads even the most overtly male presentation to attract little attention. A trans man is likely to be read as a butch lesbian or tomboyish woman. The effectiveness of testosterone HRT to fully masculinise many trans men means that those trans men not read as lesbian/tomboy tend to get read as cis men. This is not always the case, and I can cite myself as an example of someone who has taken testosterone for over three years and routinely still gets read as a woman, but for most assigned female people, testosterone effects similar changes to a boy's puberty – voice lowers, facial hair grows, body fat redistributes, muscle mass increases, and if the person is under 25, a gain in height and foot size may also be seen.

Historically, trans men tended to 'go stealth', i.e. keep their trans history secret, and allow people to read them as cis men. Often the male privilege trans men gain is contingent on them being read as cis. In a society that treats women badly and trans people worse, the desire to be read simply as a man is attractive, especially if you see yourself as simply a man.

It is perhaps worth mentioning the myth that being 'authentic' means being 'out'. If you experience yourself as a man in a society that delegitimises trans identities, a 'stealth' persona can be much more authentic. If people treat you as the man you are when stealth but start using female pronouns and treating you differently when they know you are trans, then your 'out' identity is a far greater mismatch with your authentic self than your stealth identity.

Because of the invisibility of trans men combined with the extra stigma of transmisogyny affecting trans women, and their added visibility in society, it used to be believed there were significantly fewer assigned female trans people; however, up-to-date analysis suggests there is greater parity, and that non-binary trans people outnumber more binary-aligned trans men and women (Government Equalities Office 2018).

Increasingly, assigned female people are more open about being trans and are expressing identities at odds with their birth assignment. They may signal this incongruence through their language, for instance by adopting gender-neutral pronouns, or a bigender name such as counsellor and writer Meg-John Barker's. They may try to express identity through clothing, although the spectrum of what someone assigned female is able to wear makes this tricky. Many assigned female non-binary people find themselves forced to conform to stereotypically masculine clothes to convey incongruence with their birth assignment, even if they do not feel at all that their gender is 'masculine'. If they wear 'women's' clothes, they risk having their identity dismissed. Of course, while these norms are true in Europe and the US, gendered clothing varies across the globe – in some cultures, clothing rules for women are as rigid as for men, in others, clothing rules for men are more relaxed.

Due to the narrow spectrum of what is acceptable for a man to wear in European/US culture, an assigned male person can signal a divergent relationship with their assigned gender with as little as a pair of earrings or some nail varnish, if those things feel appropriate to their gender. Gender neutrality, though, is harder to express. Even slight displays of femininity in assigned male people are deeply stigmatised and can be met with violence.

As counsellors we can at times be quite unconsciously judgemental of the way our clients present themselves. We may have unconscious rules about how someone must inhabit or perform their gender. Our clients will be navigating very complex cultural stories to try and show (or conceal) aspects of their gender identity. How these stories might fall on an individual will vary from person to person.

A butch lesbian might 100 per cent identify as a woman, wear entirely masculine-coded clothes from the men's section, but see this presentation as 'neutral'. A trans man might wear make-up and flowery prints and feel strongly that this is within the range of what a man should be allowed to wear. A non-binary person might wear dresses some days and trousers on others but consider themself to be neither male nor female all the time. Ultimately, clothes do not have a gender, they are only coded for gender. Some people will conform to those codes, some will challenge and play with them and some will ignore them.

It can be hard for us to take identities and experiences seriously, especially if they fall outside of our typical understanding of what it is to be a man or a woman. We might think clothes don't matter, but we are heavily programmed to judge people in all sorts of way based on what they wear. We might also have ideas about what clothing is 'appropriate' and 'professional' and this is likely to align with existing social hierarchies, so that, for instance, clothes from other cultures, clothes that are too feminine, clothes that do not conform to binary gender, clothes that are too 'young', are often seen as less appropriate and professional.

For some trans people, living their truth is vital to their wellbeing. For others, hiding some of the truth is vital to wellbeing. The discriminatory, ridiculing and violent behaviour of society towards trans people will obviously be a material consideration to be weighed against the inward suffering of stifling a trans identity. I talk about that kind of suffering – gender incongruence – in the next section.

GENDER INCONGRUENCE

Gender incongruence is the term now used in ICD-11 in place of gender dysphoria (World Health Organisation 2018). The experience of gender incongruence has also been removed from mental health into sexual health, reflecting research evidence that there is nothing inherently mentally ill about being trans (Robles *et al.* 2016). Many trans people will still use the term dysphoria, the opposite of euphoria, for unbearable feelings associated with being trans. Some of these feelings can be alleviated by social adjustments, and others are more medical and physical. It is important to note that neither of these experiences is more or less serious. The amount of incongruence experienced varies from person to person, from day to day.

While I will try to use the word incongruence throughout this book, this does not mean that I am underplaying the distress for some trans people surrounding those feelings of incongruence. However, as these feelings are so variable, we should not assume that well supported trans people with ready access to medical treatments *if* they need them will necessarily suffer, or that suffering is an essential ingredient of being trans.

Physical incongruence

Some people seem to be most interested in the process of trans people altering their bodies, although this is a very small part of trans existence. I will go into a little more detail later in the book, but for now, I want to just take a moment to reflect on the reasons we might modify our bodies, when this is seen as okay and when this is seen as 'outside of nature'. It is important to remember all medicine is outside of nature, in fact most of what we do is. For instance, when somebody types on their smartphone and sends a message over the internet that someone is 'unnatural', it is worth remembering that the internet and smartphones are also 'unnatural'.

The 20th century revolutionised our lives medically in many ways, and it opened up possibilities for some members of a pre-existing trans population to ease the distress their bodies caused them. Hormone Replacement Therapy (HRT) and trans-related surgery are the most obvious changes that medical advancement brought to trans people. In many cases, the treatment was life-saving, because gender incongruence drives many trans people to suicide. But we need to remember that trans people existed before this treatment was possible, and that although body modification has also occurred throughout history, it is not a surgical process that defines a person's identity.

Some trans people experience incongruence with their bodies that may have nothing to do with the social labels projected onto their physical selves. We cannot know what life would be like in a genderless society, but I suspect that physical incongruence can exist outside of social influence. However, the powerful social narratives projected onto bodies will naturally affect how people experience those bodies.

Physical incongruence is just one aspect of gender incongruence. It appears to be a way that the brain instinctively maps onto the body in atypical ways. There are things that should be there that are not; trans guys sometimes liken this to having a phantom limb. Or there are things there that should not be there, that the brain cannot make sense of. I have heard of cases of children as young as three trying to remove their body parts or asking when their penis will grow, as if they are instinctively anticipating a body different from their own.

Not all trans people experience physical incongruence, or experience it to the same degree, or about the same areas of their body. Some people who would not necessarily identify as trans experience intense physical incongruence. For instance, I know of women who wish to get breast cancer, so they can remove their breasts, but feel so strongly woman-identified it would feel like a sin for them to have chest reconstruction surgery for 'no reason'. I know of women who have taken testosterone to make themselves look more masculine, but do not identify as trans. *The Rocky Horror Picture Show* writer Richard O'Brien came out at the age of 67 about having taken female hormones, but still uses the same name and pronouns and has voiced strong opinions against trans women and lower surgery, although he does identify as third gender (Bellot 2016). People like this would be welcome under the trans umbrella but may or may not think of themselves that way.

As a side note, we need to separate feelings of incongruence from other reasons assigned female people might be uncomfortable with their breasts – related to the way they might be treated for having a bigger chest, or the way growing breasts restricted an active lifestyle in their teens. Misogyny and the objectification of breasts is going to play its part in any person with breasts' attitudes to their body, but equally misogyny may also become an excuse or cover for physical feelings of incongruence.

Physical gender incongruence is different from the dislike of being objectified or restricted by large breasts. It is the difference between wanting to hide breasts, or perhaps reduce them, and wanting them to not be there or indeed feeling strongly that they should not be there. Unless we have connected with a person who has this experience, it is easy to underestimate the power and intensity of it. For many, it is an intense sensation that can be both physically and emotionally painful.

For many, the feeling of incongruence with their body is so strong and so difficult to make sense of or act upon, it triggers dissociation. For this reason, incongruence can emerge when it seemed not to be there before. Anti-trans campaigners call this 'Rapid Onset Gender Dysphoria' (ROGD) but there is no such phenomenon listed in clinical research. The only evidence for ROGD has come from a poorly designed study (Littman 2018) that has been criticised by its own university (Brown University 2018), and by Serano, who points out the 'study of ROGD is entirely based on the opinions of parents who frequent the very same three blogs that invented and vociferously promote the concept of ROGD' (2018). It has now also been dismissed by the World Professional Association for Transgender Health (WPATH 2018). What there is, as with many difficult and traumatic life experiences, is suppression and dissociation up until a safe enough time comes to explore these feelings. The 'sudden' appearance of gender dysphoria might also be associated with a child having waited a long time to tell a parent they knew might be unsupportive.

We are likely to have some ideas about what surgery we think is acceptable and what surgery is unnecessary. I am guessing most of us accept cleft palate surgery as important, life-changing and acceptable. Reconstructive surgery after cancer or an accident probably also fall into the generally accepted category. While attitudes to 'cosmetic' surgery are changing, however, we might have less of a sympathetic view of it. Often, though, if we support someone through having cosmetic surgery, it transpires their reasons are important and meaningful. It has become an available means of reclaiming and owning our bodies.

I know I have had to work to change my views about body modification, from surgery to tattoos, and to move away from a puritanical view that people should simply accept what they have no matter what. It would have been in any case a hypocritical viewpoint from someone who had extensive dental work to straighten my wonky teeth and overcrowded mouth in my teens. From the self-harmer who covers his scars with tattoos to the child sexual abuse survivor who gets breast augmentation to feel more like a woman and less like a child, I have learned that there are profound reasons why people modify and reclaim their bodies.

Trans-related surgeries are not clinically considered cosmetic. Often, they are life-saving, as they substantially lower suicide risk (Bauer *et al.* 2015; Cornell University 2017). Even when not life-saving, the freedom they provide can significantly improve quality of life and mental health (Cornell University 2017). I liken a person experiencing gender incongruence to a computer with a program running in the background that takes up way too much memory. It slows down everything, and crashes what should be straightforward processes. Physical incongruence can interfere with a client taking care of their body, doing exercise, enjoying sex, dancing, eating and many other embodied pursuits, or for that matter being able to concentrate on or enjoy something that is not physical. Body modification that assists the client to feel more embodied and have more of a sense of ownership of that body can have major positive health benefits. In long-term studies, we learn that transition regrets are exceptionally low and satisfaction is high (McNeil *et al.* 2012; Wiepjes *et al,* 2018).

Trans-related surgery and HRT for those who require it is increasingly understood to be non-elective, non-cosmetic and as essential as any other healthcare procedure that significantly improves health, quality of life, and can save lives (Cornell University 2017; Endocrine Society 2017). But not all trans people experience physical incongruence, and the physical incongruence they do have can range in intensity or apply to different parts of themselves, including to parts for which there is no available surgery.

We tend to assume it will be genitals that cause the most concern, but I suspect there are as many different experiences as there are trans people. Discomfort and incongruence might be related to face shape, or voice, be around the testes/ovaries but not the actual genitals, might be around secondary sexual characteristics such as body hair, chest, hips, hairline, height, shoe size or fat distribution and muscle mass. Our job is to allow the client to explore their relationship with their body without judgement, and that means we must challenge any beliefs we may have about what they should, or should not, change.

There will be trans people who experience physical incongruence who for many reasons do not have surgery. Perhaps the incongruence is mild, and they are managing it. Maybe they have a health concern or disability that makes accessing surgery risky or impossible. Maybe they cannot break through the negative messages about trans-related surgery they have internalised. It could be that there is not a surgery available to address their specific incongruence, or that the surgery that would address it is not available through the NHS or health insurance, or they have no recourse to public funds and they cannot afford it.

Most importantly, but often forgotten, hormonal treatment (as well as hair removal treatment) effects far greater visible changes for many trans people than surgery, and therefore many trans people will only take hormones. A trans woman may become softer and curvier and grow breasts, and this might ease her incongruence sufficiently. A trans man may grow muscle, lose curves, grow more body and facial hair and develop male pattern balding. He may also get enough clitoral growth through testosterone to ease any lower incongruence. Trans men and other assigned female people are more likely to access chest reconstruction surgery than any other procedure, and many assigned female non-binary people opt for chest reconstruction without any other treatment.

While society focuses on our genitals, for many trans people what is in our pants is an irrelevance. However, some trans people do have severe 'lower dysphoria', or a clinically distressing sense of incongruence with their genitalia, or an aspect of their genitalia. For example, there are assigned female people out there who are comfortable with their breasts but in urgent need of lower surgery. There are assigned male people out there who do not care how society sees them but cannot live with the way their lower body is configured.

A personal example of this is that I have experienced quite significant gender incongruence specifically around having a womb, pregnancy and giving birth for as long as I can remember. Not all assigned female trans people have this, in fact I know trans men who have long since transitioned who have happily conceived and given birth. Having this highly specific form of incongruence is quite different from the need to have a penis or not have breasts, but it does not make me any more or less trans. It might, however, be quite difficult for a younger non-binary person to access medical treatment to alleviate this form of gender incongruence without having HRT and other lower surgery. For some, a hysterectomy is the lower surgery most needed and desirable.

It is highly important that we understand there is not a single trans healthcare pathway or trans experience, and that we allow our clients to get in touch with what they personally need to feel congruent with their body and identity. Some pathways may be available on the NHS, some may not, but it is also true that trans people are pushing back the boundaries of what is possible all the time. It is only in the past decade, for instance, that it has been possible for a non-binary person to access chest reconstruction without hormones. This development has meant that nobody is going through unnecessary medical changes to alleviate unrelated incongruence. Fifteen years ago, a person could not access top surgery without also taking hormones and planning to have lower surgery.

Social incongruence

Physical incongruence is not the only kind of incongruence, and social incongruence is much more of a constant in many trans people's day to day lives. Many trans people simply do not experience physical incongruence.

Social incongruence is what trans people experience due to being assigned into a social gender but not being oriented towards that gender. It is not related to our bodies, except in that it is our bodies that have led us to be socially categorised in a way we cannot live with.

Social incongruence is triggered every time you hear the wrong pronoun or get told 'you'll always be a man'. It happens when your voice on the phone causes the person on the other end to make assumptions about you, or not allow you past the banking security system because it does not fit their expectations of the name on your account. Unaddressed social incongruence can be every bit as excruciating and distressing as physical incongruence.

It is perfectly legitimate to want to physically change yourself to be more socially accepted, if the way you are being treated causes constant distress and discrimination. Unfortunately, it is much easier to change yourself than it is to change society. Society still cannot wrap its head around a man with a vagina or woman with a penis, and it is a reality that some trans-related surgery happens because of social incongruence rather than the trans individual's relationship with their own body. For many of us, these two things are so intertwined it is hard to pull them apart.

Therefore, it is important for us as counsellors to take a neutral stance towards surgery – unfortunately, transphobes tend to create a negative double-bind – they call surgery 'mutilation' but at the same time they demand that if trans people are to be accepted at all, we must have surgery before we get civil rights. For trans identities to be accepted, they must be accepted however we look, whatever we have done with our bodies. Currently, there is very much a push for trans people to conform themselves and their bodies to cis-normative standards.

Experience tells me that people who are unaware of the trans community generally believe that a trans person is just an ordinary person who goes through a surgical procedure to 'become' the opposite sex. They cannot separate our identities from the surgeries we may or may not have. This can be devastating for sick or disabled trans people, who may not be able to have surgery. Healthcare workers and carers have a particularly bad habit of treating people socially according to their genitals – and this can be humiliating for trans people who need intimate personal care.

Ultimately, social incongruence could potentially be alleviated by society accepting that we cannot gender someone according to how they appear, and that people's self-experience is more valid than our superficial appraisal. Counsellors can alleviate this incongruence by affirming our client's stated gender and clearing away our expectations and preconceptions about how they should appear, act, dress and be embodied.

Internal incongruence

The third type of incongruence, outside of how we feel about our bodies or how we are treated socially, is related to who we know ourselves to be, and our own internal relationship with gender. Sometimes, we may be fighting with learned behaviours and transprejudice we have internalised. If we expressed our trans identity from very young, it is likely it was belittled, dismissed or repackaged, and we will have internalised this negativity and misdirection. For example, a trans girl might have said she was a girl but had this repackaged as 'sissy'. This may have been accompanied with violent policing of her gender.

We will have also been bombarded with messages meant for our assigned gender, but may have more easily and instinctively internalising messages for our identified gender. When we unconsciously replicated socialisation meant for our identified gender, or stumbled over the rules meant for our own, this is likely to have been met with resistance, correction and gender policing.

Trans children have very different socialisation experiences to their cis peers, and this is often misunderstood. Some state inaccurately that assigned male trans kids were 'male socialised' and vice versa. When children instinctively replicate gender socialisation intended for them, they fit seamlessly into society, but children who transgress these rules often meet with abuse and violence, and at the very least a strong resistance to their self-expression.

For instance, as a child I instinctively was into whatever boys were into, or whatever was being marketed to boys. When I was given girly toys they internally felt incongruent and transgressive – it was not that I hated them, I just instinctively felt they were not for me. If boys had liked make-up, I would have felt okay to like make-up, but the female relatives who tried to force make-up on me and bully me for not wanting it were coercing me into feeling congruent with female socialised pastimes and I struggled with this.

I do not think, therefore, that my socialisation was anything like any cis child's, and arguably the childhood of the average trans woman transgressing male rules and internalising misogynistic messages about female inferiority is considerably harder.

We have our internal sense of who we are, and we have people around us eroding and attacking this, or even abusing us for it. We may have a stronger or weaker sense of self depending on how traumatic this has been, whether we dissociate from our experience, whether we had allies, support or affirmation, whether we were given words like trans or non-binary that validated our experience, or whether we were coerced into believing our experience was wrong, deluded, mad or bad.

When we come out, transition or articulate to a counsellor our true sense of self it will be constantly buffeted by internalised messages that are unlikely to be positive. Many trans people, in fact, deliberately seek out anti-trans literature to try and contain their identity or force themselves to stay cis. Some trans people, even in the act of coming out and researching their identity, stumble upon anti-trans sites that convince them their identity is anti-feminist or anti-God or anti-nature and that they must renounce it. Often, such people struggle against a trans identity for many years as a result, and the psychological consequences of this are profound.

It is not for anyone to decide when is the best, safest time for a person to reveal such a deep and personal truth about themself. However, we can categorically state that the abuse, negativity and conversion attempts aimed towards trans identities are deeply damaging of that self-actualisation process.

From this chapter forward, each chapter will contain a case study to draw out some themes and issues the chapter raises. All case studies are fictional, based on generalised composites from my broad experience of working with trans people clinically and organisationally.

CASE STUDY

JJ is a 35-year-old assigned female non-binary person who has come to therapy to explore whether to transition medically. After months of therapy, they remain undecided.

They have very strong, distressing and persistent physical incongruence, particularly regarding their face, voice, chest and hips, but they feel complete ambivalence about the clothes, roles and other social attributes of being a man, and feel frightened they might feel socially trapped in a binary identity by transitioning. They think of themself as an 'agender transsexual', in that they feel they wish to change *sex*, but do not have a gender.

Their mood seems to be dipping continuously and they express suicidal thoughts. They tell you that they are struggling to feel supported at their local support group because it is mainly 'binary' people who don't like the way they dress or identify.

How can a counsellor help JJ? First, we need to fully accept JJ's self-description and experience. That means accepting they feel physically male, but are not a man, and that distinction is meaningful to them even if it would not work for everyone and might be very unhelpful and even triggering for others. Their self-description of being 'transsexual but agender' is an idiosyncratic use of language, but it tells us a lot about the gap between their embodied and social experience. This is not an uncommon experience. If we project other trans narratives onto JJ, as the local group has done, we are in danger of erasing their authentic experience. Why should we doubt them just because this is not the dominant trans narrative, where social and physical incongruence neatly align?

Support from other humans is likely to be vital for JJ. They are only going to feel supported when their authentic self-experience is validated. Getting the hang of they/them/their/themself pronouns is crucial; using them in notes and supervision as well as with JJ face to face. Slip-ups of using gendered language should be quickly apologised for. Has JJ explored any more non-binary friendly spaces? They may benefit from support online or off, and a bit of research may be in order. Trans spaces that do not support non-binary identity will not be helpful.

JJ may struggle to get treatment, particularly lower surgery, as an openly non-binary person. However, this is beginning to change, and increasingly non-binary people are getting the treatment they need. Often people like JJ go through medical transition presenting as a trans man, and then live as agender. This may be one source of fear – being put into a box by clinicians and having to enact a role that may cause social incongruence in order to alleviate the physical incongruence. It is up to JJ whether to take the risk of being fully understood by clinicians. JJ may feel there are very few spaces where they will be fully 'seen'. No wonder they are in despair!

Although we may know that on paper transition is generally beneficial and life-enhancing for those who want it, we need to sit with JJ's indecision – they may take a long time to decide. There may be trauma and transprejudice that are also getting in the way of them deciding. Being affirmative of trans identities and signalling your acceptance of who JJ is *whatever* they decide to do may help alleviate prior negativity from others. Being knowledgeable enough to challenge any transprejudiced ideas JJ may have introjected is also crucial.

Suicidal thoughts are so common in trans people they can almost be expected. Sometimes, they represent the impossibility of returning to an old life, and the terror of pushing forward. Having someone there to say it is going to be okay and you are still a valid human is crucial. JJ may have heard nothing but extreme negativity both about trans people and non-binary people. 'I identify as an attack helicopter' is a regular dismissal of non-binary identities; hearing this can be a weekly occurrence. The support of other non-binary people and bibliotherapy of good non-binary sources can be a remedy to this.

The counsellor needs to both be able to sit with suicidal thoughts and explorations, but also be tuned into a change in risk. Finding trans-friendly mental health support is another challenge; we do not want a mental health service to make JJ feel worse, as sadly many do, due to lack of training and a history of the pathologisation of trans identity.

JJ's misery may seem to conflict with the idea that transition makes things better, but it is useful to think of being *in transition* as a struggle. The weight of cissexism, transprejudice, and all the rules of gender JJ has introjected cannot be shaken off easily. We as counsellors need to boldly and confidently abet this shaking off so JJ can live as closely to being authentic as possible. Yes, they will have to make compromises in a world that does not accept non-binary identities, but we do not need to tell JJ that, they will already know.

CONCLUSION

It is hard in just one chapter to give a full taste of the huge diversity of our community. I hope the take-home message is that, given the complexity of our internal, social and physical experiences with gender, there will naturally be as many different gender configurations as there are human beings. As Bellot (2016) says, 'Is it so hard to understand that my map of my mind, in terms of gender, was simply drawn differently from yours, that what is cognitive dissonance for you is the simplest of body-music for me?'

For some of us, our bodies are the most important thing about us, whether we feel congruence with them or not. But others find their bodily configurations take backstage in their self-experience, and social aspects of identity figure larger, or their own internal sense of who they are. Many if not most of us will have a combination of physical, social and internal incongruence.

If we can move away from a sense of what is normal and acceptable and what is not, towards a sense that there are rarer and more common experiences, but that they are all normal, okay and acceptable, then that will be an achievement. But such a shift takes a lot of work, as much for trans people as it does for anyone else.

PERSONAL REFLECTION

Once again, please record your answers to the following questions in a journal.

1. What has this chapter brought up for you? Please notice any areas of discomfort, resistance. What challenged you? Name the things that still feel difficult or unresolved for you.

2. What questions do you still have? Write them down.
3. One of the greatest stigmas in society is around men transgressing masculinity. Think of how film and the media portray femininity in men and crossdressing, and what messages are given out. Notice over the next few weeks whenever you see a man or boy doing something female-coded in the media or real life – is this person respected? Laughed at? Sexualised? Think about how these attitudes feed into attitudes to trans people.
4. Watch what happens when women or girls transgress – do something masculine-coded or fail to do something that is expected of women. Are the rules the same for all women and girls or do they change across geography, class, race, age or other differences?
5. What are the stories you have heard/seen about trans people? Do they reflect the diversity of the community? Which stories are missing? What is emphasised? From now on, take note of the way in which trans people are portrayed, and the stories that are told about them.

Chapter 3

IS IT THE RIGHT THING TO TRANSITION?

I want to start by talking about the opposite of gender dysphoria: Gender euphoria. As hard as it is to be trans, the exhilarating feeling of *rightness* we can get when our gender feels better aligned is an enormous compensation. Think of the 'aaaaah' feeling we get when we slip out of an uncomfortable pair of shoes, get into a warm bath when we ache, finally get to the toilet when we are busting, and then magnify it by several factors.

Is gender euphoria just the absence of gender dysphoria? I do not know, but probably not. I imagine that cis people also sometimes revel in their own bodies or feel a surge of warmth when their identities are affirmed, it is just less noticeable when there is not the backdrop of negative and incongruent feelings.

For every trans person, there will be a set of things that align with their sense of self and a set of things that undermine their sense of self. These can be internal ideas and attitudes, our relationship with our body, the way we express ourselves and the way others relate to us. Sometimes, these things can be very straightforward, such as the consistent sense that a body part should not be there and that the brain does not map onto it, so it feels alien. Many people report waking up from chest reconstruction surgery with a sense of deep euphoria that cannot entirely be explained by the pain medication. Being able to swim in just a pair of shorts like any other guy can be a euphoric feeling for trans men. A trans woman might feel that same sense of straightforward rightness of her brain mapping properly onto her body when her breasts begin to grow on HRT.

But gender euphoria does not always neatly align to the binary. A self-identified cis woman might be happy being called a woman and use she/her pronouns, but simply cannot bear gendered titles (e.g. Miss, Ms, Mrs) and switch to using the gender-neutral title 'Mx'. The discovery of the option 'Mx' might bring peace and rightness, where no other gender incongruence exists.

This is, of course, a transition, and this person would be welcome under the trans umbrella, because she cannot bear one of society's gendered impositions. At the same time, she would not necessarily feel she had significant enough issues around her gender to claim the title 'trans'. Most inclusive trans communities reject the idea that someone must be 'trans enough' as if there is a scale of transness. We allow people to self-select whether they need community support. Feeling that you cannot bear a way in which society genders you to the extent you need to change it to a less socially accepted and established title that is more meaningful to you is a gender transition. Attempting to require gender neutral language from others is no easy task.

I will use myself as an example of the complexity of dysphoria/ euphoria. As a non-binary trans person, I require gender neutral language, but I rarely receive it – people find it impossible not to gender me one way or another, and at the current stage of transition I tend to get an even mixture of 'he' and 'she'. And for me, and for some other non-binary trans people, a balance in this constant misgendering alleviates it and neutralises it to some extent.

I find now I can bear 'he' and even 'she' is less painful to my ears but when people who know me call me 'they' I experience gender euphoria. For me, this is a sense of relationship with that other person that goes much deeper. This person *sees* me. They understand the importance of calling me by gender neutral pronouns. When someone calls me he or she, their preconceptions about me or their social training around gender are superseding my own self-experience. As it happens over and over, this can be dispiriting, undermining and ultimately damaging.

As a counsellor and trauma therapist with a background working with abuse survivors, I have looked at the specific impacts on non-binary mental health of being constantly misgendered. I use the term *gaslighting* to describe its impact. For those unfamiliar with it, the term derives from a play in which an abusive husband undermines his wife's mental health by claiming she is hallucinating when he dims the lights (Cukor 1944).

'You are not experiencing what you believe you are experiencing' is at the heart of the manipulation that underlies gaslighting. The more people you can co-opt into casting doubt on the person's experience, the less certain they will feel, and the more they will begin to feel unbalanced.

This is key to understanding much of the mental health impact on trans people. It may be slightly worse for non-binary people, who are likely to be misgendered more, even in trans spaces, but it is a phenomenon that affects all trans people. In the press and online it is still perfectly acceptable for people to say that trans people are insane, that their self-experience is wrong, and that 'we know better'. The people who say this generally have no real connection to trans experiences and fail to empathise with what it is like to be trans.

Because language is all socially constructed, everyone will have their own subjective experience of the language that others use to describe them. Sometimes it will seem accurate, and other times wide of the mark. Language is relational – we use it to communicate with one another, to deepen our understanding – but it is also cultural, in that different languages will encode certain values and assumptions, making it harder to move outside of them. Some languages, for instance, do not have gendered pronouns or the gendering of language in the same way we do. In those languages, it would not feel like an almost insurmountable task to speak about a person gender neutrally, and this will inevitably change how people think about gender and the social acceptability of gender shifts.

Despite my own need for gender neutrality, I found it hard to train my brain to use singular *they/them/their/themself* pronouns after a lifetime of being trained not to. It has taken hard work and practice to change this, but that work was important to do. Even though I know how much it matters not to label people without their consent, I continue to label people, and keep apologising for doing so. A sincere apology and moving on quickly are so important when this happens. Acknowledging the error is essential, and challenging each other – our supervisees, our friends – when they misgender someone is also essential.

Misgendering is often entrenched within social cultures where it happens freely behind a person's back, and nobody challenges it. Because language is so socially encoded, it can quickly become the norm to only indulge a trans person to their face. Demonstrating disrespect for their identity behind their back through unapologetic misgendering signals that not accepting trans identities is a kind of social correctness.

For us as professionals, how we gender our trans clients to our supervisors, our trans colleagues to other colleagues, our trans students in the staff room, is as telling of our attitudes as how we treat them to their face.

TRANSITION GOALS

I hope that it is beginning to emerge that a lot of the problematic experiences for trans people are relational, and so our transitions are in many ways relational too, and our surrounding culture to a greater or lesser extent dictates what is possible. It is impossible to separate how we feel about our bodies from the social labels and cultural expectations that get applied to them. Although we can sometimes be hell-bent on demonstrating transness is in part biological, that is quite dismissive of the cultural impact of gender. Money is a social construct, and yet it rules our lives. Borders to countries are social constructs too, but that does not make them 'not real'.

Travelling from England to France before and after Brexit, for instance, will be a different experience, even though the border between England and France is a social construct. People can *die* crossing borders. The rules and boundaries and legal paraphernalia we draw up around gender have a consequence for trans people, even though these rules may differ from culture to culture, or over time.

A good way of understanding this is to watch the film *I Want What I Want* (Dexter 1972). In 1972, trans people had no legal protection, and there was little social acceptance. At that time, transition would only be permitted for trans people who would not be visibly trans, and who would be heterosexual after transition. Quality of life was dependent on 'blending in' with cis women. There was no concept of it being okay to be visibly a trans person, whereas in other cultures being visibly gender divergent has had a position, a name, a social and even a spiritual role in many places and times.

In the UK or USA in 1972, a trans woman who would not 'blend' would not have access to medical transition, and if she did find the means to transition she would have faced prejudice and violence.

> Back then, surgical candidates were encouraged to not associate with other people in the trans community because the whole goal of surgery was to be able to assimilate into the gendered world. So those of us who had been able to get surgery were supposed to be able to live and function in non-trans circles and worlds and not have people know. (Joanne Keatley, quoted in Michaelson 2015)

Things are better now, but not that much better. Non-blending trans women still bear the brunt of societal prejudice and violence. Blending is still a preoccupation, and an unwritten social expectation for trans people. How well they will blend is still an issue that many trans people wrestle with in deciding whether to transition, and much as we might not want it to be so, blending in or not blending will have a material impact on the person's level of acceptance, safety and recognition as their gender. This will also impact their employability, their access to services and many other factors.

Some people refer to 'blending in' as 'passing', but there are reasons why that is not a helpful term. The term 'passing' comes from the black community, and it is short for 'passing as white' – it means literally being read as something you are not. A trans woman read as a woman is not passing as something she is not, she is being recognised for who she is. It is more accurate to say that before she transitioned, she may have been passing as a man.

It is also worth remembering that trans people often *do not* pass prior to transition, that their difference and their transness are often quite noticeable, and impossible to hide. As Joanne Keatley says, 'even without my having to claim an identity, people were already imposing a more feminine identity on me because of my behaviour, my speech, the way that I looked—all of it' (Michaelson 2015). 'I have lived as both a man and a woman while at the same time never being accepted *wholly* as either', is how Juno Dawson puts it (2017, p.22).

Many trans people prior to transition do not pass for cis. I know assigned female people who are consistently read as male, for instance, without any hormonal transition. If they dress in feminine ways, they are read as trans women. Leslie Feinberg talks about wearing a wig and earrings because, prior to transition, zie could not get a job with hir usual presentation (zie/hir were Leslie's preferred, gender neutral pronouns). The disguise did not work: 'The more I tried to wear clothing or styles appropriate for women, the more people believed

I was a man trying to pass as a woman. I began to understand that I couldn't concealed my gender expression' (Feinberg 1996, p.12).

Masculine-looking assigned female people also get a lot of assumptions made about them. It is assumed they will only be attracted to women; it is assumed they will wear more masculine-coded clothes. 'You look like you're wearing drag' is an accusation I have heard more than once levelled at a masculine-looking woman who has chosen to wear something feminine. Of the masculine-looking assigned female people I have encountered, some are trans, some are cis; some are lesbians, some bi, some straight. There may be an overlap between masculine features and being LGBT+ but we cannot tell a person's gender or sexuality by looking at them. People's experiences are heterogenous and do not align neatly to one narrative based on how their facial features formed, although how we are read by others does have an impact on how we experience our gender.

Sometimes people who blend and do not reveal their trans history are treated as if they are engaged in a deception. The idea that 'it is better to be open and honest' is a commonly held idea. I remember a lesbian supervisor I had years ago telling me that sometimes she chose not to come out, because: 'If I came out the person's prejudices about lesbians would be a barrier to our relationship, not help it.' In other words, being open is only as useful as the other person's ability to genuinely understand our difference. Telling the truth when the truth is stigmatised risks the person knowing us *less well* because of their own prejudices and biases.

If a person believes that trans women are women and that's that, revealing a trans history might enhance that person's understanding, but sadly many people still overly project maleness, male socialisation and masculinity onto trans women. Knowledge that a woman has a trans history might become a barrier to her being seen and understood for who she is. I know of many cases where trans women have been valued and celebrated until their history was revealed, at which point attitudes towards them have completely changed, and characteristics seen as positive before were now seen as negative.

Trans feminist writer Julia Serano has this to say about the double standard with which trans women are treated:

> When you're a trans woman, you are made to walk this very fine line, where if you act feminine you are accused of being a parody, but if you

> act masculine, it is seen as a sign of your true male identity. And if you act sweet and demure, you're accused of reinforcing patriarchal ideals of female passivity, but if you stand up for your own rights and make your voice heard, then you are dismissed as wielding male privilege and entitlement. (Serano 2013, p.28)

If a person is unable to see us clearly and without prejudice, what responsibility do we have to reveal ourselves to them? And how safe would it be to do so? Having said that, if we do not reveal ourselves and then we are outed, that is also a risk.

The social experience of a trans person who blends is going to be very different, before and after transition, to that of a trans person who does not. For the person who blends, difficulties and bullying may have been greater prior to transition, for the person who does not, and who managed to pass for cis prior to transition, more difficulties may lay in the future. This will vastly depend on where they live, how old they are, what job they do, whether they are white, family acceptance/non-acceptance and all the other factors that determine how accepting people around them are going to be.

WORKING WITH FEAR AND LOSS IN TRANSITION

There will be trans people who decide not to fully transition because they are fearful of how they will be treated. Some things that influence that are: societal attitudes towards trans people; how visible they are as trans people; how available the specific kind of medical treatment/social transition they need is. Sometimes these fears are overblown, but often they are realistic, or even optimistic, and it can be hard as a counsellor to be both affirmative of transition but also fully holding and accepting of trans people's very real fears.

I personally only decided to transition when I thought I would be able to retain my career whilst doing so. This was considerably harder to do than anticipated. I encountered frequent acts of discrimination and general unaware attitudes that made it difficult to apply for jobs or exist within organisations. Fortunately, I had the wherewithal to go self-employed as a counsellor, supervisor and trainer. I do not regret taking the steps I did, but it is important to understand that transition can come with an enormous amount of loss and challenge. And this was for a middle-aged, middle-class, white, assigned female professional.

My own transition woes, including the moment someone spat in my face in the street, are small beer compared to others.

As a counsellor, holding the possibility that my clients may be putting themselves in the way of abuse and trauma yet still be doing the right thing is tricky, not least because we can never know what is in store for them. Most trans people fear coming out as trans, but the responses they get can be enormously varied, from out and out rejection to overwhelming acceptance, or even 'well, duh, I already knew'.

Knowing the complex mix of trauma, loss, discovery and euphoria clients are in for can feel both wonderful and challenging when working with someone around transition. As a therapist, my neutrality around my client's choices is essential, but that does not mean that I will remain neutral in the face of negative conditions of worth around being trans. It is up to the client how they proceed, but I am 100 per cent affirmative of being trans and everything that goes with being trans, and that is important in anyone supporting trans people. I am not going to just neutrally reflect my client saying 'maybe my dad's right, and I am just a deluded girl', but I will remain as still as possible when my client is fighting with himself over whether it is safe to tell dad he is trans.

Counsellors can often be quite mistaken about how other people will react – either be naïve about how unaccepting some folks can be or project their own fears and assume that loved ones will be upset when in fact they will be supportive and loving. The client is likely to know best how they will react, but even they may be surprised. Even when family and partners seem accepting, they are the most likely people to throw up obstacles for the client.

Part of being affirmative is to be appropriately celebratory and congratulatory about steps our clients are making, but it is also important to understand that even with a transition that is wanted and going well, there will be loss. Clients may deal with grief over many things, over friends and family lost along the way, over health changes relating to treatment, over loss of fertility if they are unable to afford gamete storage, and over the way the world is relating to them differently.

Just as someone who leaves a marriage may not feel entitled to grieve for it, so trans people may feel they have invested so much in telling the world transition will be good for them, they cannot have any difficult feelings about it. Of course, this suppression can exaggerate difficult feelings.

Stifled feelings of loss, grief and anger need to be given space and permission in the therapy room. The reality is, for many trans people, transition is a demanding, exhausting and stressful time. NHS waiting lists, which are currently about two years long just to be seen by a clinician, can add to this stress, and trans people's mental health can break down for all sorts of reasons during the transition process. While it is statistically highly probable that in time the person will be happier post- than pre-transition (Cornell University 2017; McNeil *et al.* 2012), the process itself can take an enormous toll for some, and this naturally varies according to the person's finances and support network, as well as how treatment progresses.

Adapting to the way the world treats trans people, becoming aware of the scale of transprejudice in the media, on the street and online, and having our eyes opened to the inequalities and differing expectations between men and women are just some of the issues trans people face, alongside navigating possible medical and surgical impacts.

Trans women may find themselves suddenly being listened to less and not taken seriously, as they lose the privilege of being read as male (assuming they ever were read completely as male, which is often not the case as previously stated). Trans guys report being suddenly worried about smiling at women or looking at children, because it might be read differently from a man than a woman. For all trans people, coming out can cause a loss of status, although trans men can sometimes regain this status eventually if they are read as cis men. Scientist Ben Barres tells us: 'By far, the main difference I have noticed is that people who don't know I am transgender treat me with much more respect... I can even complete a whole sentence without being interrupted by a man' (Vedantum 2006). After he underwent gender reassignment aged 42, another scientist who was unaware of it was heard to say, 'Ben Barres gave a great seminar today, but then his work is much better than his sister's' (Vedantum 2006).

Trans guys often get read as younger than they are, and this can bring frustration. Early in transition, I was on the way to a funeral and so wearing a suit and tie. Due to my fibromyalgia, when I got to the bus stop I sat down in pain. Despite plenty of seats, a man was standing there on crutches. As I sat down he started to have a go at me. 'Tired, are you?' he shouted and, 'need a rest, do you?' I was confused, until it became clear he thought I was a young man, rather than a 45-year-old assigned female person, and then I got it. Because he was not allowing himself to sit down, he was attacking me for sitting, and possibly for the pained look on my face. It was my first taste of how men police the masculinity of other men, especially younger ones.

But trans women often have by far the more difficult time during transition. Prior to transition, trans women are still absorbing sexist messages due to the way they are oriented, and they are more likely than cis men to be aware of sexism. However, being visible as a trans woman can lead to verbal abuse and sexual harassment they may not have experienced before, or not to the same extent. The caveat of this is that there is evidence that trans women are victimised much more than cis men even prior to transition and are vulnerable to sexual abuse as children at a higher rate even than cis women (Cook-Daniels 2015; Scottish Trans 2010). This is likely to be due to the fact socially marginalised children are easier to groom and isolate and therefore more easily preyed upon, alongside the misogyny-rooted abuse that is directed at assigned male people who express feminine-coded behaviours. I explore prejudices that arise from these statistics, such as 'sexual abuse makes you trans' in Chapter 8.

In general, trans people tend to be infantilised, and for non-binary people this is even more common. We are viewed as exclusively young, new and 'trendy', and often attract the pejorative label 'special snowflake', an indication that we are identifying in this way for attention, because it is 'cool' or the new thing. There is a sliver of truth in that, because I know I would not have come out as non-binary had there not been an increasing acceptance of this identity. People like Leslie Feinberg and Kate Bornstein fought for non-binary recognition back in the 1990s, and folk like CN Lester are taking up that fight today. We now have the emergence of a visible community and language to articulate our experiences, but as yet no legal recognition.

In other words, acceptance and visibility do indeed change what is possible, and more people will live openly as trans or non-binary in an accepting (or more accepting) society. I did not jump on a trans bandwagon, but I did make a choice to be more open about who I am at a time when that felt more possible. And even so, transitioning brought considerable loss – of status, privilege, financial security, career opportunities, friendships, family relationships. And it was still worth it, because I would much rather be rejected for who I am than accepted for who I am not.

DETRANSITION

There is an anxiety at the heart of every exploration of transition; what if I make the wrong decision? This is something that faces us all, at any fork in the road, but because trans identities are constantly doubted and delegitimised, it is extra hard to feel certain about making any transition-related change. Coming out to family; coming out at work; changing name, title, pronouns; getting a referral to the gender clinic; deciding whether to take hormones; have upper surgery or lower surgery: at each stage, no matter how unbearable the distress and incongruence related to keeping things the same, there is doubt.

I am about to let the reader into a big secret, which I trust will be treated respectfully: Trans people are rarely *completely* certain of anything. Often unsure of quite how our identities are configured, seldom 100 per cent sure of the treatment we are about to embark on. But often we dare not tell anyone. It is hard to admit at times, or even regularly, we wonder if the transphobes are right; we fear what we are embarking on; we worry if it will undermine our identities even more than they are already undermined. We might also be scared that our uncertainty makes us 'less trans' than other trans people who seem more certain.

> We've been conditioned not to express doubt. It's true of American society as a whole, but it's especially true for trans people. Too often when we let ourselves become vulnerable by sharing how we really feel, our doubt is weaponized and used to hurt us. (Roman 2018)

Anti-trans campaigners groom vulnerable young trans people, trying to convince them being trans is wrong and 'show them a better way'. As I research this book, I find that for every trans-related issue I research on Google, the first few hits are anti-trans campaigners presenting false 'evidence'. For a while, many trans people are won over. They are held up as proof that being trans can be overcome, much like the 'ex gay' Christian movement in the USA. I have worked with survivors of this grooming and tried to help them overcome the self-hate that it engenders. I cannot sufficiently overstate the emotionally abusive tactics used by some anti-trans campaigners, or the psychological harm they inflict on trans people.

Conversion therapy, that is attempts to 'cure' people of being trans, has now been banned by all the major psychological bodies in the

UK (COSRT 2017). Anybody working with trans people, or their partners, relatives and friends, needs to be absolutely clear both that there is a more than sufficient body of evidence to prove that trans experiences are real, not a sign of mental illness (Endocrine Society 2017; Robles *et al.* 2016; World Health Organisation 2018) and that transition is beneficial for those that want it (Cornell University 2017; McNeil *et al.* 2012). If we still have doubts about the genuineness of trans experiences, then how is a fearful trans person, indoctrinated by the anti-trans myths they read everywhere and the anti-trans attitudes that are still so prevalent, going to be enabled to connect to their authentic experience? Trans as much as cis counsellors may still be beset by doubt, and this needs to be worked through.

Detransition is held up as the bogeyman, is held against trans people. Our transitions must be sure, and certain, and final, otherwise they are not legitimate. But of course, real life is much messier. As a therapist, a big part of my job is to be able to stay with client's uncertainty and hold quite opposing desires and needs.

Trans people detransition. And retransition. And alter trajectory. And change their names and pronouns more than once. All this is entirely valid. We can know that transition benefits the people who undertake it, but we can never know if transition is right for us, or the person in front of us. We cannot cure someone of being trans, but what they do about being trans is up to them. However, society will have a heavy bias towards 'gender transition is bad', so we should probably worry less about a trans person being unduly influenced into transition, and more about all the trans people being unduly influenced to *not* transition.

Unfortunately, there seems to be a disproportionate level of concern around trans people making the wrong choice *towards* transition, perhaps because there are still underlying social attitudes that it is never the right choice. The extent to which trans people are subject to gatekeeping, having their decisions questioned, or having barriers placed in their way, is quite extreme.

There are many things we can do with our bodies – start smoking or drug-taking, have unprotected sex, get a full body tattoo, take up base jumping or horse riding – that may put us at risk or change us forever, without any outside interference. But even the smallest aspect of gender transition (e.g. changing our name) is seen as far more extreme than any of these things. This is particularly the case with children, who are often barred from exploring being trans, even in terms of impermanent changes such as names, pronouns and clothing. The underlying anxieties appear to be: 'what if the person changes their mind?' and 'what if we make it *too easy* to be trans?' The anxiety related to the latter is that people who are not trans will dip their toe into trans waters and somehow be lured in.

The reality is, if a cis person tries to be trans, they will experience much the same gender incongruence as trans people do, and they will change back, having learned something about themself. I think it would be amazing if lots of little boys had tried being a girl for a bit to see what that is like, or vice versa, but it is highly unlikely they would stick with it for any length of time. There is no evidence to suggest that trying out being trans might somehow convert or alter a cis person. But might 'slightly trans' people be lured deeper into the trans web by too much acceptance? I'll explore that in a bit, but it is important at this point to have a think about whether even when we are trans accepting, we have a default assumption that trans people should only transition *if they really must*.

Let us look at some of the reasons detransition happens, because we need to be as accepting of detransition as we are of transition. I would assert, though, that it is effectively impossible to 'detransition', because that implies the person goes into reverse, and in fact we never can return to the start of a journey unchanged, but only move forward somewhere new or return to where we were with a very different outlook. Nevertheless, detransition is a word that gets used, and we need to look at possible reasons it might apply or be applied.

Non-binary transitions

Non-binary transitions are often recorded as a detransition, particularly by clinics. There was a time when it was only possible to be treated for gender incongruence if you presented in a binary way, and equally there was a time when non-binary people were not really accepted within the trans community. This meant that there was less of a chance for a non-binary person who knew they were trans and had physical incongruence to identify themself as non-binary or to be open about it.

This still happens to a certain extent, but it is getting easier now for non-binary people.

A non-binary person might go through a medical transition process that was needed, but socially not identify in a binary way. After a more binary transition, many trans people undergo a further social transition to live in a non-binary identity. This can sometimes include returning to accept a name and pronouns associated with their assigned gender. The key here is they are not experiencing incongruence from the medical procedures they underwent, and do not seek reconstructive surgery, and therefore they have not truly detransitioned.

I have encountered, for example, women who experienced severe incongruence with their breasts, presented as trans until they were able to have chest reconstruction surgery, and afterwards claim not to be trans, but do not seek to reconstruct their breasts. I would suggest that in fact they alleviated their physical incongruence sufficiently through surgery, and that following this, it was socially easier to present as a cis person, or they simply had no social incongruence, only physical.

Others have taken testosterone, either prescribed or self-medicated, until their face has masculinised, and voice lowered. They have been happy with the changes, but do not desire to take things further. This is a transition, and just because they live as a woman, that does not change this fact. For a certain age group especially, it should also be noted that it is easier to live, work and date as an apparently cis person. Transgender pioneer Leslie Feinberg says: 'Shaping my body was something I had long wanted to do and I've never had any regrets. But I started taking hormones in order to pass' (1996, pp.12–13). Zie later revealed 'I long to live openly and proudly as a transgendered [sic] person – not as a man' (1996, p.15).

Some trans people are *genderfluid*. This means their gender has changed over time. For some, this can be day to day, for others over months, weeks, years. We do not know why this happens but given the complexity of influences on our genders it is not perhaps surprising that people's genders can change and are not always a fixed entity from birth to death. This means that a transition that is right for someone at one point in their life may need some alteration later. This does not negate the prior transition. However, for people who know they are genderfluid, there is sometimes a preference for less permanent alterations, though genderfluid people may also require medical intervention.

Lack of safety and support

It is tough out there and some trans people detransition for safety or due to lack of support. Where I live, I know there are places within an hour of me that are unsafe for trans women to walk down the street. Not everybody is able to simply move. Poorer people face obstacles to changing housing area, and unfortunately, trans people in the UK and elsewhere are much more likely than cis people to be on a low income (Grant *et al.* 2011, p.2; Totaljobs 2016, p.9) or homeless (Stonewall 2018a, p.6). Homeless trans people might temporarily detransition to be safer on the streets or in shelters. If you are homeless, you also may not have access to the grooming processes that would enable you to present as trans. If you have no money, a razor is a luxury, for instance. In the USA, there are people detransitioning because of the Trump election, fearing being visibly trans (Riedel, 2016). For black and minority ethnic trans people, safety issues are compounded by racism (Choudrey 2016, pp.7–8; Grant *et al.* 2011, p.2).

Some people detransition to try and save a relationship or protect their family. If you do not want to leave your whole life, but people where you live are putting dog muck through your letterbox and calling you a pervert or harassing your family because you are trans (this actually happens), transition may feel impossible. There are many trans people who have reversed their transition due to unsupportive family members, awaiting a time when transition would be easier, or sometimes living a double life. 'I did not detransition because I wasn't trans. I detransitioned because cisgender people physically and mentally beat me down until I gave in' (Kanner 2018).

Not having transitioned or having detransitioned does not necessarily mean the person's concept of their own gender identity has changed. For example, there are many trans women out there who still live mainly as men for safety or acceptance. Relatives in particular can put a lot of pressure on a trans person to not transition, or to detransition.

Temporary detransitions

A trans person may also detransition temporarily. They might come off hormones to conceive a child, for instance. While HRT can affect fertility and clients wanting children should explore this risk before starting, it is possible for some people to conceive or produce viable sperm once the body's natal hormones have reasserted themselves. Other reasons for temporary detransition might be social or for safety, to visit relatives they have not come out to, or to travel on a pre-transition passport.

Permanent or long-term detransitions

While some permanent detransitions can be traced to lack of support, safety or options, a small minority of people find after transitioning that it is just not right for them, and they are not happy, e.g. on hormones, or living as a different gender. Upon detransitioning, they find they are happier. This group of people is very small and should never be exploited to delegitimise the trans community as a whole. Some detransitioners are supportive of other trans people, but others feel their individual experience should be a warning to everyone not to transition.

We can only say that transition is right for most people who want it, and that there are very few regrets (Wiepjes *et al.* 2018). Even when it comes to trans children, notions of larger numbers of 'desisters' have now been laid to rest, and it is understood we can trust children's self-understanding (Temple Newhook *et al.* 2018), that trans children's gender identity is as stable as cis children's (Olson *et al.* 2015) and that for trans children who take puberty blockers and go on to transition, their 'well-being was comparable to same-age peers' (de Vries *et al.* 2014, p.1).

When we take Bauer *et al.*'s (2015) research showing that social support and access to transition were key factors in improving trans mental health, we can feel confident that supporting trans people, including children, to identify themselves and have access to treatments that only they ask for is the best course of action. Equally, we should support detransition as fully as we support transition, and trust that clients know what is right for them, whatever the reasons. Even when social stigma and violence or family attitudes are a reason for detransition, we need to remember that as we cannot change the world, the client has the right to adjust in whatever way they need to survive.

Families

A final note on families of trans people. As Bauer *et al.* (2015) demonstrated, family support is a significant factor in the wellbeing of trans people. The major US survey report *Injustice at Every Turn* tells us 57 per cent experienced 'significant family rejection' due to being trans and this substantially impacted on the likelihood of them being homeless, suicidal, misusing substances, smoking and other welfare issues (Grant *et al.* 2011, p.7). UK's Stonewall *Trans Report* shows that here trans people fear coming out, delay treatment because of family attitudes, and in some cases have completely unsupportive families or even experience abuse for being trans (2018a, p.14).

Individual families can surprise in either direction, but there remains a desperate social fear of having a trans child or being seen to have a trans child. Estrangement is very common for trans people. Family are generally the last to get on board with acceptance and correct names and pronouns. This inevitably will influence a trans person's trajectory.

McConnell, Birkett and Mustanski (2016) found that lack of family support had a significant impact even when other social and community support was readily available. The implication for us as counsellors working with family members is clear; trans-affirmative counselling is as important when we are working with cis people as with trans. If we can signal our acceptance of trans people, this can alleviate relatives' anxiety around being seen to be accepting of something that may be socially transgressive in their understanding.

We can also help them understand that their lack of support is damaging. I have encountered relatives outside the therapy room that were deliberately being hard on their trans relative because they did not want to 'make it too easy' and wanted to indicate how hard it was going to be to be trans. This is often done with the false understanding that trans is something a person 'does' rather than 'is' and that people can be talked out of being trans, or that their 'decision' to be trans was selfish. When I have helped relatives to understand how crucial support is for their trans relative's mental health, and that we cannot in fact stop someone being trans, only encourage them to be suppressed and miserable, things can turn around for the trans person, and for the family too. It cannot be nice for all concerned when a family are locked in a semi-abusive or even fully abusive pattern because somehow, they believe this is the morally correct course of action.

TRANSITION OPTIONS

It is hopefully clear by now that there are as many ways to transition as there are trans people. I just want to recap on *some* of the generalised ways in which people transition, as a reminder of the ways in which people can be trans. Not everyone will use the term 'trans', but I use it here to indicate those who are welcome under the trans umbrella if they wish to be there.

- Some trans people do not have medical interventions, but rather socially transition. This could be because of cost, health, or simply because there is no right treatment for their incongruence. It could also be because they 'blend' with others of their identified gender without any treatment.
- Some trans people decide not to transition at all. This could be for safety, because their gender is expressed and acknowledged in other ways, because of family, because their gender is fluid, or for other reasons.
- Some trans people present as different genders in different spaces. They may be bigender or genderfluid, they may be protecting family from their transness, they may feel they cannot continue their career openly trans. They may not be safe to be openly trans in some situations.
- Some trans people knew they were trans when they were three and some only realise they are trans later in life. This might be because their identity has changed over time, but it might also be because of dissociation, suppression of the identity, or it being masked by trauma. Some trans people's gender changes over time and some people's gender has remained static throughout their lives. Remembering that trans experiences are biopsychosocial, we cannot separate out the influences of nature and nurture.
- Some trans people only have social incongruence and are comfortable with their bodies. They may or may not medically

transition to alleviate their social incongruence, for instance if they have internalised the message 'you can never be a woman with a penis'. Some trans people experience physical incongruence but not social incongruence – they may socially transition to be eligible for medical treatment, then detransition afterwards. Most trans people experience a mixture of social and physical incongruence, as well as an internal experience of gender that is neither social nor physical and may have its own transition requirements.

- For some trans people their social incongruence does not match their physical incongruence – e.g. an assigned female person needing to be read as male-bodied but non-binary femme. There are also trans people who cannot separate their physical incongruence from their social incongruence.
- Naturally, some trans people do not neatly fit any of the narratives above or any other available narrative. There will also be people whose experiences overlap with some of the above but who would not consider themselves to be trans, who might be intersex, or have other terms for their experiences, particularly if raised in other cultures.

CASE STUDY

Pete is a 50-year-old trans man, who has been transitioning for three years and has been through HRT and chest reconstruction surgery. He wants to discuss whether to go through phalloplasty[1] and is weighing up the burden placed on his aging body of a complex series of surgeries, versus the distress he feels at the thought of other people not seeing him as 'complete' or 'a real man' if he does not have the surgery, and he does not consider the results of the more straightforward metoidioplasty[2] procedure would be right for him. 'If I'm going to do anything at all, it has to be phallo.'

1 Phalloplasty: construction of an average-sized penis using material taken from arm, thigh or stomach.

2 Metoidioplasty: construction of a small penis from the clitoris (after clitoral growth due to testosterone HRT).

He did have severe physical incongruence relating to chest and facial hair, which has now been alleviated. But he does not have physical incongruence related to his genitals and feels okay with his body as it is when he is alone. Having recently supported a dying friend who was in a care home, he is particularly preoccupied with how he might be treated if he is ever dependent on intimate personal care in the future. He believes he may be significantly less safe if he does not have the surgery.

Pete does not fit the standard trans narrative because he had strong physical incongruence but not related to his genitals. Some trans guys find lower incongruence makes itself much more apparent after having chest surgery. Others do not have lower incongruence at all. Some have it so strongly that is drowns out any other incongruence they might be feeling. Incongruence around hairline, face shape, hair, hips, bum, muscle strength, height, body fat distribution, skin softness and internal reproductive organs or menstruation are just as likely to trigger distressing incongruence as genitals. Even when genitals do come into it, there are many ways they can feel uncomfortable.

It is common to have an initial reaction that 'he must not have surgery!' when faced with people like Pete. We need to notice these reactions and ask if I have a hierarchy of what is and is not legitimate trans need. Do I minimise the impact of social incongruence compared to the traditional 'born in the wrong body' trope I am more familiar with? On the other hand, do I still harbour that penis=male bias that might be largely what is influencing Pete to go through very serious surgery?

Yes, Pete is grieving and may be carrying trauma around ageing, death and incapacity, and Pete may want to explore these. Nevertheless, putting Pete's thoughts about lower surgery down to grief is dismissive. Is Pete wrong to believe he may be mistreated if he ever needs care in the future and is not seen by others as really a man? Witten and Whittle present the case of James, an older trans man who has not had lower surgery and is housed in a home for women, and his identity disregarded, much to his distress (2004, p.513).

Unfortunately, I can attest this is not as unusual as it should be. Though trans people's identities theoretically have protection under the Equality Act 2010 whether they have had lower surgery or not, the public by and large are unaware of this and treat trans people according to their genitals, calling a trans man 'she' if they discover he has not had surgery. Will things be better when Pete is older? Only time will tell. Given the cyclical nature of history, they could be worse.

What Pete needs from a counsellor is neutrality in the face of what choice he should make, and an affirmative attitude to either choice. The counsellor needs to be affirming of his gender whether he has surgery or not and affirming of his right to have surgery – his body, his choice.

CONCLUSION

Transition can mean many things. Hopefully, we are moving away from an idea that a trans person is a regular person who suddenly decides to 'turn themself into' someone else via a medical process. This is the myth, but the fact of transition is much more complicated than that. Transition is a process of making oneself more congruent or comfortable with self and others. It can be as simple as changing clothes, or it can be a long and protracted surgical process.

Life is full of transitions, and the usual human processes that go alongside transitions apply here too, as well as experiences that are specific to trans people. The main difference is that many of the changes trans people make are viewed as transgressions, and it is useful to reflect on what is and what is not seen as transgressive, and why.

When Margaret Thatcher transitioned her speaking voice to a more male register to be listened to by the men of the House of Commons, she was not scrutinised in the same way a trans man would be – her voice was mainly praised (Hill 2013). When the gender non-conforming singer Prince changed his name to a symbol that incorporated the male and female gender symbols, he was not labelled 'trans', but the ridicule and scrutiny the change elicited reflects the way trans people's changes can be perceived (Lussenhop 2016). The direction of travel must also be noted – becoming more masculine is always favoured over perceived femininity.

A person can change their 'look' if their look remains cis/heteronormative but changes that cross gender lines or go outside of other social norms are often remarked on and seen as less authentic or more *performative*. Judith Butler (1988) introduced the idea that we *all* perform our gender, but cis people's gender performing is often seen as more 'natural', even though it is just as copied and culturally invented.

Cis men and women will undergo all kinds of gender transitions in their lives. A cis man might bulk up in the gym or wear plaid shirts to communicate 'manliness'. Another may grow his hair out or wear 'guyliner' to indicate being 'in touch with his feminine side'. A cis woman might get a makeover or a new wardrobe that makes her feel sexy, another might see her bright dresses and lipstick as a kind of 'armour'. One woman might wear masculine-coded clothes to turn away the male gaze. Those same clothes may make another woman feel attractive and desirable to any or just one gender.

But Thatcher illustrates the complexity of our ideas about gender. She succeeded by making changes to herself to fit in with masculinity, but sometimes at the price of not being perceived as a 'real woman'. In some ways this was to her advantage, in that she was perceived as an exception that could achieve what other women could not, of having 'transcended' womanhood. In other ways she was accused of being a traitor to her sex by lacking the 'softer' qualities we like to associate with women. Either way, this is illustrative of the ways in which we socially perceive women, and how we have two (at least) different stories playing about what makes a 'real woman'. In one story, it is all about biology, but in the other, there are a fixed set of gendered behaviours and ideals that must not be transgressed. Both the binary biological ideals of womanhood and the gender roles and qualities expected of women are problematic in the way they exclude much of humanity.

Ideas of what it takes to be a 'real man' and how easily a person falls short of this are also important to take notice of. Transgressing the idea of being a 'real man' can be done all too easily – by not eating meat and dairy (see the insult 'soyboy'), dancing, wearing a flowery shirt, drinking a soft drink at the pub, working as a nurse or with children.

Given how tricky it can be for cis people to live up to the ideals of being a 'real' man or woman, the obvious panic that sits at the back of most trans people's heads is 'nothing will ever make me real enough in other people's eyes'.

So why bother? Why go through the pain and stigma of transition? Well, the answer is, some trans people never do. I know several people who are women in their hearts but living as men, and men who are living as women. For some, the decision to transition never occurs to them and this can often be influenced by whether they have seen positive representations of trans people. It is hard to feel resonance with a negative portrayal of trans people, but positive stories will often bring other trans people out of the woodwork.

A trans-affirmative approach makes being trans possible, but it does not make people trans. The fear of being trans-affirmative is related to the idea that trans people ought not to come out unless they absolutely must, that trans feelings are better suppressed and it is cis people's job to assist this suppression. But the rates of trans suicides discussed elsewhere belie this. If so many trans people have attempted suicide, then we are forced to assume that many trans people complete suicide as an alternative to coming out. Bauer *et al.* (2015) reinforce the fact that the damage to trans mental health can only be alleviated by allowing transition (where it is wanted) rather than blocking it, as I explore further in the next chapter.

PERSONAL REFLECTION

Once again, please record your answers to the following questions in a journal.

1. What has this chapter brought up for you? Please notice any areas of discomfort or resistance. What challenged you? Name the things that still feel difficult or unresolved for you.
2. What questions do you still have? Write them down.
3. Think about the ways in which you yourself have made changes to your appearance, behaviour or other aspects of your life that relate to gender. Was it accepted or rejected by others? In what ways did it help your path in life and why?
4. In what ways do you conform, or not conform, with the gender you were assigned into or the gender you identify as? Have you experienced praise or resistance from others for these attributes?

5. Think about the big transitions in your life and the toll they took on your mental energy, whether positive or negative – going away to study, changing career, leaving a bad relationship, moving to a new town. How long did it take to settle into your new life and find your feet? Was there a period of grief, even though it was the right decision? Did you ever doubt or question whether you were doing the right thing?

Chapter 4

TRANSITIONING AND ITS IMPACTS

Transitioning, as we saw in the previous chapter, can mean many things. For trans people, even the smallest changes can have an emotional impact. 'Do I make the change and not tell people why I am making it?' is a question sometimes asked by a non-binary person as they change their name to something more gender-neutral. 'I've decided Sam suits me better' would certainly have been an easier conversation to have than 'I identify as a non-binary trans person', but it would have revealed less about me as a person.

There is often a dilemma between the psychological tension of concealing and the danger of being visible. Each trans person decides for themself what course is best amid a plethora of non-ideal options. The ideal would be that being trans is perfectly accepted, an identity is completely respected, and changes, whether medical or social, are affirmed but not insisted upon. We are not there yet.

I hope, though, we are past the point where trans people only transition if they could not have continued as they were without killing themselves. We are at the point where there is the potential not just to be alive, but to have a better life. But it needs to be understood that transition is a difficult and psychologically demanding process, and trans people will often have periods of low mood and doubt. It is in fact rare for a trans person not to express doubt and fear at times, particularly prior to hormones or surgery. We may know from multiple studies that the outcomes for trans people who transition are largely beneficial (Cornell University 2017), but what if we are the exception?

With what feels like the whole world poised to leap on any sign of uncertainty or distress as proof that we are making a terrible mistake, it can be hard for trans people sometimes to own up to just how hard transitioning is. In this chapter, I briefly outline the types of transition and some of the hurdles that come alongside. For a fuller account of trans people's medical transitions, I recommend Ben Vincent's book *Transgender Health* (2018).

SOCIALLY TRANSITIONING AND CHANGING RECORDS

Legal sex turns out to be a much more complicated entity than people imagine. A person may decide to transition their social identity at any time, and this is a largely self-determined process. Many gender clinics like to see that a client has socially transitioned prior to referral, and it can speed up the process. However, some trans people wait until treatment has effected physical change prior to social transition, as Caitlyn Jenner did, or even wait until medical transition is complete. Many different factors contribute to this, and it is an individual decision.

The World Professional Association for Transgender Health (WPATH) *Standards of Care* recommend 'Real Life Experience' living in role for one year prior to lower surgery, although some UK gender clinics still ask for real life experience prior to hormonal treatment (Pearce 2018, p.226; Vincent 2018, p.31). This requirement is controversial, as it relies on stereotypes of what it means to 'live as' a man or woman (Vincent 2018, p.31). There is also a double standard – trans women tend to be uncomfortably hyper-visible and trans men invisible. For non-binary people real life experience presents further challenges – lack of appropriate gender-neutral clothes and facilities, for example.

It is important that counsellors have no expectations or judgements of how clients present themselves. Therapy is a place where we should be able to be ourselves, unfiltered. Trans people do not need to be living 'in role' before a clinic referral, and they should not have to conform to standards of what a trans man or woman wears or does, even though they might choose to present more stereotypically in certain situations, such as when accessing healthcare or work. NHS clinics may want proof of social transition before initiating treatment. Private patients do not need to socially transition prior to treatment and may wait until they are more comfortable with their appearance.

Some trans people cannot wait to socially transition and are happy to do so without a physical transition in sight. Many trans people only socially transition. There are different factors in this: the person's natural appearance; the environment they are in; the acceptance of people around them; and the nature and/or severity of their incongruence. For some, being 'out' as themself is a matter of survival – one second longer in hiding could have led to a breakdown or even suicide. For others, there is no such distress but being out brings profound peace and joy.

In the UK, a person can change their name by deed poll at any time, and there are sites on the internet that can do this for free for UK nationals over 16. Titles like Mr/Ms have no legal significance, nevertheless trans people find putting a change of title on the deed poll alongside a change of name can help smooth the way through the ensuing bureaucracy. Many institutions are now also accepting the gender-neutral title of Mx. A deed poll is all that is necessary to change name with DVLA, council, utilities and most systems. Banks also will accept a deed poll, but it tends to help if other systems are already changed and supporting evidence can be shown.

Medical records can also be changed, but it is less straightforward. However, a patient can request that their gender marker be changed from male to female, and vice versa, or even removed completely. This necessitates getting a new NHS number. It also means there will not be automatic reminders for some sex-based health screenings – a hormonally transitioned trans woman, for instance, will need prostate checks and mammograms, but will not be reminded of the need to check her prostate, and may receive reminders for a smear test she does not require.

For registry documents, such as death, marriage and birth certificates, a gender recognition certificate (GRC) is needed. There is currently no option to certify non-binary identities. For taxation and benefits services, an individual can change name and title but without a GRC their old name and gender marker remain on file. They can be added to a special category to maintain their privacy from day to day employees, but this can cause a certain amount of hassle. For a passport, the gender marker can be changed to an M or F based on a letter from a doctor confirming this is a permanent change. Again, there is no option to remove the gender marker or have an X, as they do in some other countries.

Many trans people do not get a gender recognition certificate, because it is an expensive and onerous process. Trans people have the right to use the facilities of their identified gender, such as toilets and changing rooms, under the Equality Act 2010, and this has nothing to do with whether they have their gender legally recognised. Exceptions under the Equality Act are for single-sex accommodations where excluding trans people would be a 'proportionate means to achieve a legitimate aim' (2010, p.150) – this means prisons and single-sex services can exclude some trans people, although it is rare now for domestic violence and sexual assault services to still exclude trans women given that they are a group at greater need of these services (Scottish Trans 2010; Stonewall 2018b). Prisons rarely allow a trans woman into a woman's prison without a GRC, and this puts trans women at high risk in men's prisons (Burns 2018).

GENDER IDENTITY CLINIC REFERRALS

In the UK, a Gender Identity Clinic (GIC) can offer support, services and advice to any trans person with recourse to UK public funds, although generally people do not refer to a clinic unless they are considering some sort of medical change. Waiting lists are currently exceptionally long, at least two years for an initial appointment at the time of writing. Many trans people wait to ask for a referral until they are certain about what they want to do. With waiting lists so high, this is not a sensible option, as two years of waiting for something you are sure of can be absolutely excruciating.

If a client is considering medical transition, it does no harm for them to get on the waiting list straight away and use the waiting time to consider their options. In England and Scotland, doctors should make a referral directly to a gender clinic for anyone over 17 who asks. If a GP resists this, sometimes it is helpful for patients to go armed with a copy of the General Medical Council guidelines for GPs (2018), or even a letter from their counsellor supporting the referral.

Gender Identity Clinics are conservative about allowing people to transition, but some GPs and other professionals imagine that anyone referred to a clinic will be propelled towards a medical transition. They can take it upon themselves to get in the way of a referral or try to assess the patient despite not having experience to do so. For young people or Welsh patients, who must be referred to psychological services first, the danger is that ill-informed psychologists will want to decide for themselves whether the client is or is not transgender, rather than referring them immediately on to the professionals best placed to make that decision. Sometimes they also want to address other issues prior to referral, rather than alongside a referral. This delays a long process even further.

Gender Identity Clinics are not perfect, but there are no legitimate concerns about them being too quick to allow anyone to transition. The opposite is the case, and academics like Ruth Pearce (2018) and Ben Vincent (2018) are advising that we need to move over to an informed consent model. Vincent suggests that this would empower trans people to be responsible for their own healthcare decision and that nobody else can be held responsible if they later experience regrets (2018, p.190). There is a parallel here with us as counsellors; we need not to be invested in, or have an opinion of, what our clients should do about their trans feelings. While we are affirmative of trans identities *and* healthcare, we need to learn to shy away from feelings about what our clients should or should not do.

Currently, a diagnosis of gender dysphoria is required for the NHS to provide trans-related healthcare, but with the ICD-11 removing gender dysphoria as a diagnosis (World Health Organisation 2018), we may be moving away from a model of compulsory psychological assessment for trans people, and towards a model where psychological assistance is only provided to those who require it.

Because of the gatekeeping nature of the current system, there are genuine barriers to trans people being honest with the psychologists who assess them (Pearce 2018, pp.140–142). Mental health issues can slow down a person's transition, even if it is the wait for change that is exacerbating those mental health issues. For this reason, it is unreasonable to expect that Gender Identity Clinics have much of a role in supporting client's mental health, particularly as they will be having few and infrequent appointments. Because clinicians are not held accountable for psychological damage or suicide caused by delays to treatment, this can lead them to always err on the side of *not* treating. In my experience, delays can be a considerable cause of psychological injury.

As counsellors we have a duty to be quite neutral in the face of this. We cannot encourage our clients to lie or withhold information from our fellow professionals, but equally it might go against our duty of care to our clients to tell them it will benefit them to be open and honest. The answer, then, is to trust our clients' judgement, and to trust the judgement of the other trans people they consult about this, which is generally nuanced and non-directive.

Because the waiting list for the gender clinic is so long, many trans people look at alternatives. Going private and obtaining medication off prescription are two of the alternatives available. Private health care for hormones is within the means of many people, and it is sometimes helpful to point this out to clients if they are not coping with waiting and especially if they are considering self-medication.

People living in the UK but with no recourse to public funds are in the same position as people in the USA and many other countries of having to go private. Equally, many trans people cannot bear the wait for surgery, and some desired surgeries (such as facial feminisation surgery) are not available on the NHS. If they have health insurance, they may be able to get treatment, but this is still uncertain with many providers. Otherwise, many trans people will turn to crowdfunding or other ways of obtaining the large amounts of money required for trans-related surgeries. For chest surgeries, the cost is over £6000, for lower surgery tens of thousands of pounds. Some trans people will go to other countries for cheaper surgeries, and this is often safe and successful, but it is important that they have properly thought through the necessary after-care.

ASSIGNED FEMALE TRANSITIONS

Many, but not all, assigned female trans people consider taking testosterone. Ordinarily testosterone is taken on its own but sometimes a blocker is prescribed to block the female hormones, for instance if periods have not stopped. For many trans men periods can trigger distress and stopping them can be a priority.

Because testosterone is used by bodybuilders it is a banned substance and therefore self-medication off prescription is illegal and risky. Much of the black-market testosterone is counterfeit. Without proper blood monitoring there is also a risk of liver damage. It is perfectly legitimate to remind clients of these risks if they are not aware of them, but we still must stick to the position of *their body, their rules*. We can trust our trans clients to be weighing the risks of self-medicating against the risks of what will happen if they don't. There are guidelines for doctors supporting the prescription of bridging hormones where there is a risk of harm through self-medication, but many GPs are reluctant to do this (Pearce 2018, p.74). Private prescriptions of hormones are also relatively affordable and accessible, and often a good GP will agree to 'shared care' in which the NHS monitors bloods while the private GP prescribes hormones.

The kinds of incongruence that testosterone potentially alleviates are many. Face shape, voice, fat distribution and muscle mass change similarly to a cisgender boy's puberty. If the person is under 25, foot length and height may also change. For many the clitoral growth that occurs on testosterone can alleviate feelings of incongruence around the lack of a penis, although it is also possible for these feelings to increase or at least make their presence felt when other feelings of incongruence are alleviated.

It is not possible to pick and choose what changes you get on testosterone. A massive increase in body hair is a usual side effect that for many is unwanted. The body hair tends to appear on legs and belly long before face and chest and this can be frustrating. Head hair loss is also a side effect of testosterone. For non-binary people this can be a concern as hairiness and hair loss is a distinctly masculine rather than neutral feature. Some non-binary people will take a reduced testosterone dose or only take testosterone until desired changes occur.

Some testosterone changes are reversible, such as fat distribution and skin softness, but many are not. Thus, taking testosterone and then coming off it can sometimes achieve a certain amount of androgyny. Some trans men have also, after a long time being on testosterone, come off it again to have a child and successfully conceived. However, hormones can affect fertility and younger trans people will be expected to consider this, and the storage of gametes (currently not available on the NHS for trans patients), if they want to have children in the future.

The speed at which changes occur on testosterone is entirely down to genetics. It is likely to take about seven years for full masculine maturity. Sometimes an oestrogen blocker is also prescribed in the early days of taking testosterone.

The usual course of treatment for a trans man is hormones followed by top surgery, then lower surgery if desired. Trans men who have problems binding their breasts have been known to ask for top surgery prior to hormones although the results are better if hormones are taken first. Many people desire top surgery and no other treatment. This is now possible on the NHS under some non-binary friendly clinicians.

Many assigned female trans people who have chest incongruence will attempt to bind their breasts. There are various chest binders available online. There are also many risks associated with chest binding. The most severe risks are associated with using bandages, which is an unsafe practice that can lead to injury. However, many people bind their breasts for too long or too tightly and this can restrict breathing and even damage the rib cage, as well as causing heat exhaustion during hot weather. Binding also damages the breast tissue and this can impact later surgery. However, this is not to suggest we should discourage clients from binding, but it is entirely appropriate to talk through safe binding and make sure they have accessed up-to-date advice about this (Vincent 2018, pp.9–10; Ira 2017). There will be some assigned female trans people who develop little or no breast tissue, either naturally or because they were able to take puberty blockers, and will have no need of top surgery.

There are various forms of lower surgery including a straightforward hysterectomy and oophorectomy, sometimes including closure of the vagina. Metoidioplasty is another option, which uses the enlarged clitoris to create a small penis, urethral lengthening if wanted, and insertion of prosthetic testes. Some will go for a more simple 'clitoral release' that simply frees the clitoris from surrounding tissue, thus lengthening it. Phalloplasty is a more expensive and challenging procedure. Phalloplasty uses tissue from the forearm, belly or thigh to construct an average sized penis, along with urethral lengthening and the insertion of testes and a device to help create a simulated erection. It is a series of at least three operations and is quite liable to complications and risk (Vincent 2018, pp.184–186).

Many trans men do not have any lower surgery, and some non-binary people do. There is not a neat formulation for who will want this. Each person will weigh up factors such as the toll it will take on their body, other health issues and time off needed against the amount of and type of physical or social incongruence they are experiencing.

The complications of surgery and the amount of surgery required are one way in which some trans men are at a disadvantage compared to trans women, but the necessity for surgery will be hugely variable from person to person. The amount of time off can impact on health and career and when things go wrong can have a considerable impact on mental health.

ASSIGNED MALE TRANS PEOPLE

Assigned male people who have been through puberty often have the disadvantage of some irreversible changes such as height, foot size, voice depth, hair loss and thickness of body hair and facial hair. Hormones for trans women can still make some significant changes such as breast growth and fat distribution. Skin becomes softer, the face rounder and the body curvier, and there is a certain amount of body hair reduction for some.

For trans women there are far fewer risks regarding hormones, however the dosage is much more variable, thus requiring someone to oversee the dose to achieve the best effects. Most trans women will be prescribed androgen blockers and oestrogen. These hormones are not banned substances off prescription and neither are they likely to cause long-term damage, so the risks of self-medicating are lower than for those taking testosterone. However, getting the right prescription is quite individual and can have a big impact on successful outcomes, so self-medication without any monitoring is still inadvisable (Vincent 2018, pp.152–160).

For many trans women voice training and facial hair removal achieve the greatest impact in terms of transition. These are both available on the NHS but to a limited degree. Some trans women will need breast augmentation, but this is not available on the NHS. Neither, as mentioned before, are the various types of facial feminisation surgery. Vocal cord surgery and tracheal shave are other non-NHS procedures some trans women opt for. Assigned male people might also 'tuck', meaning conceal their genitalia using tape or special underwear. Prolonged tucking carries risks to fertility due to heat, and infection risk due to warmth and moisture from sweat, so it should not be done continually (Vincent 2018, pp.169–170, 177–181).

Some but not all trans women and assigned male non-binary people require lower surgery. There are various possibilities. Removal of the testes is the most straightforward procedure. Many trans women will request the construction of a neo-vagina from the penis. If this option is taken the vagina will need to be dilated for the rest of her life. Not all trans women desire to have a vagina. There will be some who will keep everything and others who will have penis and testes removed but not have a vagina constructed. Many factors will play a part in this decision, from the ease with which they will fit dilation into an ongoing schedule, to cost, if they are not able to get NHS treatment or cannot cope with the wait. It should also be noted that fertility and the ability to get an erection are lowered or eradicated when a trans woman has a typical female hormonal profile (Vincent 2018. pp.182–184).

ATTITUDES TO BODY MODIFICATION

The counsellor's attitudes towards body modification are crucial here and need to be explored. Undesirable attitudes come in two varieties. Some consider trans people to be incomplete without lower surgery and have a fundamentally reductive belief of gender, that penis=male. A challenge to this view as I suggested previously is to reflect on whether a cisgender man who loses his penis or testicles, for example to cancer, immediately becomes a woman. Obviously, the idea that penis=male is biologically simplistic, even ignoring the complications of social gender and gender identity.

Others have the opposite view, that all body modification is undesirable, and that people should love their bodies the way they are. No amount of developing self-love is going to alleviate gender incongruence. However, being affirmed in their gender without the need of surgery might just save somebody from having surgery to alleviate social incongruence. Nevertheless, it is normal and usual for some trans people to use medical treatment to alleviate social incongruence and this is not a lesser kind of incongruence than physical incongruence.

INTERSEX PEOPLE

Some intersex people have found it hard to access gender identity services due to pre-existing intersex conditions. It cannot be assumed that the pathway will be straightforward if someone has an intersex condition, particularly if they have had prior medical treatment.

Having an intersex condition does not make somebody non-binary or necessarily put them outside of the social binary of gender. Many intersex people are comfortable with the gender they were assigned into by their parents and doctors when they were children, or that society assumes them to be.

However, proportionately more intersex people than non-intersex people do experience incongruence with the binary gender they found themselves socially placed into (Reiner 2005). Whether these people consider themselves to be trans or not is complicated and variable, as there is sometimes friction between the trans and intersex communities, and a person assigned 'sex indeterminate' at birth might insist their current gender identity is congruent with their assignment at birth, making them technically cisgender. This, by the way, is why I talk about the binary gender people were assigned into, rather than 'sex assigned at birth', because not everyone is assigned into a binary gender when they are born, and 'gender' denotes the social apparatus that is imposed upon us, rather than a simple appraisal of our biology, particularly true for intersex people. But intersex people who go through gender transition certainly experience many similar things to trans people, with the addition of often having to undo surgical or hormonal treatment that was administered in their childhood or youth without their meaningful consent.

Many intersex people wanting to transition will therefore seek out the support of intersex-aware trans spaces. It is also common for people to discover they are intersex only when they embark on gender transition. It is common, for instance, for assigned male people to discover they have PAIS (partial androgen insensitivity syndrome), where they do not respond typically to testosterone, or KS (Klinefelter's syndrome), where they have XXY chromosomes and can have certain feminised traits, including symptoms that echo the sideeffects of menstruation.

PCOS (polycystic ovarian syndrome) is very common in people assigned female, and only sometimes described as an intersex condition. Some consequences of PCOS are hirsutism, higher levels of testosterone and hair loss. While most women with PCOS are entirely cisgender, PCOS is very common among trans men and non-binary people (Baba *et al.* 2006).

HORMONE MYTHS AND ISSUES

There are many myths about hormones, and trans people are not immune to these. Testosterone particularly gets a bad rap, and sometimes the stress of transition can bring out difficult behaviours that testosterone then excuses. For a comprehensive debunking of all the myths and bad science on testosterone, I thoroughly recommend

Dr Cordelia Fine's *Testosterone Rex* (2017). In it, Fine demonstrates that the evidence for aggression, including sexual aggression, risk taking and violence being caused by testosterone is more tenuous than we realise.

Many trans men report being calmer on testosterone. If they are experiencing mood swings, it may be more to do with hormonal fluctuations than testosterone itself. Highly sensitive or autistic people may struggle with hormone fluctuations. If they experienced PMT, they are likely to experience something similar towards the end of a testosterone shot and may find daily application of gel more stabilising than bi-weekly or twelve-weekly shots of the injected forms of testosterone.

Trans men do report finding it harder to cry on testosterone, and trans women find it easier on oestrogen, so I will not claim hormones have no effect, although these effects are reported rather than proven. Clearly, hormones have enormous physiological effects, but we need to take care about the sex stereotypes they engender and be wary of how known stereotypes will influence our own and our trans client's reading of their behaviours. Changes in libido are known about – testosterone is prescribed in lower doses to improve libido in cis women (Davis and Tran 2001). Trans women, despite libido decrease and loss of erection, often talk about significant improvement in their sexual experiences and sensations (Serano 2007, pp.69–71).

It should be clear by now how individual each of us is in response to our physical self as well as the gendered world. Trans people will take hormones for slightly different reasons, from experiencing incongruence with their natal hormones to desiring the effects hormones bring. Sometimes, it is an experience of taking cross-sex hormones for another reason that gives trans people clarity in their identity. Many trans people express a sense of 'rightness' about their new hormonal profile.

But for some, getting the hormonal profile right, fluctuating levels and atypical responses can be challenging and painful, while the changes can bring a mixed set of gains and losses. A non-binary assigned male person, for instance, might love their softer skin and shape but experience incongruence with their growing breasts, and the strength of these feelings will need to be weighed against each other. There are some trans people who come on and off hormones, either through genderfluidity or balancing conflicting needs.

TRANSGENDER YOUNG PEOPLE

The only treatment available to young people on the NHS is reversible puberty blockers, once puberty has begun. Cross-sex hormones are available from 16, surgery from 18. For trans children with strong physical incongruence, the development of secondary sexual characteristics in puberty can be torture, and those children can be at risk if not allowed to access treatment. Like adult gender care, the process of accessing care is extremely slow and conservative. Children in the UK are referred through CAMHS (Child and Adolescent Mental Health Services) and unfortunately many CAMHS practitioners will gatekeep their patients rather than referring them. 'Let's address your depression/autism/eating disorder before we refer you to the clinic' is a story I often hear, and it is unhelpful as these issues can be addressed alongside a clinic referral.

The false belief that pausing a young person's puberty will somehow stop them from learning to accept the changes often stems from a general disbelief in the reality of trans experiences, or a tendency to disregard adolescents' ability to make decisions for themselves. Most of the children treated in this way will have Gillick Competence – a legal ruling that allows adolescents over 13 to make their own decisions about things like abortion and contraception.

Puberty blockers are a reversible treatment also used for treating precocious puberty in cis children (Vincent 2018). This is when puberty starts much too young and it seems sensible to delay nature for a while. For trans young people, the clinicians use increased distress at puberty as a diagnostic criterion (Vincent 2018). This means adolescents with only social incongruence, or gender incongruence that is not triggered by secondary sexual characteristics are unlikely to be diagnosed or treated and will have to wait until they can access adult services. In my experience, many people who accessed gender services as children but did not transition will return to services again as adults.

One of the conflicts between trans and intersex people is over the treatment of children. Intersex people, aware of what has happened to them, fear children might be 'corrected' according to a parent's will. It is important to be aware that most parents are extremely resistant to their child being trans, and there is no issue, despite reports from anti-trans campaigners, that adults are 'transing' children. We absolutely cannot make a child trans any more than we can make them not trans through conversion therapy. However, there may be a risk that when a child says they are trans a parent might wish for the neatest possible trans outcome, for instance pushing them towards being male or female rather than non-binary.

Children need to be given room to explore their gender and given options. The current alarm around talking to children about trans issues for fear of putting ideas in their heads echoes a similar history around LGB issues, for instance where Section 28 stifled discussion of sexuality in schools (Ashenden and Braidwood 2018). With enough information, children can make sense of themselves, and ideally should be allowed to socially transition. Evidence suggests that trans (and cis) children generally understand their gender at a young age (Vanderburgh 2009; Olson *et al.* 2015).

CASE STUDY

Agan is a non-binary person who was assigned male. They experience severe incongruence with their hormones and gonads, but not their genitals. They are androgynous rather than femme, but their face structure is read male rather than androgynous. If they go on oestrogen, they will grow breasts, and they fear this will feel incongruent. If they take a hormone blocker without oestrogen, there are serious health complications.

Agan has very heavy body hair and this also triggers incongruence, but funding for hair removal is very limited on the NHS. They would like to be as 'ahormonal' (low in either testosterone or oestrogen) as possible, but it is difficult to get such non-standard treatment, and it would have health implications. Until they are on a successful hormone replacement treatment, their desired orchidectomy (removal of the testes) cannot happen. Facial feminisation surgery, another procedure that might help, is also not funded on the NHS. Agan is finding their current situation unbearable, where they are read simply as male with difficulty giving clues to the contrary without presenting overtly femme, which also causes incongruence. They are in despair that there is no clear pathway forward, and at times suicidal.

It is likely that any steps forward for Agan will be experimental, and contingent on a supportive medical practitioner. If Agan has not been referred to a gender clinic, they should be encouraged to do so. Given the waiting lists are two years at least, it is essential we don't consider a trans person needs to be certain of what they want to do before referral. They can refer on the basis they are trans and need to talk through options. Some (but not many) clinicians will have experience of non-binary, non-standard hormone treatments (Vincent 2018, pp.165–166). Agan is well advised to ask on forums which clinic doctors are good with this sort of thing and ask to see those doctors. They may also want to ask what other non-binary people have done.

However, Agan may decide there are no realistic options for them, or get through those two years of waiting and still be uncertain what to do. The distress they are feeling makes them a suicide risk if they do nothing, but they may feel any treatment is too experimental to attempt. They may also try various hormone regimens, either self-medicated or under a sympathetic endocrinologist, but not discover anything that suits them.

For the counsellor, our job is to believe that Agan wants and needs what they say they want and need, and to ensure they get appropriate support. We need to use Agan's non-binary pronouns consistently, and indicate that whatever they look like, their identity is valid. We need to be able to communicate a sense of valuing and prizing Agan's identity in its complexity. Those trans spaces that will respect Agan's pronouns and identity may also alleviate some distress.

More importantly, we need to be prepared to hold the distress. At times there is no workable solution or resolution, and yet Agan's experiences are as strong and as valid as any trans person's. The possibility that there are no answers, and that suicide is the only way to alleviate the distress is hardly an unreasonable feeling and cannot simply be dismissed. We need to be able to stay with that feeling without losing our own sense of hope for the discovery of a way forward. Although there are possible options for Agan if they talk to enough non-binary people and find the right gender doctor, Agan's presentation is one of the more complicated trans experiences and is exacerbated by the narrow treatment options available for non-binary people, and lack of non-binary civil rights.

CONCLUSION

Being trans is, as should be obvious by now, a multi-determined experience with a great diversity of ingredients. While all trans people share that sense of incongruence with a binary assigned gender, this picture can be made up of many different facets of gendered experience or embodiment. It is useful to know a little about what is possible for trans people, but it is equally important not to assume anything about what a trans person will need.

Some trans people agonise for years about even the slightest transition, doing everything by tiny increments. Others throw themselves in at the deep end. I trust that each process is right for the person having it, and that there is no right or wrong way to transition. Some transitions are linear, and some are all over the place, and that is how it needs to be for the individuals concerned.

PERSONAL REFLECTION

1. What has this chapter brought up for you? Please notice any areas of discomfort, resistance. What challenged you? Name the things that still feel difficult or unresolved for you.
2. Close your eyes and take a few breaths. What do you *feel* about all this? What is your body saying to you right now? Notice what comes up.
3. What questions do you still have? Write them down.
4. Think about the different ways society thinks about the medical treatment of trans and intersex children. What stories about gender do these contrasting approaches hold up?
5. Think about the potential changes a trans person may choose to make or not make and examine your own feelings about this. Do you think it is possible for a man to not have a penis,

or a woman to have one? Is it okay for men to wear make-up, for trans women to wear jeans and a T-shirt? How much do you expect trans people to perform their gender, and blend in? Or do you judge trans people for performing gender? Do you apply the same standards to cis people who perform/resist performing gender?

Chapter 5

DIVERGENT PEOPLE

A long time ago I mentioned to someone at an arts event that I was (at that time) a lesbian, and she responded, somewhat bizarrely, 'Oh? Do you have ME?' My bewildered face was her only answer. 'It's just every lesbian I meet seems to have ME', she added, rolling her eyes in obvious disapproval.

I did have ME, or at least that was what it was diagnosed as then. Now they tell me it is fibromyalgia, but it is clear they are just guessing. What I know is my body responds differently than average to things, even the weather. I am beginning to understand that lesbians having ME was one clue to a very interesting cluster phenomenon. In the trans community, ME and fibromyalgia are also very common. But it gets a little more complicated than that, as it always does.

Some of the people reading this will be already making psychosomatic assumptions about this incidence of ME and fibromyalgia in an obviously stressed and traumatised population. I have spent much of my life working on the assumption that my own physical symptoms were psychosomatic. We like to connect things together. Traits that are *divergent* must have causes, even though nobody seeks for causes of more normative traits.

It turns out a lot of physical issues – migraines, ME, fibromyalgia, IBS, sleep cycle problems, coincide with the LGBT+ population. All these are easily dismissed as psychosomatic, but provably physical conditions such as joint hypermobility (being 'double jointed'), postural orthostatic tachycardia syndrome (POTS), arachnodactyly ('spider fingers') and Ehlers Danlos syndrome (EDS), also coincide with this population group. In fact, many people diagnosed with fibromyalgia,

ME, or simply 'Medically Unexplained Symptoms' have turned out to have one of these syndromes.

It does not serve our clients if we collude with dismissive GPs in assuming for instance that our client's IBS is related to stress or unresolved anger, rather than a genuine physical symptom. Naturally, stress can aggravate any symptom, and as one GP once said to me, 'all illness is psychosomatic', but when we work with trans people, we need to be prepared for a lot of divergent traits and learn to challenge the assumptions we might make about them or causal links we might assume.

It turns out that when human beings are divergent in one way this increases the odds of them being divergent in another way. A number of divergent traits cluster together in the population – non-heterosexuality, left-handedness, joint hypermobility, genius, synaesthesia, ME/CFS/fibromyalgia, physical conditions like EDS and POTS, gender variance, certain facial features, dyslexia, ADHD, high sensitivity, autism, dyslexia, dyspraxia and other body and brain quirks (Baeza-Velasco *et al.* 2016; Crespi 2016; Dickerson 2016; Erickson-Schroth 2013; George and Stokes 2018; Polderman *et al.* 2014; Posserud *et al.* 2018; Skills for Action 2018; Van Der Miesen, Hurley and de Vries 2016).

Why does this happen? We do not know, and I recoil at the idea of anyone trying to discover the cause, because they might want to prevent divergent people from existing, and I believe divergence is important. Holistically speaking, even if some aspects of divergence can be difficult, I believe divergence overall benefits society.

What is important to me is to invite the reader to note their responses to each of these differences. We may not realise how we are harbouring inaccurate pet theories about many divergent traits, particularly when we see them occurring together and link them in our minds. I know I have spent a lot of time undoing my own assumptions and urges to link, for instance, transness and autism together.

WHAT ALAN TURING CAN STILL TEACH US

Alan Turing is my go-to guy for exploring responses to the various divergences in this population cluster. Alan Turing was the genius who cracked the enigma code during World War Two. Nobody, as far as I know, has coined the term 'genius disorder' or tried to 'solve the problem' of why some people's brains are 'abnormally' clever.

Turing was also left-handed, at a time when left-handedness was finally seen as just a part of natural human diversity, rather than the sinister mark of the devil it had been taken as in previous times (Anything Left-handed 2017). Scientists have not been preoccupied with the cause or the cure of left-handedness, and I do not imagine anyone is proposing that Turing used his left hand because his autism made it difficult to conform to right-handedness, even though more autistic people are left-handed than in the general population. Still, we imagine that people *just are* left-handed and do not consider causation, at least not in a problematising way.

Turing was, almost certainly, autistic, although undiagnosed (Hickling 2016). Attitudes towards autistic traits were, and remain, hostile. Autistic people process information and respond to it very differently from neurotypical people. Turing's difficulty with social relationships, or perhaps we should say others' difficulty with Turing, might have contributed to his downfall.

But the aspect of Turing that was most judged in him was his sexuality, and we see that very differently today. Turing was attracted to men, and ultimately arrested for a same-sex relationship (Hickling 2016). He saw no wrong in his actions, which proves he was wiser than the conventions of the time, that condemned him to a pernicious choice. Turing could go to jail or be 'treated' to cure his sexuality. The cure he opted for was called 'chemical castration'; he was treated with female-typical hormones to reduce his libido. His body began to feminise, and he could not bear it. It is likely that he experienced what trans people experience *before* taking hormones, his changing body may have given him a sense of gender incongruence. Turing ultimately took his own life (Broomfield 2016).

The course of attitudes towards same-sex attraction over the last century are mirrored in attitudes towards the trans community – from criminalisation and pathology to slow acceptance. There was a time that the psychologists tried to make something of the higher incidence of autism in the LGB population (George and Stokes 2018), and alas we are currently beset with much negative speculation about the coincidence of transness and autism. Chief of these is the popular notion that trans and autistic people do not know their own minds, that they are claiming to be trans because of a problem in perception due to autism. In one sweep, both trans and autistic people are thrown into suspicion.

AUTISM AS AN IDENTITY

The reason we say 'autistic people' not 'people with autism' is because autism is an identity aspect, not an accessory or worse, an illness. I am a trans person, an autistic person, a short person. I am not a person with transness, shortness, or autism. I may *have* a headache, but I *am* autistic.

The problem with so many issues co-occurring in the same population is that we do not knows where 'autism' ends and other issues begin. There are a cluster of neurodivergent traits – autism, ADHD, dyslexia, dyspraxia and others that have many overlaps. As an autistic person myself, I remain bewildered by the vast differences in perception of what autism is. The neurotypical experts who study autism seem to have hold of many radically differing ideas, and this gets worse when they try to link together different divergent traits under one cause (Milton 2014).

I only realised I was autistic when a friend of mine, a counsellor, was diagnosed. I had been so bombarded with the 'autistics lack empathy' myth that it never occurred to me that my deeply empathic self could be autistic. There are more myths about autistic people than truths. Many things seen as 'traits' are merely the habits and defences some autistic people develop to cope in a world that does not try to accommodate our divergence (Milton 2014).

The bias in autism studies has let down a lot of people who are not cisgender men (Andrews 2015; Begeer *et al.* 2009; Furfaro 2017; Lawson 2017). Autism appears to be much more common in trans people than cis (Glidden *et al.* 2015; Van Der Miesen *et al.* 2016; Dickerson 2016), but is also often undiagnosed in both assigned male and assigned female trans people. Typically (white) cis male presentation of autism is influenced by the socialisation experiences of autistic cis men. More marginalised people are much more likely to mask their autism symptoms or have them interpreted differently (Begeer *et al.* 2009; Westwood 2017). In other words, autism symptoms are less tolerated in people who are not white cis men. If screening processes in studies exclude anyone who displays a complicated profile, to get a 'clearer picture', this could add to the problem of how autism is conceptualised.

There was a point where autism in trans men was theorised as 'proof' of the association between autism and maleness (Subbaraman 2014), but that does not explain why so many trans women are also autistic.

Lists of autism traits still often include 'gender confusion', but gender diversity is neither a symptom of autism, nor is there a known causal link; they simply co-occur.

Speculating about causes

I have heard people theorise that autistic people are more immune to gender socialisation and therefore more likely to come out as trans. This certainly does not reflect my own experience of absorbing male socialisation quite easily and instinctively as a child. I was not at all immune to gendered messages, I was just orientated towards the wrong ones. Later, I learned to mask things so well, my queerness got masked along with everything else. I am not sure autism helped me out of the closet.

Some people are highly immune to gender socialisation messages or a sense of having a gender identity. These people are called *agender*, not autistic. Not all agender people are autistic and not all autistic people are immune to gendered socialisation or a sense of having a gender identity.

It is as inappropriate to imply gender non-conformity is caused by autism as it is to imply autism causes left-handedness. These phenomena co-occur, but that does not mean they are causally linked. It is important to notice the way we theorise and create associations as soon as we see divergent traits alongside each other.

One of the people who trained me in therapeutic work with children perpetuated a damaging myth about autism. This teacher was convinced that autism is caused by child abuse and is merely a trauma presentation that can be helped with therapy, rather than a genuine difference in neurology. This is a common notion in 'anti-diagnosis' circles. While it is true that neglect, as with the Romanian orphans, can cause 'autism-like' symptoms, they are not the same thing, and this is well established. Unlike autism, these autism-like symptoms quickly repair under favourable conditions (Rutter *et al.* 1999).

While pretending to be 'anti-diagnosis', this *was* a diagnosis. The notion that autistic traits are damage from trauma and not a part of natural human diversity is inherently judgemental. It implies that there is just one kind of 'natural' human and anything that deviates from this is problematic. Some naïve notions of the 'organismic self' can lead into a judgemental version of what a 'natural' human ought to be, and this can lead us into judgements we do not even know we are making.

What is particularly problematic in this viewpoint is the enduring notion that autism is damage to be fixed, rather than a different way of experiencing the world. Counsellors who promote the idea that it is not 'natural' to experience things in an autistic way are perpetuating the stigmatisation of a group of people who have always existed. The orientation towards curing autism is every bit as abhorrent as curing people of being gay or trans.

Myths about autism

Much of the 'pathology' associated with autism is down to neurotypical people's expectations. Lack of empathy, for instance, is not a symptom of autism. It is very common, as Dr Luke Beardon proposes, for neurotypicals to lack empathy for autistic people (2017). If, as Mary Gordon claims, empathy is 'caught, not taught' – then children who are not empathised with will not learn to empathise (Bennet 2015).

Milton (2014) challenges the common notion that autistic people 'lack sociality', while Jaswal and Akhtar (2018) add: 'We believe that some influential accounts of autism rest on a questionable assumption that many of its behavioural characteristics indicate a lack of social interest—an assumption that is flatly contradicted by the testimony of many autistic people themselves.' They go on to talk about the common behaviours of autism being misinterpreted by non-autistic observers (Jaswal and Akhtar 2018). Sasson *et al.* (2017) found that it is statistically probable that neurotypical people will make negative and superficial snap judgements of autistic people that lead to rejection; in other words the deficit in social interactions comes from the neurotypical person, not just from the autistic person.

Chown *et al.* (2017) discuss the problem of autistic people having been studied in a medicalised way by non-autistic researchers, and state 'there is little point in researching autism unless the forces creating and sustaining the barriers to autistic people living fulfilling lives are tackled' (p.729). Wheeler (2011) proposes that, based on evidence, autism be viewed as a social difference to be accepted, rather than as a medical problem to be fixed. Like trans people, we see that autistic people have improved mental health when they are socially accepted (Cage, Monaco and Newell 2018; Miltona and Sims 2016).

The experience of many if not most autistic people is of being told that everything they think, say or do is wrong, rather than just different.

If most people do not have a problem with scratchy clothes, for example, the autistic person who has a more intense sensory experience is simply told they are over-sensitive. I remember a client who could not bear to be in the same room as a ticking clock. Without any training to understand how differently people can experience sound, how could I not be puzzled or even judgemental about his experience?

I am not certain where autism ends, and other divergences begin. Autism is just a word for what is possibly in itself a cluster of traits. It is known to be a heterogenous and varied condition (Milton 2014; Wheeler 2011). There is also overlap with ADHD (Polderman *et al.* 2014), and again with ADHD there is a 'no labelling' approach in some counsellors that can cross a line into erasure. ADHD should not be pathologised, but that does not mean it does not exist, and is not common, once again, in the same cluster of the population. Intellectual disabilities, much like left-handedness, can also co-occur with autism (Posserud *et al.* 2018), where they used to be understood as part of autism.

Accommodating autism

At the trans support group I help facilitate, autism is so common we make allowances for it by default. This means that considering the sensory environment is essential – brightness of fluorescent lights, echoing carpet-less floors, everyone talking at once, can create significant access issues. We pay attention to making what is going to happen in the space explicit, rather than expecting people to infer this. There is a clear structure and ground rules and sensitive challenging if anyone goes off track.

When someone has difficulty turn-taking, or speaks too loudly or quietly, we set boundaries but don't problematise this. Talking too much or too loudly tends to correlate with other autistic traits, so we reject gendered assumptions about these behaviours. All too often trans women in other spaces find themselves labelled as 'masculine' based on their autism.

I have not seen a difference in the behaviours of autistic trans men and women. Although some people imply trans men have 'female socialised' autism, my experience is that we cannot make such neat gendered assumptions about autistic presentations or make a binary out of our complex socialisation experiences. As with other life experiences, the presentations of autistic trans people do not map neatly onto any of their cis peers. We are simply trained to look for examples in trans people that correlate with their assigned gender, and we need to unlearn this.

It is best not to make assumptions about what autistic people may need, but it is great if we start to become aware of the sensory environment, the information we give out about how we work and what will happen, and any other information, sensory or otherwise, we are expecting our clients' bodies to process. If we are doing mindfulness, for example, we need to be aware of how sensory-based tasks might impact some autistic clients in unexpected ways.

More than this, though, all counsellors need to learn more about autism and neurodivergence. We need to learn from autistic people, not the 'experts' and not parents who still see their child's autism as a 'problem'. We need to challenge our ideas about autism, especially if we hold onto narratives about causality or pathology. Noticing these, where they come from, and why they are clung to is vital. If we put that effort into *accommodating* autism instead of imagining it cured, what a different world this would be.

I think the hardest request of some person-centred people is to challenge any resistance to people 'labelling' themselves. By calling autism (or transness, or anything else) 'labels' we are casting these things in a negative light. We use all sorts of words to describe the richness of our experience. They only get called 'labels' when seen as bad things to attach to someone. These words are useful descriptions that many people find freeing.

Some people who have been through medical diagnosis in the past may have had a difficult and problematic experience of having that label applied to them. People diagnosed as children have found it particularly restrictive and pathologising and may reject it for those reasons. Ultimately, our identity descriptors should be something for us to self-discover. If our client says they are autistic but has not been diagnosed, we should believe them. They may not look or sound the way we imagine autistic people all look and sound.

Misdiagnosis

Autistic, gender atypical people with a history of trauma often get less helpful labels attached to them. Emotionally Unstable Personality

Disorder (EUPD, formerly Borderline) is a label I have frequently seen attached to trans or LGBT+ autistic people. The label can be useful for some people, however Complex Trauma (CPTSD) is a diagnosis not used in the UK that I believe is much more useful in many cases, because it acknowledges the root of many issues attached to EUPD relate to trauma, rather than just focusing on behaviours that are generally a result of trauma (and sometimes autism as well). When people get diagnosed with a personality disorder they are often not considered for an autism diagnosis, although it could be helpful if it applies. Autistic people, like trans people, are vulnerable to abuse because of marginalisation, but if someone is autistic, it is going to be much easier to address trauma once their underlying communication and sensory needs are addressed.

One of the many reasons for the over-diagnosis of Emotionally Unstable Personality Disorder in LGBT+ people and mistreatment of those with a diagnosis is that the everyday 'behaviours' of LGBT+ people can be viewed under the lens of 'attention seeking' and 'poor impulse control' by prejudiced clinicians (Rocks 2016), while the overwhelm and meltdown of autistic people are also seen as signs of someone who cannot manage their emotions. Instead of seeing that the autistic person is experiencing differently, the assumption is they are *reacting* differently to the same experience.

It should also be noticed here that there is a known correlation between undiagnosed autism and eating disorder, and this important aspect of neurodivergence may be missed by practitioners intent on finding past trauma or abuse in the client's history or using other approaches that do not take neurodivergence into account (Huke *et al.* 2013).

SENSITIVITY AND SYNAESTHESIA

The sensory issues of autism overlap with another phenomenon, *sensory processing disorder* and the term Highly Sensitive Person (HSP) (Liss, Mailloux and Erchull 2008; Tomchek and Dunn 2007). There have been some interesting studies showing that sensitivity to environment is biologically variable, that is, sensitivity is not something we can choose (Aron, Aron and Jagiellowicz 2012). The way other people respond to that sensitivity is crucial for a sensitive person's development (Liss *et al.* 2005). For instance, parents who cannot tolerate the irritability of highly sensitive babies (perhaps because they are sensitive themselves and have not been well soothed) can impact how the developing child learns to process and integrate their experiences. Many people learn to dissociate from or wall up their sensitivity if it has not been appropriately responded to by caregivers. There may be gender norms at work in how sensitivity is responded to also.

Not only do many people in this population cluster experience the sensory environment in a heightened way, there are also many people who process sensory information in unusual or even painful ways. Misophonia is a condition that overlaps with autism, in which sound is experienced as painful, and can trigger quite aggressive reactions. If you have ever had someone bite your head off for chewing too loudly (or been the biter), that could be misophonia.

Synaesthesia is a condition where people process their senses in ways that overlap or diverge from the norm. For instance, hearing colours or tasting names. Some people propose other perceptual differences are separate from synaesthesia, but Marks and Mulvenna (2013) suggest that, for example, hearing voices, a non-pathological experience in 13 per cent of the population, could also be a form of synaesthesia. Again, hearing voices is common in this subset of the population, and perceptions of voice-hearing are integral to the wellbeing of the voice-hearer.

Until I stumbled on the above-mentioned article, it had not occurred to me that the kaleidoscopic auras I see when I get migraines are in fact visual hallucinations. These could also fall under the banner of synaesthesia, as could other visual hallucinations. Because I had not thought of them as hallucinations even though they are, they had not particularly troubled me. The pain that comes after is much more troublesome. If someone had told me I was having visual hallucinations, I might have associated that with mental illness and been more distressed or anxious as a result.

My migraines in themselves are curious, as their main trigger is weather. Since I was a child, people could tell if a storm was coming because I would be completely immobilised. This sensitivity may be more common than we realise, hence terms like 'under the weather'; however, I suspect most people do not get mind-splitting, vomit-inducing migraines when the barometer drops.

Being sensitive can be amazing, but it invites constant criticism. Terms like 'over-sensitive' are common currency. When I was growing up, the word 'precious' was used to describe sensitive (and therefore perceived as feminine) men, and it became synonymous with 'gay'. There is a gendered aspect to people's perception of sensitivity, where women are thought to be more sensitive, and sensitivity is seen as feminine/effeminate, but also an undesirable quality. Over-sensitive is also a term thrown at minorities when they raise their discomfort about discriminatory behaviour that they are expected to just 'suck up', so this social hierarchy extends beyond simple sexism and ableism.

This cultural tendency to be dismissive of other's experiences if they do not chime with our own is something we have to consciously unlearn. It is helpful if we bite down that learned response and develop our ability to accept how our clients experience the world, even if that turns out to be quite unusual, or outside our experience.

Perfect pitch is another trait common in this cluster, so is a heightened perception of colour. These perceptual differences can be disabling, particularly in a world that makes no adaptation for them, but they are also important. I cannot help thinking evolution might be doing useful work creating divergent people.

CASE STUDY

Alicia is 25 and has been self-medicating with oestrogen and androgen blockers for three years. She is self-diagnosed autistic, asexual and polyamorous. She is suffering from depression and anxiety and hears voices. Alicia is estranged from an emotionally and physically abusive family. She struggles to work and has frequent meltdowns, but she is also constantly feeling pain and fatigue. She self-harms by cutting to cope, and controls her eating when things are bad.

Alicia considers herself to have fully transitioned to live as a woman, but others struggle to accept this as she mostly wears joggers, T-shirts and no make-up. Alicia tells her clinician that all her clothes are from the women's section, and lots of girls don't wear dresses or make-up, but they tell her she is not making 'enough of an effort'. Alicia becomes upset, saying she really struggles with the sensations and textures of clothes and make-up. The clinician decides that Alicia's gender, sexuality and relationship style as well as other 'over-emotional' traits are all part of a pattern of 'attention seeking' behaviour. They dismiss the autism self-diagnosis and propose that Alicia has EUPD.

I wish Alicia was unusual, but she is a composite picture of a common presentation; someone who has so many things going on that they complicate the picture. Clinicians are used to trying to find patterns and causes, they take all the unusual information about Alicia and try to wrap it up into one diagnosis. Until Alicia finds a professional who is experienced working with LGBT+ and autistic people in a non-pathologising way, she is not going to find the interventions offered particularly helpful. Clinicians, just like everyone else, are susceptible to bias towards youth, disability, unconventional relationships and LGBT+ people.

A counsellor working with Alicia needs to learn to trust her self-experience and the labels she chooses for herself. If EUPD feels right to her, then go with that, but if it feels like an imposition, trust her self-diagnosis of autism. We need to notice the fatigue and pain. It could be part of her depression, but it is just as likely to be a co-occurring physical issue. Expecting random co-occurrences, rather than trying to tie everything together, will serve us well with Alicia.

Self-harm and eating issues are common in this cluster, particularly with undiagnosed autism (Westwood 2017). Many autistic people stim, that is engage in self-stimulatory behaviour as a self-soothing process. Most stims are benign, but they can cross into more troublesome behaviours such as dermatillomania (compulsive skin picking) or trichotillomania (compulsive hair pulling). I wonder if self-harm and eating issues also serve similar functions in which case we may have less success directly addressing the behaviours than we have in exploring the triggers.

We need to remember that while exposure therapy can decrease anxiety in some situations, no amount of exposure is, for example, going to make Alicia more able to wear certain texturally problematic clothes. When you are autistic, avoidance of some things is as necessary as avoidance of stairs is necessary for mobility impaired people. Our job then is not to cure Alicia of her feelings, but to take them seriously and help her find ways around her worst triggers. Eventually, we can address her trauma (if she wants to) as an issue in itself, rather than trying to tie it in to everything else.

CONCLUSION

There is not space to go into an exploration of all the other issues trans people might have that set them apart from the average person. What is important here is to not mould these different characteristics together, but to understand them as separate kinds of divergence that just tend to co-occur.

People are not trans because they are autistic, nor autistic because they are trans. Transness and autism are not signs of abuse, they just happen to be two groups which are likely to experience abuse. Our client is not complaining about the fluorescent lights because they are a 'snowflake'. Physical pain may well not be psychosomatic, but a sign of a co-occurring medical problem. Their wheelchair or their stick are not signs of attention-seeking behaviour, but in younger people especially they are often seen as such. Their loud voice and interruptions do not make them male. Their oddness or social exclusion may be a sign of undiagnosed neurodivergence, not just their transness.

When we question whether people are trans, or gay, or polyamorous because of their autism, we need to immediately ask ourselves – would we have questioned whether they were straight, cis or monogamous because of autism? It is possible for autistic people to develop rigid thinking, and therefore also possible that an autistic person might carefully follow the social rules and have difficulty exploring the possibility of living outside of them. But equally, some autistic people find it easier to discard social rules that do not fit them. In other words, it is no more likely that they are trans because they are autistic than it is that they are cis because they are autistic. But clinicians will try to tie these things together, even calling gender incongruence an autistic 'special interest'.

Sometimes, it is helpful to signpost clients to information about autism, sensitivity and sensory processing differences, ADHD, and sometimes it is important to hold those thoughts, and just take the divergence into account in our interactions. It is important to remember how prejudice works subtly to undermine relationship with people who are different. We need to learn to examine our dislike, irritation or judgement in supervision. These negative feelings when they come up can be all too easy to justify and hard to work through.

Above all, when working with trans people, we need to expect divergence, but not assume it. People are endlessly surprising.

PERSONAL REFLECTION

1. I would be surprised if this chapter did not challenge some myths and assumptions. Journal about the parts of this chapter that surprised you. Which parts do you disagree with and want to reject? Mark those for further exploration and study.
2. What has been your model for autism up to now? Where did it come from? Did your training include neurodivergence as a topic? Have you done training since? Was it from a neurotypical 'expert', or an autistic person? Is there room for more learning?
3. Consider the above questions with respect to ADHD, hearing voices, medically unexplained symptoms and other divergences.
4. Where are you with labels and diagnoses? Finding a comfy place in between 'all labels are bad' and 'the medical model is perfect' can be hard thing to do, but it is worth some work.

Chapter 6

MINORITY STRESS AND ITS CAUSES

In this chapter, I explore the concept of *minority stress* as it applies to trans people. We look in more detail at the reasons why, although being trans is not in itself a mental illness, mental health for many trans people is profoundly compromised because of the way society is structured.

I also introduce a model I use called the 'web model', which demonstrates additional pressures some people experience as fundamentally *relational*, and therefore resolvable through supportive relationships. The web model is a simplified concept I drew together that ties in what we know about the influence of relationship on mental health. We have long known that there is substantial evidence that social support profoundly impacts both physical and mental wellbeing (Uchino, Cacioppo and Kiecolt-Glaser 1996; Broadhead *et al.* 1983). We also know as counsellors that the quality of the relationship with our client is the most influential factor in therapeutic outcomes (Lambert and Barley 2001). When I train, attendees find this a particularly useful way of drawing together threads from both social justice and psychotherapeutic theories into a coherent framework that is fundamentally person-centred. When working across difference, relationship can be compromised, so it pays to bring it into focus.

Therapy, and particularly person-centred therapy, has often been criticised as overly individualistic (Merry 1995, pp.114–115). I personally find it frustrating that much of what my clients bring to therapy is trauma caused by others, and we are left to pick up the pieces for someone else together. Many counsellors who have not spent time considering the social model of disability will view their clients purely through a lens of individualised issues, where there is nothing barring them from success but a positive attitude. Counsellors orientated this way can cause untold damage to minority groups, who are often groomed into taking more than their fair share of blame for what happens to them. In addition, an individualistic approach comes from the global north western white culture and ignores the more community, collective-based cultures around the world (Merry 1995).

The social model of disability suggests that people are disabled not only by their individual medical conditions, but by a disabling social environment (Oliver 2013). If we look at what we learned about autism, we can see that an environment where all people are expected to have similar neurotypical responses to sensory information is disabling for neurodivergent people.

Humans use all sorts of adaptations to the natural environment to make their lives easier – we build shelter to keep us dry and warm, steps and ladders to gain access to heights, forks to eat our food, diaries to assist us with remembering. Somehow, none of these is stigmatised, and yet many disability aids come with a stigma attached, even though they often provide similar functions to the everyday tools we already use. Why is a wheelchair more stigmatised than a bicycle? Because we socially stigmatise the minority that use them. Why do we have smooth and step-free roads and cycle paths that ease the progress of certain kinds of wheels, while still falling short on providing level access for wheelchairs? Adaptions that suit the majority are readily embraced, while adaptions that help minorities are an imposition. This is how an *environment* becomes more disabling than the condition itself.

MINORITY STRESS

Meyer's (2003) theory of minority stress was originally introduced for lesbian, gay and bi (LGB) people. It is now widely used to describe the experiences of different minority groups. Meyer proposed minority stress as a model to explain the increased prevalence of mental illness within LGB communities in a non-pathologising way:

> The author offers a conceptual framework for understanding this excess in prevalence of disorder in terms of *minority stress*—explaining that stigma, prejudice, and discrimination create a hostile and stressful

> social environment that causes mental health problems. The model describes stress processes, including the experience of prejudice events, expectations of rejection, hiding and concealing, internalized homophobia, and ameliorative coping processes. (Meyer 2003, p.674)

Work like Meyer's helped the world shift from a perspective where same sex attraction was viewed as a mental illness towards an understanding that there is nothing inherently mentally ill about being lesbian, gay or bi. Increasing acceptance of LGB people should yield better mental health. Family acceptance has proved a crucial factor in the wellbeing of LGB people (PACE 2015, p.6).

There is naturally a positive feedback process associated with this phenomenon. As LGB people start to function better in society; build better and more trusting relationships with their surrounding community; rely less on drugs and alcohol to cope with their distress; find themselves better housed and better employed; gain better access to services and healthcare; appear increasingly on television or in parliament; their wellbeing becomes positively reinforced by these supportive structures and greater positive visibility.

I am not suggesting that the fight for LGB acceptance was fully won with the advent of same sex marriage, but it is true that we have come a long way from the days when homosexuality was partially decriminalised in 1967 or declassified as a mental health condition in 1990.

The fact that Meyer wrote a study about LGB rather than LGBT people is also significant. If we look across history and cultures, LGB and T have always been an intermingled community. Not a homogenous one, because gender and sexuality are not the same thing, but a blended community where there have always been LGB people who also experience gender incongruence, and trans people who are also LGB. These experiences are on a continuum, with no hard borders. The artificial division between LGB and T has somewhat left trans people behind in the 50 years since gender divergent and trans people kicked off the modern-day Pride movement at the Stonewall riots (Equality Archive 2015).

The model of minority stress has now been applied to populations other than LGB, and it is particularly useful for trans people. In the next section I look at how things are now in the UK and across the world specifically for trans people, and the factors that might create minority stress.

THE PRESSURES ON THE TRANS COMMUNITY

I am going to start this exploration not by looking at hate crime that happens to trans people at street level, but at the influencers who use words to create the troubling conditions trans people find themselves in. Hitler once said 'words build bridges into unexplored regions' (Bullock 1953, p.45), indicating how it was language itself that paved the way for what followed. There is currently a passionate cultural debate about the necessity of 'free speech', but unfortunately hateful and manipulative speech costs the people it impacts. Speech influences people, and speech that is supported and amplified by a media platform, or an academic or political position, can normalise all kinds of toxic ideas. Trans people rarely have such platforms and are rarely in a position to challenge the narratives that are created about us, even when we are called by the dehumanising term 'parasites' within the walls of Westminster itself (Lander 2018).

Hate crime does not just spontaneously happen because the individuals perpetrating it are 'troubled' or 'disaffected', although people under stress are perhaps easier to manipulate. Nor can hate crime be individualised. If it could, there would be no explanation for the ways in which hate crime figures rise and fall in sync with what is happening in popular discourse, such as the 147 per cent rise in LGBT hate crime in the months after the Brexit referendum (Townsend 2016). What rapper, author and activist Akala says about race is relevant here:

> All this nonsense about people being racist because they're frustrated about their lives is totally classist, what we're saying is only working-class people are racist...racism was not invented by working class people, it was invented by elite academics through pseudo-scientific nonsense and perpetuated as part of political policy – from the top down, not the bottom up. (BBC 2013, 13:37)

Words are not powerless, as any advertiser will tell us. It is the people who make films, write in newspapers and books, and speak in parliament and on television who can influence the level of acceptance different groups experience.

Representation

Understanding and empathy grow through hearing about the experiences of a minority community or seeing them represented as just an ordinary part of society. Are one in every 200 people we see on TV or in film trans? Because that would be normal representation. Are they living their lives, just existing as part of humanity? Except for rare occasions, the answer is no.

It is widely believed that the sympathetic character of Hayley Cropper in *Coronation Street* paved the way for the Gender Recognition Act 2004 to come into being (Wallace 2018, pp.208–210). Nadia Almada, the trans winner of *Big Brother 5*, also had an impact, as did trans woman Paris Lees being the first openly trans person on *BBC Question Time*, Eddie Izzard explicitly talking about being transgender. These have been important moments of progress, but we have a long way to go until trans people are accepted on our screens as more than just 'zoo television', as Belcher puts it (2018, pp.317).

There is suddenly a good deal of interest in our community, but the interest is not always helpful. It is hard to watch a comedy show without hearing an off-colour Caitlyn Jenner joke, a gag about men dressed up as women or someone dropping the unacceptable slur word 'tranny'. The jokes are often at the expense of trans women, rather than other trans people. They are designed to ridicule any expression of femininity in assigned male people. This preserves social ideas about masculinity and the gender binary.

There is also another media tradition of making trans women (or trans-coded people) seem dangerous or unhinged. This dates to films like Hitchcock's *Psycho*, in which the killer dresses up as his mother, or the film *Silence of the Lambs*, in which a serial killer uses dead women's skin to make himself a 'woman suit'. Sadly, the trend continues to this day, in recent films like *Insidious 2*, with its disturbing trans-coded serial killer of women (Mey 2013).

Trans representation has been consistently problematic in drama, horror and comedy. Remember that moment in *Crocodile Dundee* when Paul Hogan's character grabs a trans woman's crotch (that is sexual assault, by the way) and proclaims loudly 'that was a guy dressed up as a Sheila!'? Or the moment that Ace Ventura discovers romantic interest Einhorn is 'really a man' and vomits copiously? So many narratives portray trans women as deceptive 'traps' rather than as human beings just being themselves (Weslynn 2016).

The abiding misconception of trans women is that they are 'really men' and the ongoing tendency to use cis men to play trans women perpetuates this. It portrays transness as a costume that can be put on, reducing trans women's selves to their outward appearance. Studios seem to go to great lengths to repeat this trope, despite repeated concerns raised by the trans community. Eddie Redmayne in *The Danish Girl*, Jared Leto's fabricated character in true story *Dallas Buyer's Club*, Jeffrey Tambor in *Transparent* (Fury 2016).

If you see a story about a trans women, look out for some clichés. You will see her putting on make-up, to indicate her identity is a façade. At some point you will see her presenting as a man, and this will be easy for her, just a matter of taking off her wig and make-up. In print media, they will include a 'before' picture, and her deadname (her previous name), to indicate 'who she used to be'. Every effort will go into portraying a transformation and delving into medical processes. The emphasis is that trans women are no more than a series of operations and some clever make-up techniques.

Meanwhile, trans men and non-binary characters are rarely seen at all, and when they are, similar tropes to those above abound.

Are things better now, though? Do trans people get to tell their own stories? Well, we have some more sympathetic portrayals, but very rarely do we see trans people telling trans stories, and I would genuinely advise anyone to seek out the words of trans people themselves, however hard they are to find.

For the last few years, there has been a slew of misinformation in the media about trans people, and national news making a thing of minor crimes committed by trans individuals that would not make any headlines if the perpetrator was not trans. Violence against trans people, including the murder of Naomi Hersi in 2018, is barely noticed and, if noticed at all, badly reported (Stonewall 2018c). When trans woman Kate Stone was gored by a stag in 2013, the press showed a prurient interest in her trans status, even questioning whether the stag hag gored her because she was trans (BBC News 2014).

Misinformation about the Gender Recognition Act (GRA) and Equality Act have abounded since the government announced their intention to reform the GRA. In one instance a *Sunday Times* article claimed trans women who had not had gender reassignment surgery could be given access to toilets in important tourism venues in London after Gender Recognition Act reform (Braidwood 2018). The implication being that this would be problematic. Trans people have been legally protected in using the toilets for their assigned gender from the moment they decide to transition since the Equality Act 2010.

They have legally used toilets for much longer, as there is no law in the UK to state who should use which toilets. Meanwhile, getting up to anything inappropriate will remain illegal. *The Times* were creating a panic about something that has been happening for years, and never been a problem. It also completely misrepresented what GRA reform means. This article was one part of a slew of almost daily misinformation from many news sources.

For an antidote to all this, I recommend shifting media consumption and adding in some trans voices. Reading or following writers like Janet Mock, CN Lester, Paris Lees, Julia Serano, Ben Vincent, Ruth Pearce, Natacha Kennedy, Roz Kaveney, Meg-John Barker, Leslie Feinberg. Watching trans produced series like *Her Story*, *Pose* or *Sense8*, or films like *Tangerine* or *A Fantastic Woman*. Following people like Alok Vaid-Menon, Travis Albanza, Sabah Choudrey, Munroe Bergdorf, Laverne Cox, Rae Spoon. We cannot begin to change things without dialling up the amount of time we hear trans voices directly, rather than filtered through another's gaze. In fact, we need to listen to those voices until they become human to us. Until we believe what the voices are saying.

Trans exclusionary feminism

CN Lester, in their incredible book *Trans Like Me*, mentions an incident when they were interviewed, in which they were described as a 'trans activist' and pitted against a 'feminist' (Lester 2017, p.177). This narrative has been imposed for a while now, but it obscures the true story. CN Lester is, like me and most of the trans people I know, a passionate feminist. Feminism is, by and large, trans inclusive. And yet there is a small but vocal element within feminist organising that is very focused on the idea of trans people being a 'problem'.

Most feminists find these fringe groups a nuisance, but they get a suspicious amount of funding and bolstering from outside of feminism, especially from right wing and Christian groups that are also opposed to trans people, groups like Hands Across the Aisle (Southern Poverty Law Centre 2017). They also get a lot of space within media, more than other feminist causes get. For this reason, these voices are often heard more loudly than others and have greater influence. An oppositional 'debate' will always get more ratings than a fact-driven, educative piece of journalism.

For many trans people, this fringe group are in fact one of the main contributors to our distress and marginalisation. We expect Jeremy Clarkson or Piers Morgan to say awful things about us, and we are not very likely to want to enter social spaces where we are going to encounter people with such extreme views. But these fringe feminists have been given such an enormous platform their views have taken strong hold within the void of accurate information about trans people. As such, it is hard for trans people to go into any space, particularly online, without encountering somebody who has absorbed these views. Their main tactic is to weaponise some women's justifiable fear of male violence to attack trans people. 'Trans women are men and trans men want to be men' is the inaccurate stereotype to taint the whole trans community with a sense of being 'anti-woman'.

These campaigners often use bogus or wildly misinterpreted research to further their aims. One case of this happened at the end of 2017, when one of these groups, *Fair Play for Women*, published a report that was widely shared in the mainstream media, which falsely claimed that 41 per cent of trans prisoners were sex offenders (2017). Inevitably, the rich discussion debunking this figure, eventually including a piece on the BBC News website (2018), reached a far smaller audience.

It is inevitable we will encounter people, including some trans people, who have been swayed by this factory of misinformation. Without an awareness of facts and research, their propaganda can be highly persuasive. I do not have the time to debunk everything these anti-trans campaigners say here. More accurate information is out there, but it might not get as wide a readership. One way to test the trustworthiness is to investigate whether the writer is a committed anti-trans campaigner. Often these 'feminists' do not talk about much else than trans people. If the propaganda was true, more reliable research would back up what they say, and it never does. 'Search the person who has written the piece. What angle have they previously been coming from? What articles are there about them?' advises activist and graphic designer Lee-Anne Lawrance (Levesley 2017). I find a search for the person's name, plus the word 'transphobia' highly enlightening.

Groups like *Transgender Trend*, *Fair Play for Women*, *4th Wave Now*, *We Need to Talk*, *Woman's Place UK*, *Gender Trender*, *Parents of ROGD Kids* and *Gender Identity Watch*, are all single-issue groups campaigning against trans people accessing civil rights and treatment, and they present manipulative and falsified arguments that gain respectability simply by being too often repeated. Sadly, the online forum Mumsnet has now also been substantially radicalised by these groups (De Gallier 2016).

Some of these groups actively recruit trans people, young ones especially. Pre-transition trans people are told they are really gay or lesbian, even if they are in fact asexual or attracted to the opposite gender to the one they were assigned. This tactic is akin to conversion therapy, which we know is ineffective and damaging, and has been condemned by all major UK psychological bodies (COSRT 2017).

> I came out as lesbian aged 13 whilst struggling with my gender identity. I then came out as trans but went back to identifying as a butch woman when I became immersed in TERF theory and 'detransitioning'. I nearly didn't survive this far. I was filled with internalized transphobia and self-loathing which led to multiple suicide attempts. I believed that I must be a misogynist if I am trans. (Latarche 2018)

Trans people experience great suffering while trying to repress their trans identity. Post-transition trans people are persuaded to campaign against other trans people by various manipulations. When trans people extricate themselves from these group's webs, they need a lot of support to deprogramme themselves and re-integrate with a trans community they may have been extremely hostile to. Dana Taylor, a trans woman who joined with anti-trans campaigners, talks about how they showed a semblance of acceptance to 'transsexual separatists' who split off from the rest of the trans community. They are lured by the false promise of being accepted into womanhood. 'Even though some of the most vile hate I have seen before was on their websites, I told myself they weren't talking about me, they are talking about the transgender community, of which I was not part.' Eventually, Taylor began to listen to trans people and see the hate, which she had assisted in, for what it was:

> The relentless attack on trans women by this group of radical feminists made me realize that I was acting just like they were. After intense soul searching, I began to listen to my sisters. Once you get sucked into sucking up to this nasty group of bigots, it is hard to leave it. I was terrified at the thought that I could end up being shamed and humiliated on one of their sites. It was debilitating and oppressive to me and it was of my own making. (Taylor 2013)

Those trans people who cannot be recruited are often bullied and harassed, as Taylor describes. The extent of this harassment is rarely believed by others, who have been in their turn groomed to believe that trans people make a fuss about nothing. If a trans person says or does something awful, it will often get in the newspapers but there is silence when trans people are harassed or assaulted by members of these groups, have their employers contacted with false stories, or have their photos and personal transition information paraded on websites as objects of ridicule.

Many trans people are understandably angry about this targeted campaign against our validity and civil rights. These campaign groups have swayed trans equality legislation before and are currently going all out to stop the forthcoming Gender Recognition Act reforms and reverse our provisions under the Equality Act 2010. Many trans people call these campaigners *TERFs*, an acronym for Trans Exclusionary Radical Feminist that was coined by cisgender radical feminists to distinguish from their own brand of trans inclusive radical feminism. 'TERF' has now been labelled a 'slur' by the people it is directed at, meaning it is hard for trans people to even articulate our misery about this bullying without being accused of aggression.

The counsellor who is unable to hold the extreme hurt and anger trans people feel about the psychological and social damage these campaigners do is going to be difficult for us to trust. The counsellor who blames trans people for not always being able to maintain a calm and patient response to this onslaught is failing to absorb the enormity of the suffering these groups inflict. The counsellor who can 'see both sides' in a scenario where one side is fighting against a minority group's civil rights is not going to be much help to a trans person. Someone buying into the idea that words like 'TERF' or even 'cisgender' are slurs just because sometimes trans people are very, very angry when they say these words, is not going to be able to hear their legitimate hurt. Someone who spends more time absorbing the words of these anti-trans groups than legitimate trans positive academics, writers or speakers is simply going to be unable to make full psychological contact with a trans client and should not try.

Meanwhile, trans feminists and cis feminists are working out brilliant, creative ways that spaces can be safer for *all* women and gender minorities, and their voices are rarely heard. For good trans feminist writing, go to CN Lester, Julia Serano, A. Finn Enke, Andrea

Long Chu, Susan Stryker, Leslie Feinberg, Kate Bornstein, Eli Clare, Jin Haritaworn, Syrus Marcus Ware, Ani Datta, Laxmi, Janet Mock, Patrick Califia, C. Jacob Hale, Talia Bettcher, Cristan Williams, Sally Hines, Emi Koyama, Otter Lieffe, Viviane Namaste.

Coming out and the internet

Trans people are especially vulnerable when they first come out as trans or are exploring their identity. The internet has made it possible for a tiny community to organise in a way it never could before. We can find words for what we experience, and other people who share these experiences. Finding other trans people on YouTube and watching their stories can help a young trans person find themself. For me, reading an article about a genderqueer person my own age finally nudged me to express my identity. Folks will say we were *influenced* by these articles. To those people I say, I spent my life being influenced into being cisgender. Learning about people liberated me from a pervasive erasure of trans existence. There is a huge resource out there, and I encourage trans people to explore it widely, and not just settle in one small trans group but see the real diversity that is out there. However, there are many online triggers and challenges, as described above.

Sometimes, well-meaning people suggest we just stay offline, but that is of course the point; trans people are discouraged from participation in public spaces, be they toilets or internet forums. The anti-trans lobby will go to great lengths to make spaces uncomfortable for us, and they often achieve their aims. For example, I no longer open my copy of *Therapy Today* or engage in anything BACP-related because they have on more than one occasion published deceitful propaganda from the anti-trans organisation *Transgender Trend* (Hope 2017a). It is not that I decided not to do so, I simply am gripped with anxiety every time it drops on my mat, and somehow, I never manage to pull it out of its plastic wrapper.

The relationship between the trans community and pervasive transprejudice reminds me of what I learned working with domestic violence. Abusers (or abusive groups and systems) have the power to deceive with impunity, because nobody sees what they are really like but the victim. Abusers also co-opt other unwary people to assist with the abuse. The abuser, all charm, will convince everyone the victim is crazy and how they suffer from it. The overwrought, traumatised victim will, naturally, display behaviours that confirm this. These abusive relationships rely on the hierarchical power dynamics that exist between men and women, able and disabled people, older and younger people, white and BAME (Black, Asian, and minority ethnic) people, cis and trans people, etc. It is in the interest of those not affected to not see the abuse. If they allow themselves to become aware of the abuse, they may have to act, and that would mean putting themselves in the abuser's path.

> It is very tempting to take the side of the perpetrator. All the perpetrator asks is that the bystander do nothing. He appeals to the universal desire to see, hear, and speak no evil. The victim, on the contrary, asks the bystander to share the burden of pain. The victim demands action, engagement, and remembering. (Herman 1997, pp.7–9)

Counsellors working with trans people displaying trauma related to this psychological abuse should consider the same issues as they would working with survivors of any kind of abuse. Herman (1997) is an excellent resource on such trauma.

Statistics on trans lives and welfare

I already shared some alarming statistics about suicide in the Preface. Here, I am going to focus on some key studies, a few among many pieces of data that portray a community under duress. Let us first look at the *Trans Mental Health Study 2012*, a major UK survey by a group of organisations and researchers (McNeil *et al.*).

In the responses to the study, more than 90 per cent of participants had been told they were 'not normal'. Thirty-eight per cent had experienced physical intimidation and threats for being trans, and 19 per cent had been beaten up for being trans. Fourteen per cent had been harassed by the police. Understandably, this led to over 60 per cent of participants being afraid of going out. Sixty-five per cent feared growing old alone.

Over 60 per cent had to educate a healthcare worker and 26 per cent had been purposefully misgendered by healthcare workers. Seven per cent had experienced requests for unnecessary genital examinations while accessing healthcare and 16 per cent had experienced 'unprofessional levels of curiosity' about their genitals. For 29 per cent their gender identity was treated as a mental health symptom. The study found that Gender Identity Clinics exacerbated trans mental health. Sixty-two per cent felt distress or worry alongside their appointments, and 53 per cent did not feel safe to disclose this.

Specific data on mental health shows 76 per cent had taken antidepressants and 31 per cent had accessed a community mental health team. Rates of mental health experienced were: depression 88 per cent, stress 80 per cent, anxiety 75 per cent. Thirty-six per cent scored as having major depression. Use of mental health services lowered significantly post transition.

Shockingly, 49 per cent had experienced abuse in childhood. Fifty-three per cent had self-harmed. Eighty-four per cent had had suicidal thoughts, 27 per cent had thought about suicide in the last week, 63 per cent in the last year. Thiry-five per cent had attempted suicide, 25 per cent more than once. Elevated levels of drinking, smoking and drug use were also seen. Again, transition lowered risk.

Despite this, 81 per cent 'felt they had gained something' from being trans. Fifty-two per cent had work problems because of being trans. Nineteen per cent had been homeless, 11 per cent more than once. Seven per cent had left parental home because of reactions to them being trans. Nineteen per cent saw their children less because of transition and 9 per cent lost custody. Fifty-one per cent 'felt that the way trans people were represented in the media had a negative effect on their emotional wellbeing' (McNeil *et al.* 2012).

Worrying figures indeed, but have they been replicated? We saw earlier in the book that suicidality is consistently high across multiple countries. The US report, *Injustice at Every Turn* (Grant *et al.* 2011), shows trans people experienced twice as much unemployment, and 55 per cent lost a job due to bias. It also shows that trans people have a significantly lower income, more than four times as likely to be in the lowest income bracket. Fifty-one per cent were harassed or bullied in school, 61 per cent had been physically assaulted and 64 per cent sexually assaulted. Nineteen per cent had at some point been homeless, of those 29 per cent had been turned away from shelters and 22 per cent were sexually assaulted in shelters. Twenty-two per cent reported police harassment. Fifty per cent had to educate healthcare workers. Fifty-seven per cent experienced significant family rejection. Sxity-three per cent had experienced an act of discrimination that had a major effect on their quality of life. For black and ethnic minorities, particularly African Americans, treatment was far worse across the board (Grant *et al.* 2011).

Stonewall have released the following figures (2018a, pp.6–7): 41 per cent experienced hate crime in the previous year. Twenty-eight per cent have faced domestic violence in the last year. Twenty-five per cent have been homeless at some point. Twelve per cent have been physically attacked in work. Thirty-six per cent of university students had negative comments from staff in the last year.

A Totaljobs (2016) survey of trans employees found that: 60 per cent 'experienced workplace discrimination' and 36 per cent left a job because of such attitudes; this rose to 50 per cent for people who identified outside the gender binary.

In the UK government's *National LGBT Survey* (Government Equalities Office 2018), we find only 37 per cent of trans women, 34 per cent of trans men and 38 per cent of non-binary people 'felt comfortable being LGBT in the UK', with lower comfort for younger trans people. Fifty-nine per cent of trans women, 56 per cent of trans men and 76 per cent of non-binary people had hid their identity from fear of other's reactions. Thirteen per cent had been excluded from activities in education. All these statistics were significantly worse for trans than cisgender LGB people.

Perhaps the most alarming statistics come from the report *Out of sight, out of mind? Transgender People's Experiences of Domestic Abuse* (Scottish Trans 2010). The domestic violence statistics are stark: Abuse from partner or ex – 80 per cent; emotional and transphobic abuse – 73 per cent; controlling behaviour – 60 per cent; physical abuse – 45 per cent; sexual abuse – 47 per cent. In addition, 37 per cent of respondents said that 'someone had forced, or tried to force them to have sex when they were under the age of 16' and 46 per cent had experienced some other form of childhood sexual abuse.

We can see from these surveys, and from a large body of research data, that trans people face material disadvantages in every aspect of life. As shown previously, we know that support and acceptance as well as timely access to healthcare substantially improve trans lives.

SOCIAL HIERARCHY AND ITS IMPACT

A cumulation of the issues mentioned above can in time amount to an experience of complex trauma. Even if severe abuse and hate crime are absent, trans people can still face a daily attack on their identity that can be traumatising over time. Many trans people experience complex post-traumatic stress (CPTSD) symptoms and will be continually re-traumatised over and over by small and large incidents of discrimination in their daily lives.

As stated before, it is much like being in an abusive relationship, only the relationship is with multiple people. Trans people are more likely to be assaulted, but also more likely to be shunned, disbelieved, infantilised, have their experiences and emotions disregarded, and be constantly put down. Often abuse victims are viewed as 'the problem' or 'over-sensitive' or 'not being positive enough' and this can compound the sense of isolation. When trans people speak about their experiences, they rarely receive genuine empathy, respect and listening in return.

The relational values of the person-centred approach are crucial to helping a trans person recover their wellbeing. One of the worst parts of experiencing negative attitudes from so many people is that it becomes hard not to internalise these attitudes, particularly if they come from people close to you. The abused person will, almost inevitably, blame themself to achieve a sense of control they do not have. If anti-trans attitudes seem to be all around, particularly from family, even more reason to self-blame; 'It is better to be a sinner in a world ruled by God than to live in a world ruled by the Devil' (Fairbairn 1952, pp.66–67).

Hierarchical systems assert themselves by working to maintain everybody's place. Person-centred counsellors are committed to anti-hierarchical practice, but if we do not notice the hierarchy is there, how will we challenge it? Some people will only accept a trans person who is passive, grateful for any kindnesses they choose, or not, to bestow. If a trans person expresses anger at the injustices the community faces, they may be met with patronising voices telling them they are misbehaving. Because of the powerful narrative that trans people are *so hard* to love and accept, people can be left thinking that even a small amount of kindness or accommodation is an extraordinary effort. When a trans person says that is not enough, they are likely to be met with resentment from the person who has already exerted themself more than they care to.

Without healthy anger motivating us we cannot shift social norms – hence Pride is an event that commemorates a riot and suffragettes did things that were thoroughly disapproved of at the time. But shifts will inevitably feel uncomfortable for people who do not see why things must change. It is easy to become the good trans person who is 'not like other trans people' and never makes a fuss. Those statistics in the last section? *That* is why things need to change, and a fuss is called for.

When I worked as a school counsellor, I used to often hear two responses to bullying, neither of which is any use whatsoever. One was 'stand up for yourself' and the other 'just ignore them'. Social groups choose their victims carefully, and not at random. Bullying is a way to further establish yourself in a social hierarchy, often enacted by people who are themselves insecure, albeit more powerful than their targets. People who can be marginalised are chosen as the targets. Who gets marginalised is an ever-shifting thing – in one school I worked at, LGBT+ kids were fiercely supported and there was little bullying, but black kids were treated badly, and the school was poor in its response to racism. In another school, they seemed to have racism better licked but gay prejudice and transprejudice were rife.

What we *should* tell any person who is being bullied is 'seek support from other people', because it is our connections to other people that will both deter the bullies and help mitigate their impact on us psychologically. However, when society has you pegged as a scapegoat, seeking support is no easy task. Constant, humiliating, unjust betrayal is what scapegoats get used to. Other humans are simply less trustworthy than they are towards people who are more socially supported. This is because it feels socially unsafe to show support for scapegoats, so people will look hard for a reason not to have to. 'One trans person committed a crime? Good, that means we can stop supporting all trans people!' Sadly, targets of bullies are just as susceptible to acting as bystanders or bullies towards other marginalised people instead of building solidarity with them, in the hopes of a reprieve from being targeted themselves.

This is not the natural order of things. Evidence suggests humans are pro-social creatures who evolved to success through teamwork – that we by nature balance out our competitive, hierarchy-prone traits with collaboration and cooperation that is inherent to us (Gavrilets 2014; Loch, Galunic and Schneider 2006; Tomasello *et al.* 2012). I noticed in my school work that where the bullying was at its worst, the teachers were bullies too. The national LGBT survey stated that 9 per cent of serious LGBT bullying incidents in school were by teachers and went on to say that trans children fared worse (Whittaker 2018b). Where I worked, the staff were unhappy and feeling bullied by their superiors, who in their turn were under pressure from government policy change. Often these schools were also underfunded and in deprived areas. Going back to what Akala said, about the 'top down' nature of oppression (BBC 2013), sometimes behaviours at the bottom have causes. Why else would hate crime have increased after the Brexit referendum? It is the very nature of hierarchy that the jostling for position and safety among people at the bottom is instigated by the people at the top.

THE WEB MODEL

The web model I use is a simple theory. Humans are pack animals, who develop, learn, heal and thrive through relationship with other humans. As counsellors, we all know relationship is at the heart of what we do (Lambert and Barley 2001). People heal in relationship – they heal *through* relationship. Yet we still individualise our clients' problems far too easily.

We label our client's ability to trust in relationship and form relationship as a precondition for therapy (Rogers 1957) but are often oblivious to the fact that we represent, and in many ways enact, the very untrustworthiness our clients are fearful of. As a white person I have been marinated in racism and racist thought for my whole life, and so of course I represent and sometimes enact untrustworthiness with my BAME clients. Davies (1996, pp.28–29) talks about the work straight people must do to be trustworthy for their LGB clients. Hunt (2014, p.295) found a lack of counsellor understanding and client satisfaction in a study of trans experiences of counselling.

The more a person is marginalised in multiple ways, the less there will be solid social threads that connect them to other human beings. When I walk into a shop, because I am not black, or homeless or otherwise profiled as a likely criminal, I know the security guard will not be suspicious of me. That is a solid thread built between me and another person, a positive human interaction. But when I go to the counter, it is quite likely the cashier will call me sir or ma'am, because we are trained from a young age to gender people into the binary. That is the cissexism we have all been marinated in. My interaction with the cashier will more likely be a broken thread – the cashier has met their belief system, they have not met me.

One broken thread may be trivial, but if you repeat this process over and over it has a chip, chip effect, especially when people are eroding the very thing you are fighting to establish – social recognition of your gender.

Minority groups (and women) have their social threads 'cut' in their interactions with other people in multiple ways, sometimes many times a day:

- **Less likely to be believed** – after an assault, when describing your experiences, when sharing your knowledge or wisdom or simple information.
- **More likely to be blamed for any misfortune** – 'you shouldn't dress like that', 'you should keep your head down/be more polite/not go to those places/be more patient waiting for rights'.
- **More likely to be invisible or hypervisible** (visible in uncomfortable, objectifying or attacked ways) – erasure in literature and onscreen, and when people like you appear it seems 'forced' or 'politically correct'. Violence towards your group is expected, it does not make the news. Your category gets erased completely – like bisexual Freddie Mercury being a 'gay' icon, or trans men being told they are just lesbians. Unable to blend in anywhere, your identity stands out and is judged, rather than accepted and understood.
- **Less access to employment** – unemployed, underemployed, lower waged, or not seen in upper management.
- **More likely to live in poverty** – due to employment issues, lack of social network and support, estrangement, slipping through nets in services, less access to benefits (because of systemic barriers and biases in staff).
- **Barriers to accessing services** – lack of diversity training; unconscious bias of workers; not represented within the services; lack of cultural awareness/competence; more likely to be written off as 'difficult', 'hard to engage' or 'the problem'; more likely to be viewed as 'unsuitable for this service'.

  For many minorities, there is also a fantasy among some staff that specific services or community resources are available that cater to them and will look after them (e.g. the myth that trans people are well supported by LGBT+ services, or that all BAME people have good in-community support).

- **Fear/stress accessing services** – many marginalised people approaching services fear that they will be mistreated. This is especially true for some groups approaching the police, due to ongoing police brutality and harassment towards certain groups, including BAME and LGBT+ people.
- **Problems dismissed as 'part of the group's culture/lifestyle'** – an example of this is the Stephen Port murders, where four gay men were murdered using a recreational drug, and police assumed despite significant evidence these were just young gay men accidentally overdosing as part of 'the lifestyle' (De Simone 2016). Domestic violence within South Asian communities and sexual assault or exploitation of trans people are other things often dismissed in similar ways.
- **Housing issues** – trans people can be denied housing, housed in unsafe areas, experience harassment within housing/from neighbours, be evicted/thrown out by family or housemates, experience homelessness or sofa surfing.
- **Social or familial exclusion/estrangement and isolation** – existing support networks such as friends and family can be very unsupportive when someone comes out as trans. Complete rejection, mistreatment and bullying, or distancing and marginalising are very common.
- **Higher risk of sexual assault/abuse/exploitation** – sexual objectification and fetishisation of trans people is common, particularly but not exclusively trans women. People can exploit a trans person's marginalised status to groom or sexually assault them. Many trans people have also engaged in survival sex work for safety or shelter. Many trans people willingly choose sex work, and that's a separate thing I will discuss later.
- **More likely to be demonised** – by politicians or the media when scapegoats are needed – clearly there are points in history where society has sought scapegoats, and trans people among others have been those scapegoats – in Germany in the 1930s, in Greece in 2013 where trans women were profiled, detained and harassed en masse (Williams 2013), and currently in Russia, the US and increasingly, the UK.

- **More likely to experience hate crimes** – abuse, harassment or violence because of identity.
- **No margin for error** – socially safe people tend to be given the benefit of the doubt, and let off for small transgressions, or have excuses made for them. Marginalised people are often held to account for everything, given the most severe sentences available and rarely excused for a small transgression or mistake.
- **One person transgresses, we're all to blame** – when a socially safe person commits a crime, it is individualised, when a marginalised person commits a crime, the whole group is implicated.
- **Health inequality** – due to issues with accessing services and lack of cultural competence/awareness of health staff; due to more demand for services in poorer areas; due to minority stress and trauma; due to health education and screening programmes not being good at engaging minorities; due to the impact of hate crime and domestic violence; due to co-occurring conditions as mentioned in Chapter 5; due to the physiological impact of isolation and loneliness.
- **Discrimination** – the simply unequal treatment many socially marginalised people experience that tends to go unnoticed by less marginalised folk.
- **Expectation of a lower position in hierarchy** – e.g. not expected to be among board members, parliament, judiciary, A list celebs. This can be both an external and internalised phenomenon. Trans people may see themselves as less likely to be loved, accepted, housed, promoted, represented and included, and more likely to be abused, excluded and put down by others.

Trans people and other minorities are generally faced with multiple issues from this list daily. It soon mounts up to enormous inequalities between people, and tenuous relationships with the world around you. We tend to wish it was a fair world and like to think of it as being so; those inequalities can be hard to believe, and both cis and trans people might not notice them, but they are real.

Most of us will find ourselves on the right and wrong side of that list in one way or another, and sometimes we are guilty of noting when we get the smaller slice of cake more than when we get the bigger one. Social justice campaigners use the word 'privilege' for people that get the bigger bit of cake more often, but I think that is a tricky word for some people to accept if they were not born with a silver spoon in their mouth.

Thinking of my web theory, and how this is all about just how many safe and secure threads are woven between us and other people, I prefer the idea of 'hidden support' rather than privilege. If we go to the police and report a crime, and their first instinct is concern, rather than suspicion or blame, that is hidden support. We might expect it and not be surprised when we get it, but some minorities will not have that fortune. If we can access a service without difficulty or discrimination, that is another bit of hidden support. If we can reveal who our partner is or what our gender is without grinding the conversation to a halt while people collect themselves and try to think of something to say that is another bit of hidden support we barely notice.

But all this hidden support makes people socially secure, and it makes it that much more difficult to criticise them, bully them, attack them, accuse them, fire them, isolate them, con them, exploit them or treat them unfairly without consequences.

If we are to extend our person-centred approach beyond the individual and look at the relational networks that hold communities together, we can maintain our emphasis on relationship but see our client–counsellor thread as just one part of a larger whole. From there, we can attend in a broader way to how our clients are being held.

CASE STUDY

Melissa is a working class, white, elderly trans woman who has been referred to a women's counselling service for support around childhood sexual abuse. She is also under a service for alcoholism. She has only begun to transition in the last two years and is experiencing verbal abuse whenever she goes out (which is increasingly rarely).

The counsellor who assesses her asks about what support Melissa has, and it transpires she is estranged from her children and friends since transition. There is nobody significant in her personal life, and she goes for days without seeing anybody.

In trying to establish whether Melissa is 'right for the service', the counsellor asks Melissa whether she has had lower surgery, which she has not. The counsellor states that she is not sure the service will be able to support Melissa in that case.

It is not unusual still for workers to believe whether someone is a woman or not is down to her genitals, which can leave trans people all too often being asked what is in their pants in highly inappropriate situations. The counsellor may be asking the question because Melissa does not 'blend' and looking for reasons to reject her from a women only counselling service. It may well be that women only services are all that is available locally, meaning this is Melissa's only potential source of help to address the abuse.

Under the Equality Act 2010, Melissa is protected in her identity, i.e. as a woman, from the moment she seeks to transition. However, single sex services may exclude her if it is 'a proportionate means to achieve a legitimate aim'. Essentially, this legally enshrines other people's transprejudice, allowing trans women to be excluded if it might make others uncomfortable. This clause is being used less and less by women's services, so we do not need to assume trans women will have difficulty accessing such services, but it happens (Stonewall 2018b).

It may be that the service is on rocky ground refusing a trans woman one to one counselling under the clause. They certainly should not be asking about what is in her pants. If it is group counselling, there may be more resistance to including Melissa, however when I have worked with women's services that have included trans women, it has largely been a growthful experience for all concerned.

The counsellor may also see the lack of support Melissa has as a barrier to counselling. Ideally, when we do trauma work, we need to know the client is supported, because it can be tough going. In addition, there are those counsellors who theorise that lack of relationship is a result of the client's processes, rather than the world around the client, and this may signal an inability to form a counselling relationship. In Melissa's case, the world's transprejudice is salient to her lack of relationship, as is her age, for loneliness is a big problem among the elderly.

She may take time to trust a counsellor, but to remove a potentially transformative relationship from the client because of a lack of other relationship is cruel. Instead, it is far better to offer Melissa longer-term counselling with an experienced and trans aware counsellor who can go at her pace and consider the other service support she is getting, and ways to expand this. Therapy might become the gateway to her trusting people again, if taken at a very gentle pace.

This is not to say that Melissa cannot be experiencing fragile processes because of the lack of empathy in her formative years, therefore any counsellor needs to be patient and rock steady in their prizing of Melissa (Livingstone 2011, p.139).

It is not unusual for past trauma to resurface when someone comes out, nor for transition to become possible when somebody begins to address an alcohol problem. It is likely that Melissa needed to suppress both her trauma and her gender identity. It is also likely that she was abused *because* of her gender identity. As we have seen before, the growing up experiences of trans women are not the same as those of cis men. Rarely able to completely hide their orientation towards female socialisation, these children are marked as targets for all kinds of abuse. Because of this, they are far more likely to be abused than cis men. One survey put the rate of sexual abuse of trans women at 48 per cent (Cook-Daniels 2015), and rates are invariably higher than those for cis men, 16 per cent of whom experience childhood sexual abuse (CSA) and even cis women, 15–20 per cent of whom experience CSA (Kelly and Karsna 2017, p.9). It should be noted that the NSPCC does not divide abuse statistics by gender but notes that *disabled* children are most vulnerable to abuse (2018). It may be that our focus solely on gender with respect to abuse is erroneous.

Trauma by its nature leaves us with 'shattered assumptions' (Janoff-Bulman 1992) about the world and thoughts and feelings that are hard to process. Creating a safe enough environment is essential when working with trauma (Rothschild 2000, p.99). Undermining Melissa's identity is liable to re-traumatise her and at the very least make her feel unsafe. A counsellor supporting her after the invasive questions about her anatomy must be able to be with Melissa's distress about this, and not leap to justifying a colleague's unacceptable behaviour. Offers to look into trans awareness training and a commitment to get things right for Melissa going forward could be the start of a more trusting relationship being built.

CONCLUSION

When we look at minority stress, the ideas of therapy as a one to one, individualistic endeavour breaks down. Although our one relationship, if we weave it well enough, may be truly transformative in the context of a potentially barren landscape, what our clients really need is to be held in a much better social web. I am a trainer as well as a therapist because of this; I know that training a few hundred people to build better relationships to the trans community is going to weave hundreds and hundreds of threads that will hold many trans individuals more securely.

As a therapist it feels equally important to attend to the web that is holding, or in some cases precariously dangling, our clients. Sometimes, this is about encouraging the client to build relationships with other trans people. We may need to help break down the internalised transprejudice that might be blocking them from building those relationships. Internalised transprejudice can also prevent those relationships from feeling as affirming as relationships with cis people. It is important to help them find a space for trans people like them, though, because just like the rest of the world, trans spaces are not always perfectly inclusive.

The support of non-LGBT+ people, especially family, will be much more effective than support from within the LGBT+ community (Grant *et al.* 2011). It is not hard to understand why, because if we hold within ourselves the same biases the rest of society has, the acceptance of other LGBT+ people is not going to be as validating as acceptance from people who are themselves more socially accepted.

That is not to say that minority community solidarity is not invaluable, if not essential. But a client may need help to learn to value that support, to see the potential happiness in having trans friends and trans lovers. Depending on on the general level of awareness within a community group, trans people may find themselves marginalised even within trans spaces – as everywhere else, racism, intersex erasure, bisexual erasure, antagonism towards non-binary people, sexism, ableism and classism exist.

It is too easy for us to fail to bear the weight of all these rejections and broken threads alongside our client. While we may want to support our clients to mend the threads they want to mend, there is no benefit to our clients in us maintaining that an irretrievably broken thread is mendable. We may feel the urge to encourage a client to suppress themself to maintain a relationship. But really then we are asking them to maintain a relationship based on a fiction, and that may feel like the other party is having a relationship with someone else. It is a broken thread in denial that it is broken.

The urge to tell a client their parents may come around when in fact they might not may originate in our own need to believe that people are not that terrified of having a trans person in the family. But sometimes they really are. Some families are accepting from the first moment, some come around after time and some never do. The urge to encourage a client to 'make nice' in the face of mistreatment is encouraging submission in exchange for a relationship that is conditional. Naturally the client will, by necessity, be doing their fair share of submitting, suppressing and bargaining, but we need to resist our urges to subtly encourage this at the expense of their growth.

What we can do is support the client to notice and build contact with allies where they can be found and seek them out where they seem absent. We can also act as advocates where appropriate, assisting clients with GP referrals and introductions to appropriate services where a word from us might help build a bridge to them being listened to. We can point family towards trans-affirmative support services like GIRES, Mermaids and Distinction.

Those of us that feel able to 'offer' activities within our sessions might find the 'Where's my support?' activity useful. On a paper, we draw concentric circles or simply place a marker in the centre to represent the client, and they use buttons or pebbles or other items to map out their support network. Services, spaces, family, friends, online groups and forums – any human contact that is relational and at least partly helpful. Once mapped out, the client has a chance to think – do any of these people need to be moved closer? Do any need to be further away? Off the page entirely? Are there any 'vacancies'? What for? Cuddles, chit chat, venting, sport and recreation, challenge, acceptance, advice, mentoring, volunteering? Often by visualising more precisely what we are missing we can locate it.

The web model pays close attention to the network of relationships that holds each of us. It draws our attention towards the people for whom those networks are tenuous. It encourages us to actively attend to those threads for the strengthening of social cohesion in general. I hope any person-centred counsellor knows in their heart that hierarchical relationships are not that relational at all, they tend to be more instrumental. If we are over-attending to our security within a hierarchy, we are neglecting the webs of social cohesion that we could be spinning laterally.

Hierarchies will have us all feeling insecure and dangling by a thread. When we spin lateral threads, they are mutually holding. As we know from the enormous fulfilment we gain from our work, the relationships we build in the therapy room are mutual, and each of our clients, however isolated and outside of society they seem, has the capacity not just to be held but to be holding someone in return.

PERSONAL REFLECTION

1. Consider the way you consume and share stories about LGBT+ rights in other cultures – are you boosting the voices of people on the ground? How can we help the people concerned? Which stories get prioritised, which voices heard?
2. When was the last time you stood up against transprejudice? Note how it feels to be asked that question, and whether any fear or discomfort is there.
3. Look at the list in this chapter of ways in which minority groups can be disadvantaged. First, go down the list focusing on ways you are personally disadvantaged in each situation. Second, go down the list again, this time focusing on the social advantages you have that another might not, in each situation. An example might be a) as a person on a low income, I am excluded from a lot of safe and secure housing; b) as a white, cis, straight person I am less likely to be harassed by my neighbours or denied housing based on my identity.

4. Do the 'Where's my support?' exercise yourself – how many threads are holding you? Any repairs needed to your web? Any vacancies?

Chapter 7

A DIVERSE COMMUNITY

In this chapter, I look a little more closely at the ways in which extra difference can compound a trans person's marginalisation, and the specific ways in which different experiences complicate our lives. In addition, I invite the counsellor to look at how the narratives around their own differences interact with trans stories.

As a white person I would not want to co-opt the theory of *intersectionality* (Crenshaw 1991) to speak about my own experience. Nevertheless, for those not acquainted with Crenshaw's work, I invite you to discover it, perhaps starting with her TED talk (Crenshaw 2016) and moving onto her academic writing. The theory deepens our understanding of inclusive practice. Crenshaw used the theory to describe how we cannot view people's characteristics in isolation, because one aspect of our experience may well complicate another. Specifically talking about how black women cannot be served by looking at racism and sexism separately, she used the example of a company that employed a lot of black men as labour and a lot of white women as administrators, but did not employ a single black woman, and yet claimed it was adequately fulfilling its prerogative to diversify its workforce (Crenshaw 2016).

Examples like the one above demonstrate how an apparent commitment to diversity can be superficial, and how the experiences of minorities *within* a minority can often better signal the covert existence of ongoing prejudice. So, we may have an unrealistic view of how things are for minorities when we look at the circumstances of well off, white, middle class LGBT+ people. How things are for young, elderly, black, disabled, poor or otherwise marginalised LGBT+ people is another story.

WHO SPEAKS FOR LGBT+ PEOPLE?

When I work as a community organiser, I am often caught between two conflicting positions that hark back to the issues of hierarchy raised in the previous chapter. To get funding, to gain support from the wider community, I find myself building relationships with people who are in positions of power within the LGBT community. These people are often in middle management, in good jobs, or well-connected trustees of NGOs, and they themselves work hard to maintain a network of positive relationships that enable their work or their charities to continue to be funded and their projects to have an impact. They are often older, whiter, posher, more abled and more gender conforming than the communities they represent.

When I focus on maintaining such relationships, which are often with people who are not themselves trans, I can find myself caught between two options: do I challenge some of the things that are being said or done that are not helpful for people in my community or other marginalised communities, or do I try and keep relationships smooth by 'sucking up' to people, rather than challenging them?

The web model and person-centred ethics in general encourage me to maintain lateral relationships at the expense of hierarchical ones, but it is easier said than done. A hierarchical society requires people to know their place. Speaking up and challenging are things that someone low down in a social hierarchy just should not do. What quickly happens, alas, is that these 'LGBT+' organisations quickly become homogenous and resistant to input from more marginal LGBT+ groups. To maintain their positions in the social hierarchy, they neglect the needs of the more vulnerable elements of their communities. Often, the theory is that marginal voices may damage the overall cause and need to be silenced.

This need for a position might explain the kind of respectability developed in the modern LGB movement that thoroughly distanced itself from the trans community. The pinnacle of this is the setting up of the UK charity Stonewall. The charity was named after the 1969 riots started predominantly by trans and gender-divergent BAME people (Equality Archive 2015). Despite this, the charity did not include trans people in its remit until very recently (Stonewall 2015).

This also happens *within* the trans community, so just as we see lesbian and gay people distancing themselves from trans (and bi, and

BAME, and disabled, etc.) people, we also see certain trans narratives being favoured and others shut down as dangerous:

> What happens when the doors are only open to a handful of 'acceptable' trans lives – those that don't threaten the status quo? Is that a success? No. That is transnormativity. As transnormativity gains steam, it generates what is called respectability politics: I am ok with you being ____________, as long as it fits into the story I have of what an upstanding ________ person looks like. (Kray 2015)

Jackson (2017) talks about respectability politics as 'a politics that goes along with the status quo, never challenges structures of power', going on to point out that the structures themselves are the problem, and respectability politics does nothing to dismantle them.

What does this mean for a counsellor, raised within these structures of power and persuaded to see them as neutral and 'just how things are' rather than problematic? It means we have a lot of work to do to raise up and value voices that do not go along with these structures or suffer under the weight of them. If we truly believe in an equal relationship with our clients, if we truly want to have an affirmative approach towards differences, we need to be prepared to embark on a process of unlearning everything these structures have taught us.

RACISM WITHIN THE LGBT+ COMMUNITY

In my home city of Nottingham, about a third of the population are BAME, but in LGBT+ spaces, this ratio is not represented. The assumption is often made that this is because of the anti-gay prejudice in 'other cultures', rather than racism in LGBT+ spaces. In fact, the assumption of a superior approach to LGBT+ rights in white countries is a big part of the problem. White LGBT+ leaders, for instance, speak a lot about the plight of LGBT+ people overseas, but often we don't hear those voices for themselves. There is a kind of paternalism that can develop where we learn to think of 'other cultures' as being 'less progressive' around LGBT+ issues and we can feel some sense of superiority about our own culture:

> The danger here is that the rhetoric of 'civilisation' could take hold once again. Empire was often justified as a means of enlightening, and thereby saving, the populations of the colonial outposts. If Western

> neoliberalism and paternalism can be reframed as liberating tendencies, that false narrative will return with force. (Ahmed 2017)

For many cultures where we are now concerned about LGBT+ rights, it was colonialism that exported anti-LGBT+ laws (Ahmed 2017). I wish that full acceptance and inclusion of all LGBT+ people in British culture was part of our fundamental cultural values, but it is not so. Rights had to be fought for and they can go backwards as well as forwards over time. If seeing how much worse things could be silences UK pleas for better treatment, that would be an injustice. If two thirds of LGBT+ asylum claims are rejected, many from some of the most brutal regimes regarding LGBT+ people (Duffy 2017), then perhaps our 'concern' for LGBT+ people overseas is quite superficial. High levels of impossible proof and intrusive prejudice remain in the asylum system (Duffy 2017).

We can easily point at atrocities towards LGBT+ people as an example of a particular culture or religion but ignore the way populations are being manipulated by corporations, oligarchs or outside political influence, or living in the shadow of war. Our media can single out the atrocities that occur under the regimes that are our current political enemies but remain silent about atrocities committed closer to home.

There is a term for this, called 'pinkwashing', where countries draw a contrast between their own superficial record and others' on LGBT+ rights in order specifically to justify exerting their might over other cultures, while at the same time being complacent towards the very real inequalities that still exist for LGBT+ people. Naturally, such inherently white supremacist ploys can drive enormous wedges between white and BAME people within the LGBT+ community, and some of the political manipulations that have led a chosen few white LGBT+ people to feel 'favoured' in our society have also led to those individuals shutting down more robust discussions, and even making LGBT+ spaces feel impossible to access for BAME people and other more marginalised groups.

As counsellors, being aware of this complex arena is crucial. It can stop us from assuming our BAME clients will be welcome in all LGBT+ spaces. We can direct them to QTIPOC (Queer, Trans, Intersex People of Colour) spaces, or organisations like *Imaan*, for LGBT+ Muslims. We can also support our clients to navigate false beliefs that being LGBT+ is a 'white western' identity and help them find their authentic self through a knowledge that all global cultures have their own ways of expressing what we call LGBT+, much of which was suppressed by colonialism.

We may have to challenge our ideas of how gender is to be performed, and the way we racialise gender in BAME people, women particularly. Vidal-Ortiz (2009, p.101) tells us:

> Other women of color face stereotypes that include the (perceived) hyper-masculine African American woman, the hyper-sexualized Latina teenager, or the 'exotic' Asian massage parlor worker; they endure the subsequent negotiations that surround these images. These assumptions of racialized sexuality are also imposed on transwomen of color.

Parallel stereotypes of men also exist, naturally. We must become aware of the racialised gender stereotypes that exist, where they came from and the purpose they serve in restricting BAME people. I recall when doing my counselling training reading an article long since lost, that taught me how many of the stereotypes of black and working class masculinity had been imposed. Workers were valued for physical strength, with loose ties to family so they are easily taken away for long shifts, or even to another region, discouraged from book-learning or thoughts of betterment, reckless towards their own safety. Gender for men as well as women, in this instance, was a top-down imposition from the overclass – slave and factory owners. Looked at through this lens, we can see the dehumanising process that is utilised on men who are lower in the social hierarchy. Gender is not something only imposed on women. Nowhere is this clearer than in the indoctrination of child soldiers (Human Rights Watch 2008).

Vidal-Ortiz goes on to ask us how we picture trans women of colour, and whether we limit those images to the margins or see such women taking a place as full citizens (2009, p.102). I would encourage each of us not only to learn to see *past* stereotypes, but also to be open to understanding stereotypes and how they come about. We need to understand that sifting through and fighting free of the layers of story imposed on us regarding gender is the work of a lifetime for all of us.

When organisations consult BAME people, it is often local businessmen or religious leaders who are engaged with. This can leave minorities within the community out of the conversation entirely.

The way community groups are set up and ordered according to these hierarchies can create a sense of extra marginalisation for anyone with a foot in two separate communities. Sabah Choudrey, an important speaker on diversity issues, has this to say:

> During Ramadan, especially as a queer Muslim, it kind of highlights how difficult it can be to find community, we're not really allowed to be queer in the Muslim community, or Muslim in the queer community... I often feel a bit isolated during this time because it is really hard to find community – we really have to work for it and look for it. (Choudrey 2018)

MARGINALISED EXPERIENCES WITHIN THE TRANS COMMUNITY

In 2012, an alarming statistic was brought to light by National Coalition of Anti-Violence Programs (NCAVP) in the USA. It showed statistics of LGBT hate murders. Despite trans women being a small proportion of the overall LGBT population, 53 per cent of the murder victims were trans women. More worrying still, the percentage of BAME people murdered was 73 per cent. This was a small sample, but unfortunately similar statistics are replicated elsewhere, and not just in the USA (Giovanniello 2013).

This alarming statistic cannot be taken in isolation as it represents a ubiquitous problem. Each year on 20 November the trans community observes Transgender Day of Remembrance (TDoR,) in which we commemorate the hate murders of the previous year. The TDoR organisation compiles yearly statistics (TDoR 2007). Some people mistakenly believe these statistics are the total numbers of murders – they are not, they are only the murders where it is clear the cause of death was anti-trans hate crime. They do not include the many trans women who are victims of domestic violence murders, for instance.

Each year at TDoR we notice that most of the victims are trans women of colour. Mostly these murders happen in the Americas, however the disproportionate violence that is aimed particularly at trans women, especially if they are women of colour, is a ubiquitous problem. TDoR is a painful ritual, but it gives the community time to process the bombardment of news of deaths from in-community news sources and give humanity back to the dehumanised victims.

When Naomi Hersi was murdered, only the LGBT+ press humanised Naomi, reminding people that she was a fun woman who was well liked in her local community (Morgan 2018).

The media is influenced by, but also an influencer of, public opinion. Perhaps people are not interested in seeing trans women as victims but more interested in stories that portray trans women as a danger. Inevitably, sowing fear of trans women puts them more at risk. Transmisogyny, the way transprejudice and sexism combine, has many threads within it. It is the way trans women are sexualised, objectified and fetishised. When womanhood itself is seen as inferior, then a trans woman's need to live as a woman is held as suspect. It is the way trans women are exempted from the need to be protected from violence because they are perceived to be men, but at the same time are targets of misogynistic violence because they are women.

This is not to say that other trans people are not affected by misogyny, but that for other trans people there is not this perfect storm of transprejudice and misogyny combining in such a violent way. The sexualisation and objectification of women combined with the notion that trans people are fake and fraudulent has given rise even to the justification of murder by legislators. The 'trans panic' defence is legitimate in many US states, for instance (The LGBT Bar 2017). This is the legal notion that it is justifiable to murder somebody if you discover they are trans in the context of having been attracted to them. Underlying this is not just misogyny and transprejudice but also gay prejudice. These fears are intrinsically connected. It is important to understand how these different structures work together in complicated ways, meaning that if you are trans *and* a woman *and* black *and* poor, for instance, these experiences will work together to produce effects that are distinct from any one of these identities in isolation. In this example, your chance of being murdered goes up considerably with each aspect, especially if you live in the USA or Brazil.

In complicated ways our differences combine to give us unique and sometimes difficult paths. For many trans people, as discussed previously, transness is combined with dyslexia or autism or physical disability or mental illness. Finding spaces that support all these things can be taxing, and often these complications can make individuals seem 'too difficult' for unprepared services or counsellors to support. Trans individuals frequently fall through the nets of agencies who are unable to meet their complex needs.

Working with difference in the therapy room

Lago outlines the various structural inequalities that exist and lays out the many ways in which they affect women and minority individuals' lives. He then asks:

> What guarantee do we have, as a professional body of therapists, that we will not repeat these same patterns of discriminating behaviour in our therapeutic work with minority group clients when so many others in 'caring' services have been found wanting? (Lago 2013, p.437)

Hopefully I have given some idea of the extent of the social structures that exist around gender and gender divergence and how they trouble the lives of trans people. I am imagining that some readers are nodding and instantly accepting this information. There will be others who are finding it a struggle, or are even caught in doubt. How can such an enormous structure be so invisible? How could we have known so little about what is written here? And what is written here is so contrary to what is told elsewhere, so how can it be trusted?

Often, we retreat to the belief that treating everyone the same is the best approach. Naturally, our 'same' will be defined by cultural norms and it will fit some people much better than others. If we see all clients in the same carpetless room with a ticking clock, for example, most clients will be fine, but clients who experience sensory overwhelm from sound may find the room unbearable. If we meet in a church building, this environment is neutral for many, but clients who suffered from religious abuse, or clients of another religion, may find this a barrier. We can only learn the differing needs of diverse people by doing plenty of research – there is no easy way around this.

Another reaction to difference is to see it as divisive. The idea that to be strong together we need to focus on our similarities not our differences is a powerful social narrative. Slowly, if we do the work, we may start to be tolerating of difference, although our heads will still be full of 'why do they have to be like *that*?' when those differences are too 'in our face'. Eventually the aim is to be excited by difference, to love it and embrace it and be in awe of it. As novelty-seeking animals this should not be too hard, but we have many fears instilled in us about difference that need to be overcome.

DIFFERENCE ACROSS THE LGBT+ COMMUNITY

These challenges exist even if we are LGBT+ ourselves. LGBT+ people internalise the rules and structures of society alongside everyone else. Sometimes, these often-unwritten rules were made more explicit for us growing up. For instance, while my feminine sister took to make-up and girly things without having to think about it, I had them forced on me by certain relatives because I was unconsciously following the rules for boys rather than girls. On coming out or becoming aware of a divergent identity, we reflect on and unlearn much of what was forced on us. Sometimes this is easy, sometimes less so. Our own route for struggling free of these social expectations and our meaning-making around our new reality will be personal, unique and inevitably tangled up in all the layers of social rules about gender and sexuality that we internalised previously.

For trans people the need for social acceptance can sometimes lead to suppression of the diversity of our community. Despite non-binary people (although not that specific term) having been around for as long as trans people have been around, and in fact numbering greater than more binary-aligned trans people (Government Equalities Office 2018), we have often struggled to find a place within the community. Sometimes our needs are perceived as a 'threat' to trans people whose identities align more comfortably with the binary. There can be an assumption that we will grow into a more binary-aligned identity, or that if we are transitioning we are surely just a trans man/woman.

Non-binary people's desire to break down perceptions of gender as a binary and the need to identify outside of the legal gender binary can clash with people who want to be understood simply as men and women, without ambiguity. Some non-binary people can cast aspersion on trans men and women's identities, feeling that non-binary is a more accurate way to describe *all* trans people. While it is true there cannot be a binary if there are more than two types of gendered experience, I suggest that trans people have as much right to call themselves men and women as do cis people, who are equally unlikely to fully align with a completely binary idea of gender.

Rather than fighting over which is the more 'correct' way to be trans or LGBT+, it helps if we accept everyone's path as valid and correct for them, and ensure our language and terms are fully inclusive and equalising of all possible identities. LGBT+ people need to work as hard as any others to learn and reflect on these issues if we are to be able to fully meet our trans (or other LGBT+) clients. It is likely in working ourselves out, that we came up with a few theories and 'answers' about gender and sexuality and we need to be careful that these do not promote some identities over others.

The relationship between trans and LGB people

LGB people are marginalised for their own atypical relationship with gender. and sometimes this causes tensions between LGB and trans people. LGB people may have had to fight to be recognised and accepted as the men or women they are, hearing comments such as 'real men don't do that' or 'why do lesbians act like men?'. Some LGB people believe trans people's experiences are the same as theirs and express frustration that trans people cannot identify simply as gender non-conforming cis men and women. They might also conflate gender and sexuality and believe all trans people are or should be cis gay people. Even within the LGB community, though, relationships with gender, with the sexed body, and with sexuality are diverse.

In 'Counselling across Difference and Diversity' (Lago 2013, p.443), we encounter a quote by Julie Bindel, in which she assesses a room full of butch and femme lesbians as experiencing 'internalized homophobia' to the extent that they 'ape' heterosexual couples. Lago presents this uncritically as the 'impact of internalized oppression'. Lago's work on cross-cultural counselling is important, but this glaring mistake provides a teachable moment. Lago has taken the voice of Bindel, a lesbian, and used it to speak over other lesbians, enabling a judgement to be made about lesbians who do not relate to gender in a 'neutral' way, as Bindel does. For any counsellor reading this who has puzzled about why some lesbians 'dress like men', Bindel provides an answer that reinforces the suspect nature of butchness or female masculinity. At the same time, she reinforces a social rule found in some quarters that lesbians are expected to dress somewhat androgynously and that 'lipstick lesbians', the derogatory term for femme lesbians, are also suspect.

In this way people can, as I noted before, unconsciously use prominent members of a minority group to police other members. Lago believes he is sharing an important observation about butch and femme lesbians, but in fact he is sharing Julie Bindel's judgement of a lesbian subculture she does not personally relate to. It is worth noting at this point that Bindel is another passionately anti-trans campaigner (Minou 2010), and I do not think this is a coincidence. Bindel has very rigid views about the right and wrong ways to be an LGBT+ person.

A butch lesbian once put it to me very clearly: 'Lesbian is my sexuality, butch is my gender.' Gender and sexuality are different things, but as we learned earlier, they often co-occur. We see in the lesbian community a broad range of gendered experiences. Many lesbians, therefore, have divergent experiences of gender that do not relate to their sexuality. It is important that we do not blur these things and are explicit that we are talking about *gendered* experiences and not sexuality, for instance, when our lesbian client says she feels like she is wearing drag if she puts on a dress. Our culture tends to absorb gender divergence into gayness. Other cultures might do the exact opposite.

There can be defensiveness and confusion between the experience of lesbians and trans men on both sides. In a binary world, you can only be one of two options, but I hope by now we understand that everyone's gendered experience is different. A butch lesbian who fully identifies as a woman may constantly be having her identity as a woman undermined and questioned, while her assignment at birth and her experience as a woman may be central to her identity. Other butch lesbians openly identify as trans. Leslie Feinberg, one of the foremost trans activists of the last century, stated:

> I am female-bodied, I am a butch lesbian, a transgender lesbian — referring to me as 'she/her' is appropriate, particularly in a non-trans setting in which referring to me as 'he' would appear to resolve the social contradiction between my birth sex and gender expression and render my transgender expression invisible. (quoted in Webber 2014)

Feinberg's experience is not a model of how all non-binary people or trans men 'should' relate to the lesbian community. Feinberg's experience, as discussed earlier, was formed by being unable to pass as a woman prior to transition, and by many other things unique to hir. But it is an important note about how permeable the boundaries are between the realms of lesbian, butch and trans, and yet these are still distinct experiences.

There are those who feel identifying as a woman is a matter of 'solidarity' and that rejecting the label is a 'betrayal.' I would counter that we cannot choose where our incongruence lies, and it lies very differently with each of us. Just because one butch lesbian feels satisfaction and a sense of self identifying as a woman, does not mean that another butch lesbian is not experiencing unbearable incongruence with the same words and ideas that give another person meaning. Being trans is not an act of betrayal or forsaking of womenkind, it is an act of loyalty to oneself and authenticity.

A lesbian might ease chest incongruence by having a breast reduction, but not consider herself to be trans. Another might ease her lower incongruence by using a prosthetic, another might have a drag king persona. The word trans may not be meaningful to these individuals, even though they would be welcome under the trans umbrella. It might also depend on their age, culture and social group how they define themselves. BAME cultures may use words like *bois* or *stud* rather than butch. Many straight or bi women are also having these experiences and might even be assumed to be lesbian because of this. But although there is a population overlap here, gender and sexuality are not the same thing and can present in all sorts of ways in all sorts of people.

Those of us who are trans but once lived as lesbians may never have been butch. Butch and trans are simply not the same thing, even if they overlap. I personally see myself as more femme than butch, which a lot of people find confusing. To feel more like a femme man than a masculine woman is not unusual for assigned female trans people. Butch trans women exist also, because nothing is a binary and nothing is simple. Experiences are variable, and the meanings people attach to words are also variable. More importantly, these words have value. Butch woman as an identity and appearance is *valuable*. In her award-winning comedy Nannette, Hannah Gadsby talks about being 'incorrectly female' and the violence she received specifically for her gender non-conformity rather than her sexuality; 'if I'd have been feminine, that would not have happened' (Gadsby 2018, 58m). She also discloses that people keep saying she is trans, but she does not identify as trans. These experiences have a definite kinship with trans experiences, but they are also distinct, and 'butch' is a long-standing cultural word that stands on its own. Butch lesbians are valuable and do not need to be corrected or renamed, neither should they correct or rename trans people to 'butch'.

If this is too confusing, because the idea that we can understand and categorise people based on type is breaking down, then good – when we encounter clients, we need to be able to hold all these labels very lightly and ask our clients – what does lesbian, trans, butch, mean to you? And equally so when they say 'I'm not trans' as when they say they are, because how and why they hold a descriptive away from themselves is as important as how and why they embrace another.

Are these themes echoed in the gay community? Well yes, and no. Crossdressing in men has different connotations than it does in women. It is much less acceptable for men to publicly cross-dress, so it is more difficult for feminine men to express their femininity, but the same tensions do exist between drag queens and crossdressers (many of whom are not gay), and trans women. Some crossdressers may insist, for example, that trans women are 'taking it too far', as if they are having the same experience but responding differently to it, rather than their experiences simply not being the same. Other crossdressers and drag queens see themselves as part of the trans community and embrace its diversity.

Likewise, some trans women embrace the continuum of experience, while others try to draw a hard line between themselves and crossdressers. This is a particular issue when all trans women, drag queens and crossdressers are inaccurately perceived by some by the pejorative phrase 'men in dresses'. It is understandable for trans women to want to delineate the difference between a man who dresses for performance or pastime, and an authentic woman living her life. Trans is not a costume. However, while these sections of the community are very different, they exist on a continuum. Someone perceived by trans women as a 'crossdressing man' may be a trans woman in the early stages of discovering herself, or a bigender, non-binary person with an authentic male and female aspect (such as Eddie Izzard).

Expressing femininity in the gay community can be just as marginalising as it is in the lesbian community. Grindr profiles can read 'no femmes' or 'masc4masc' and gay men can complain about other gay men being too camp, desiring people to behave in ways that equate to stereotypical heterosexual masculinity. 'Upholding "straight-acting" behavior and masculinity to such a high standard can only lead to queer people internalizing homophobia and self-hate' says Kacala (2018). There appears to be a lack of understanding of the overlap between same sex attraction and gender divergence, so that feminine-coded behaviour is seen as 'stereotype' rather than natural difference.

In a world where gay is much more acceptable than trans, trans people may come out as gay first, or be identified as gay by others, before coming out as trans. 'Everybody up to that point assumed I was a cis femme gay man even though I never came out as a gay man' says Owl, who came out as trans in rural Iceland having never met another trans person (Roche 2018).

Counsellors need to take care about 'stereotypes' when working with LGB people. We are likely to have internalised the idea that a camp man or a butch woman is a 'stereotype' while 'straight-acting' men and feminine women will be seen more neutrally. We can even problematise gendered behaviour that veers away from what is essentially a stereotype of cis-het normativity. Some men are naturally more feminine, as they have absorbed some social cues from women. This may also mean they are orientated towards their mothers rather than fathers (and vice versa for some lesbians). Words like 'camp' and 'effeminate' often imply the negative connotations of men expressing femininity, as does 'mummy's boy'. Femme men become the caricatures of old comedies, and the trope endures. It is important to celebrate femininity in men and move away from judgements about the inferiority of femininity. We can see, though, that gender non-conforming LGB people are more likely to experience stigma for their identities than those that 'blend' with straight people, and that gender diverging experiences exists on a continuum into trans identities, whilst not being *the same* as trans identities. Think how purple and blue are on a continuum, but not the same. Also note from the old line *violets are blue* that we sometimes blur the boundaries of blue and purple in language, just as we do with gender and sexuality.

Bisexuals are, perhaps, the least likely group to be bogged down with these problems, as their sexuality does not centre around either being or being attracted to one gender. Of all the parts of the LGB community, I have found bisexuals to be the most welcoming of trans people. It should be noted here that bisexuals also tend to be marginalised within the LG(bt) community. Enduring ideas of bisexuality being a phase, or a problem, still exist among gay and lesbian people, as they do in the heterosexual population. There also exists, in the realms of the internet, a narrative that 'bi means two', and that therefore bi people believe there are only two genders. An extension of this narrative suggested that bi people do not date trans people at all. Because of this narrative, the term pansexual has been popularised but it is important to understand the two words have distinct meanings. A popular definition of bisexuality is that of Robyn Och:

> I call myself bisexual because I acknowledge in myself the potential to be attracted, romantically and/or sexually, to people of more than one sex, not necessarily at the same time, not necessarily in the same way, and not necessarily to the same degree. (Bisexual Resource Centre 2018)

Och also talks about the fact that being bisexual is not necessarily being attracted to people 'regardless of gender'. Gender might, for bisexual people, be an important factor in attraction – Och, for instance, is attracted to androgyny in people assigned both male and female (Bisexual Resource Centre 2018).

The term pansexuality is in fact more accurately used for those who do experience attraction regardless of gender, although naturally different people will use all these terms differently. What matters is what the term means to the individual using it. My caveat to that is just so long as they are not in their own definition making sweeping statements about others that simply are not true.

The trans counsellor

Minorities beset by outside attack must take care not to pull too far together into something rigid and monolithic, where nobody can breathe. I am by and large immensely proud of the wisdom and diversity to be found within the trans community. Like everyone, trans people must work at their unconscious biases. Being oppressed does not give you the automatic ability to see other forms of oppression clearly, or even your own.

Fragility in one's own identity can make it hard to fully meet an identity that is different. Exclusion of non-binary identities can come from a sense that trans people are easier to understand and accept if we leave non-binary out of the equation. However, that leaves an incomplete and inaccurate description. Some non-binary people believe trans men and women's identities 'conform to the binary'. Seeing that gender (and assigned sex) is socially constructed, they might perceive gender neutrality or an agender identity to be superior to a male or female gender identity. The tendency to see one's own identity as superior and 'the right answer' is common among many groups. In minorities it can come from defensiveness. It is important to realise that just as we are no worse than anyone else, equally we are no better.

There are many different iterations of this: Are trans people who do not experience physical incongruence really trans? Is 'non-binary trans woman' a legitimate identity? Can someone be trans if they use their assigned pronouns? If they have no diagnosis of gender dysphoria? If they love their body? The answer to all these things is yes, if the word trans is meaningful to them, then they can claim it, and many of us in the community are passionate that there is no measure of 'trans enough'. Equally, on the other side of the coin, we get: Are conventionally feminine identities genuine or just 'stereotypes'? (Yes, they are genuine); Are non-binary identities braver/cooler/more challenging to the 'cistem'? (Nope). 'Being gender variant is not about flouting the rules or making alternative lifestyle choices; it is simply about having developed differently from the majority' (Livingstone 2011, p.141).

There are certain difficulties tied to different parts of the community, for example trans women experience transmisogyny; some trans men face difficult phalloplasty surgery; some non-binary people have no legal recognition or protection. However, each path has its own obstacles and we may be more aware of those we have encountered ourselves or those that are more familiar.

Trans counsellors therefore need to be sure they have widened their experience and understanding of the community, rather than seeing being trans as a qualification. When we try to form a relationship based on shared identity, we can miss so much of our client. Equally, our client may over-identify with us, and it is important to open the window and ensure they understand just how many trans iterations there can be.

CASE STUDY

Amira is a British South Asian, Muslim, 19-year-old trans woman who has started gender transition and is living full time as a woman. Amira lives with her family. She was referred to counselling after a hate incident in the city centre, where she was spat on by two white men, who also attempted to remove her hijab.

Amira has diagnoses of generalised anxiety disorder, autism and depression. She says she no longer wants to go into town because people are always staring at her, and the threat of another hate attack is high.

There may be a lot of myths and assumptions we will need to clear away to be in full psychological contact with Amira. We may have assumptions about what it means to be trans in South Asian cultures. Some myths that abound: 'It's easier to be trans than gay in South Asian culture, so she's probably gay'; 'It's impossible to be LGBT+ and Muslim, her family will disown her or abuse her'; 'Her hijab is a symbol of female oppression'; 'Her hijab is a sign that she is aping oppressive female gender stereotypes – she's not a real woman.' If these thoughts entered our head it is not surprising, because they are out there in the media and society. What matters is that we challenge them, we have better information to draw on, and we can clear these assumptions and prejudices away.

No culture is a monolith – Amira may have had all kinds of reactions from her family, but it appears they are accepting, as she experiences home as a refuge. The main source of her trauma is *out there,* and it is from white people. If the counsellor is white, this could be overlooked or minimised. We need to be comfortable naming racism and Islamophobia and talking about its impacts. If Amira blends in, then she is experiencing the violent intersection of misogyny, racism and Islamophobia. If she does not, transprejudice will be in the mix as well.

In a culture where attacks on Muslims have increased, especially since the Brexit referendum, it can be an act of defiance to dress according to your own culture. We can use the term 'westernised' in approval of British South Asian girls who dress in similar garb to white people. In which case, clothes from one's own culture may be a throwing-off of oppressive dress expectations.

Another unequal structure that is often forgotten is age. Amira is young, and young people are generally treated with considerably less respect. This can add to the chance of them experiencing violence. Within the trans community, there can be judgement from middle-aged trans people who believe younger trans people 'have it easier now', often missing the way young people are disbelieved and taken less seriously, while their own identities are more likely to be respected (Hope 2017b). Transitioning young is still challenging, even with more acceptance than in yesteryear. And as stated previously, there is currently a backlash against trans people, and an increase in hate attacks. Young trans people have it very tough.

A counsellor may want to try exposure therapy with Amira to tackle the anxiety and help her feel safer in town. Is her appraisal of the situation correct, that she simply cannot be safe or comfortable there? She may be right, whereas we may be inclined to think she is being 'dramatic' – an accusation often levelled at young queer people. Concentrating on finding spaces where she *can* be safe may be better than trying exposure therapy – think of this more as an ongoing trauma than something in the past. Local *QTIPOC* groups, *Imaan* and trans groups that have good inclusion policies may provide safe spaces for her. There may be safe people she can go out with and visits she can make to build her confidence. Also remember that with autism in the mix, she may be easily overwhelmed and that some situations may never be within her comfort zone, no matter how much exposure therapy we do.

CONCLUSION

In a therapy world that is predominantly white, middle class and cisgender, our conversations around difference and diversity can struggle to achieve the necessary depth. We can see communities outside our own in two dimensions. We might, influenced by biased reporting, consider the Muslim world to be a monolithic entity associated with LGBT+ antagonism. How the can we reconcile our trans client's Muslim faith? Or if we challenge that monolithic perception and warm our hearts to the diversity of Muslim culture, how can we hear another client's bitterness to the particularly insular religious community in which they were raised, which seems incompatible with their queer self?

We might have seen LGBT+ people as a monolith, too, and seen trans men as an extreme form of lesbian, or trans women as 'really gay men'. We then learned that trans men and lesbians are different, gender and sexuality are not the same, and were confounded by our non-binary client who calls herself a 'trans dyke' and sees her gender and sexuality as interconnected.

It is much easier to see our own culture or identity as complex, multi-layered and diverse, while seeing the 'other' in stereotypical terms. Brits are, after all, not just stiff-upper-lip bores who drink tea at four. For us, the label 'British' might be expansive, but for someone elsewhere it may be a narrow box in which to place people. In Australia, for instance, I was labelled a 'whinging pom' and found myself shocked to discover the power of that stereotype in influencing my behaviour. Although this is nothing comparable to the structural inequality of racism, it had an effect. I became acutely aware of not wanting to be a 'whinging pom' but somehow being pulled more into behaviours that marked me that way. This was my first small experience of *stereotype threat*. Studies in stereotype threat show, for instance, that women underperform in maths tests if told previously that the test shows gender differences and perform equally as well as men if told that no gender differences are expected (Spencer, Steele and Quinn 1999).

It takes work for us to explore the rich diversity of human nature and to unlearn the stereotypes and unconscious biases we internalise. These come from narratives told by the people who have more power and influence, or a bigger platform; people who are more likely to be white, cisgender, over 30 and under 70, heterosexual, able and male. One of the ways we can reduce this is by seeking out the less-heard voices and immersing ourselves in them. Looking for the voices that are loved *within* those communities, rather than those lifted up by mainstream society.

PERSONAL REFLECTION

1. What has this chapter brought up for you? Make a note of anything that is confusing, is uncomfortable or needs more information.
2. When you think of a trans person, what is the picture that comes into your mind? Are there particular narratives that stand out, and others that are hidden? How much do you think you have heard the voices of more marginalised trans people, and how could you go about challenging this?

3. Consider how much reading and research you have done on difference and diversity, and note the gaps: disability (physical, cognitive and mental), ethnic minority, religion, gender, class, age (youth and old age), homelessness, poverty, immigration, asylum, alternative relationship setup, neurodivergence, sexual orientation, asexuality, sex work, political belief, nationality, HIV status, intersex status. Pick a couple of these that you know least about and commit to seeking out diverse voices on the subject.

4. Think about how your own differences affect your life. Can you separate one from the other, or do they interconnect?

5. If you are a part of the LGBT+ communities, reflect on the interrelationships between the different sections – what are the narratives around trans people within your social/community sphere? If you are trans, how close or distant to you feel to LGB people? And is your own social/community sphere diverse? What sort of inclusivity is there around disability, BAME people, non-binary people, etc.?

Chapter 8

TRANS SEXUALITY

Talking about sex in relation to trans people is delicate territory. Trans people, particularly trans women, are so over-sexualised by the cis gaze. Many people find it hard not to reduce trans people to their genitals, or to conflate transness with sexuality. We need to unpick the myths and stereotypes and come to a better understanding, because our trans clients may well want to talk about sex, and we need to be prepared.

Let us start with a self-reflective experiment. I would like you to picture a married couple. Go with the first picture that comes into your head and stick with that. Now, I would like you to think about what is expected of that couple's sexuality. How do they have sex, how often and with whom? What are they having sex for?

Even I as a queer person am likely to have thought of a heterosexual (probably white, able and middle class) couple when I heard the term 'married couple'. After all, same-sex marriage has only been legal for less than a decade in the UK, and in many places, it still is not legal. I also have a picture in my head of a stereotypical kind of sexuality in which this couple make love a couple of times a week, with each other. I understand that we are a long way past the belief that sex is just for having children and that we are taught that good sex is an essential ingredient of a loving relationship. I might also have some ideas that the man is more interested in sex than the woman and is more likely to have sex outside of the marriage or be the initiator of sex within it. As you can see, my received ideas about what constitutes a loving, fulfilling sexual relationship are very narrow.

Naturally my introjected narratives about stereotypical cisgender heterosexual (cis-het) sexuality are a very long way from my learned understanding of the diverse kinds of relationships and sexualities that exist. I am privileged to know and socialise with as well as work therapeutically with people who have a wide range of relationship and (a)sexuality styles and forms. The norms of sexuality in society now are no more objective or real than Victorian values around sexuality were. As counsellors, we have work to do so we can learn not to judge our client's sexualities, and this goes far beyond just LGB people.

There are some people who very comfortably and happily fit within the pattern of what society thinks of as 'normal sexuality' and that is okay. There are others who fit themselves to these norms with considerably less comfort. There is nothing wrong with being naturally monogamous, heterosexual, vanilla (the opposite of kinky), with mid-range levels of sexual desires. It is okay to be that person but where it becomes problematic is when that person is seen as the default, and anything outside of that is seen as abnormal and open to question. Barker and Hancock (2017, pp.12–14) problematise standard sex advice for its lack of talk about consent, focus on PIV (penis-in-vagina) sex and normativity; 'people are actually very diverse in terms of what they enjoy sexually, if they enjoy sex at all. What is one person's biggest fantasy will be another person's worst nightmare!' (p.14).

Natural human sexuality is highly variable. Fine cites a study in which finds participants citing '237 distinguishable reasons for having sex' and goes on to demonstrate how human sexuality is not biologically tethered to reproduction, in other words humans more than any other animals engage in a lot of non-reproductive sex (2017, pp.66–67). Like everything else about us, our sexuality is diverse, and rather than there being a fundamental male/female sexuality divide, we now understand that sexualities are more similar and overlapping than they are different (Fine 2017, pp.78–79).

HOW WE PATHOLOGISE NON-STANDARD SEXUALITY

We can often find ourselves looking for 'reasons' for somebody's non-standard sexuality or relationship set-up, in ways we do not scrutinise normative cis-het relationships. A person who has multiple sexual relationships, for example, may be regarded as emotionally deficient, particularly if she is a woman. They may even be considered 'sex addicted' although the sex addiction model is now being challenged (Kort 2017). We are less likely to scrutinise a woman's monogamy in the same way. If a woman *really* loves the movies, or shopping, and does that a lot, we have no concern, because these things fit with acceptable stereotypes. If she has sex a lot, we might worry for her self-esteem, wonder if she was abused as a child, speculate as to whether there is some *other* need not being met. We struggle to see her need as sexual, because society does not regard women as owning their sexuality or being sexual for their own benefit. We might fail to consider that any associated low self-esteem might be connected more to the way society treats highly sexual women than directly to her behaviour.

Let us say our highly sexual woman is also queer, autistic and has sexual abuse in her history. We might miss the fact that any historic abuse is connected to her being autistic. Autistic people are at higher risk because they can be isolated, vulnerable and less believed (Edelson 2010). The amount of sexual activity she engages could then be a *special interest* – in other words, she happens to have an abuse history and happens to like sex, and although both might be connected to her being autistic, they are not connected to each other and her sex life is not a problem. She may receive messages that her sexuality must be dictated by her abuse history, but it does not have to be. If the sex is safe and consensual, we should not worry about the *type* or *amount* of sex she is having.

It is not uncommon for counsellors working in abuse services to be trained that abuse survivors might go through a gay or lesbian 'phase' while healing from abuse. The narrative that heterosexuality is the 'true' sexuality and other sexualities are caused by something going wrong remains firmly part of the social narrative. Nobody ever questions whether someone got married and had children because of abuse, and yet it is just as possible that a woman who was sexually groomed into heterosexuality might take longer to recognise that she is a lesbian *because* of the abuse, or a gay man abused by another man might take longer to come to terms with being gay himself.

> When professionals ask me how to determine if a transgender man's gender identity is the result of childhood abuse, turning the question around to consider whether the same assumption would be reached in the case of a cisgender client provides a useful prompt for reflection on personal process. (Robinson 2016, p.19)

It is not that our sexuality cannot be affected by our life experiences, naturally it can. It is valid, for instance, for somebody who has been sexually abused by women to decide they do not want to date women, or vice versa. All kinds of experiences affect our attitudes towards gender and sexuality. But we tend to ignore the way dominant narratives around cis-het monogamy affect people and influence people *away* from their organismic sexuality. If we are to question influences on people's sexuality, then surely, we should question those dominant themes that assail us from our screens most of all?

Alternatively, we can simply trust people to find a relationship and sexuality type that works for them and be open to all the possible ways people are influenced and mediate their innate feelings through social norms. For instance, a naturally polyamorous woman in a social world that does not accept polyamory may find other ways to meet her sexual or relational needs. We may suspect her 'affair' with a woman says something about the validity of her marriage to a man, but it may be that both these relationships are equally important and meaningful to her. While I do not want to perpetuate the stereotype that bisexuals tend to cheat or require polyamory to be happy (we certainly don't), there will be *some* people for whom this is a reality. In a world that accepted bisexuality and polyamory or non-monogamy, we would not need to see multiple concurrent relationships as problematic any more than these days we see multiple consecutive relationships as problematic.

Within the realm of non-monogamy there are many relationship models. Some people have multiple life partners in loving relationships that interconnect either domestically or socially. Some people have partners of only one gender, some have partners of different genders. Some are monoromantic, loving only one person, but having multiple sexual or play relationships outside of the relationship. Some people do not have a sexual relationship with their primary life partner, and both are happy with this arrangement and fulfil their sexual needs elsewhere. For many people, sexual and romantic attraction just do not map onto one another, and they would not want a loving relationship with the people they sexually desire. They might fancy men but love women, for example. And some people do not see any of their relationships as either sexual or romantic in nature and may or may not choose a primary/life partner for other reasons.

Relationship success or failure in non-normative relationships rests on similar things to more socially endorsed relationships. Good communication, clear boundaries, enthusiastic consent of all parties, and honesty about what works and what does not for all concerned.

A counsellor may be called to support a client through something that is going wrong within their non-normative relationship setup. It is important that the counsellor grounds themself in the fact that all kinds of relationships go wrong and reserve their judgement about this relationship type. We need to think of why we favour or privilege some kinds of relationships, sexual activities and feelings, and explore our own narratives. If we cannot overturn these beliefs, then how can we help our clients?

A trivial example: why do we think it is creepy or ridiculous to be turned on by feet, but okay to be turned on by breasts? What is the problem with *feet*? We might have a clear double standard over the validity of somebody, say, masturbating over a normative sexual image or item, or masturbating over something that is seen as a fetish – clothes (such as leatherwear or rubber), non-sexual body parts, etc. We need to be very clear where these negative feelings around 'fetishes' come from. Richards and Barker (2013, p.177) suggests they derive from 'poor quality documentaries, police procedural dramas… which include them for sensationalist reasons' and go on to talk of the process of 'othering' what is another person's norm. Sadly, we do not have to look too hard to find someone dishonestly associating safe, ethical, consensual practices with something non-consensual, such as paedophilia or rape. It is inevitable that we will have internalised prejudices about different relationship types and sexual practices, but it is vital that we unlearn them if we are going to offer our clients the core conditions.

We may conflate BDSM (Bondage, Discipline, Dominance, Submission, Sadism and Masochism), and kink (sexual tastes, generally unusual ones) with abuse and danger, and not understand that when safe and consensual, BDSM and kinky lifestyles can be enormously important, fulfilling, even spiritual, and help people learn about themselves, as well as covering a range of practices from 'wild to mild' (Carrellas 2017, pp.7, 202–205). We may have an assumption that primary partners are for sex or that sex is an important aspect of primary partnership, or our lives in general, when this is not always the case. We may think of asexuality in all its many presentations as something that 'happens' to people that can be helped or treated, rather than a natural sexual orientation.

People naturally have a huge range of sexual desires and needs. These do not always map cleanly onto their romantic or relationship needs. Some people simply are not sexually attracted to other people but may still have sexual feelings. They may or may not have sex with other people, but they are vulnerable to corrective rape from people who will not accept asexuality (Mosbergen 2017). The existence of asexuality is only starting to be acknowledged; it has been mislabelled sexual dysfunction but is now understood as an orientation (Richards and Barker 2013, pp.106–107). In 2017, the major psychological professional bodies and the NHS signed up to a Memorandum of Understanding against conversion therapy for asexuals (COSRT 2017). Loving relationships do not always rely on sex for sustenance, and many people see sex as a hobby or play activity and do not need a relationship to engage in it. Where we have been sold a quite monolithic tale of sex, sexuality and relationship, there is, as always, enormous, exciting diversity.

It is important that we note and interrogate our prejudices and resistances to the various types of sex and relationship our clients might need or enjoy. Hopefully, we will be eventually able to satisfy ourselves that so long as it is safe and consensual, and our client is happy and fulfilled, we should not be troubled. Where a client *is* disturbed or upset by their sexuality, we need to be clear whether it is really a problem, or whether our client is reacting to social stigma and internalised prejudice. We live at a time when our clients can go to body positivity workshops, conscious touch, neo tantra, sacred sexuality, cuddle parties, play events, BDSM events and conscious sexuality events that help them develop their awareness of their sexuality and embodiment. Counsellors need to be open to these new realities and understand their potential to enhance the lives of our clients. We also need to realise the sensory differences some people have, particularly autistic people, that might make their touch requirements different. For example, light touch may be painful, but hard touch, pressure and restraint more pleasant. This ties in with the increasing popularity of deep pressure therapy for calming people with autism, sensory processing disorder and other issues. In other words, being tied up correctly *could* be therapeutic.

I hope it goes without saying, though, that unsafe and non-consensual things do happen in these spaces as they happen in all spaces. While explicit communication about safety, consent and boundaries may make BDSM spaces, for instance, safer than a lot of other places, there will always be some people who will take advantage of vulnerable, young people exploring their sexuality. Predators can pray on the marginalised and use people's fear of their own sexuality against them. The best antidote to this is confidence and support, as well as having recommendations and buddy systems rather than going into something alone and vulnerable.

Sometimes, people exploring these worlds can throw away all the old rules they had but forget about the necessity of drawing up their own rules and boundaries and learning to respect the individual boundaries of others. The more self-reflective and supported a person can be while exploring these worlds, the safer, happier and more fulfilled they are likely to be in discovering their own sexual and relationship needs. Supporting clients to negotiate their needs and boundaries with clarity and make consent clear and explicit is essential work for anyone who has the potential to be vulnerable and taken advantage of. We need to be able to tune into when our clients are *actually* unsafe rather than being so uncomfortable with what we are hearing, we blur it all into a 'culture' we cannot understand or distinguish.

Consent and awareness of power are also vital in our own practice. Therapists can push clients to talk about sex when they do not wish to, particularly in couples work, and this can be an abuse of power based on the assumption that it is *necessary* to talk about sex and always a *positive* to talk more openly about sex. Conversely, and anyone who has worked on an LGBT+ helpline will bear this out, there are some clients, perhaps not always genuinely LGBT, who seek certain spaces for their own sexual gratification, and naïve therapists and call operators may feel compelled to go along with a verbal exchange that feels uncomfortable or inappropriate based on ideas of wanting to be seen to be okay talking about sex. The therapist/operator's consent is also required for this to be a safe interaction. Our ability to negotiate and say no to something that lies outside what we are offering is paramount.

I hope it goes without saying that in LGBT+ communities that are closely interconnected, clients and therapists can be thrown together in unexpected situations. I highly recommend having a clear boundaries policy if you are LGBT+ and seeing LGBT+ clients, and I also recommend having very tight boundaries rather than being so flexible around boundaries that they can be accidentally overstepped.

TRANS PEOPLE AND SEXUALITY

I outlined diverse relationship and sexuality types in the previous section. We will come across a lot of divergent experiences within the trans community. Partly thanks to that cluster effect mentioned previously and partly because when we start to question one unnecessary social rule we can end up questioning many of them. If a trans person is engaging in socially stigmatised relationships or sexual practices, they may need support to feel safe and accepted in a boundaried and consensual exploration of their needs and desires.

There are also, though, issues that are specific to trans people around sexuality, and I will explore those here.

Medical transition and changing sexuality

While we now know enough about human sexuality to reject the idea that male sexuality and female sexuality are fundamentally different (Fine 2017,pp.46–79), it is true that hormones can have an impact on our sexuality. Menopausal women are prescribed female-typical amounts of testosterone, for instance, to raise libido. Testosterone surges related to stress can make both men and women feel more sexual when stressed. But equally, stress can turn us off sex altogether. Hormones, it turns out, are complicated and multiple, and our ideas particularly about testosterone are reductive (Fine 2017).

Many trans men report an increase in libido when taking testosterone. This may be the hormone itself, and it may also be related to clitoral growth. Trans men sometimes report hormon-related shifts in sexuality, although this is by no means a given. People who previously dated women exclusively find themselves attracted to men, and those who were attracted to men find an attraction to women. I have known of trans men who came off testosterone and found their sexuality reverted, leaving them to believe this was wholly a hormonal effect, though no studies confirm this, and it might be quite individual.

Equally many trans people feel they can explore and open out their sexuality as a part of transition. Many trans people post-transition are more open to bi and pansexuality. Many come to terms with being asexual. Asexuality is very common in the trans community. Those trans people who were perceived as lesbian or gay before transition are sometimes gay or lesbian after transition, in other words their interest switches from men to women or vice versa, but they remain same-gender attracted. Some feel their same-gender attraction, their gayness, to be a fundamental part of their identity. For others, sexuality remains exactly as before, and they transition from being viewed as straight to gay, or from gay to straight.

The myth about trans sexuality is that people will transition to be straight, and some even imply that trans people are 'really gay or lesbian' and are transitioning because of internalised gay prejudice. The evidence refutes this. In a survey by the US National Centre for Transgender Equality (2015, p.59), only 16 per cent of trans people identified as straight, and my own community work experience bears this out. This means all but a few trans people would belong in LGB+ spaces even if they did not include trans people. It is hard to disrupt your own gender without being forced to consider what the gender of sexual partners means to you, which may explain the lack of heteronormativity in our community. However, it might simply be that population cluster mentioned in Chapter 5 at work again.

When we consider the existence of non-binary people, our existing sexuality terms break down. What term exists for exclusive attraction to non-binary people? What is the sexuality of a non-binary person who is attracted to men? Attracted to women? Attracted to other non-binary people? We may find ourselves, when pondering these questions, wanting to know about the birth assignment of these individuals, which misses the point of many non-binary identities entirely. For myself, I make do with the label bisexual. I am explicitly *not* pansexual, because I am not attracted to all genders, just more than one. In other words, I am not attracted to people regardless of gender (pansexual) but am attracted to two or more genders (bisexual).

When trans people take hormones, they are effectively going through a similar hormonal process to puberty. Because teenage brains are also going through a major rewire it is not quite the same as teenage puberty (Arain *et al.* 2013), but in the context of being stigmatised it is still a challenging process. Trans people may feel, in some ways, younger than they are, and may dress that way too. For trans men who are growing their first facial hair, this can often mean being assumed to be much younger. For trans women, whose female selves may feel very young and new, the contrast between a testosterone-matured body and younger women's clothes can be a target for unjust prejudice and judgement. Trans women are given little leeway to explore their new identity and style. Their clothes are judged, sexualised and objectified, or ridiculed.

It is not unusual for people to find their sexuality awakening or needing to be explored as part of transition, and in the light of changing hormones and body, or greater comfort in social identity. This can make trans people, again especially women, vulnerable to their gender identity being conflated with sexuality. While bigots may project many false narratives onto trans women's genitals, hormonal transition and increasing bodily comfort tell a more complex story of trans women learning to experience sex in a very different, but often satisfying, way. Hormonal transition can put an end to erections, but many women report different kinds of pleasure. Shoshana Rosenberg (2018) interviewed 12 trans women about their experiences of sex and intimacy:

> My findings confirm what authors such as Julia Serano and Mira Bellwether have already stated in their own reflections and research. Not only are trans women capable of experiencing sexual intimacy and maintaining sexual function, but often our pleasure and satisfaction increases substantially following medical transition.

In her book *Queer Sex*, Juno Roche (2018) interviews many trans women, discovering a varied picture of sexuality – women who keep their genitalia but do not use them, women who have vaginoplasty but are unconcerned with accommodating a cisgender man, women who have all kinds of (a)sexualities. Roche reflects that when she transitioned there were no such choices; a trans woman was expected to have vaginoplasty (2018, p.73).

Existing relationships

The impact on existing relationships of transition can be profound, but it does not have to be a deal-breaker. Two people, very much in love as life partners, often find a way to negotiate transition. This is often easier if the cis partner is knowingly bisexual, but transition can alter a partner's perception of their sexuality. Other couples find themselves in 'mixed orientation' relationships, such as lesbians married to trans men, a heterosexual woman married to a trans woman, or a straight man married to a trans man. Sometimes, this comes with a sense of loss of identity and community for couples who were gay or lesbian (Green 2017, pp.76–77). Not changing orientation or 'label' does not mean a person is in denial of their sexuality, or that trans men and women are not *real* men or women respectively. Few people are 100 per cent of any orientation, and partners will often say that were they still single, they would exclusively date women (or men), but they happen to love *this* man (or woman, or non-binary person). While mixed orientation relationships are understandable for existing relationships, claiming a general attraction to trans men if you are a lesbian or straight man, or trans women if you are a straight woman or gay man, is considered erasing of trans identities.

For some partnerships, sex endures as a part of the relationship, or improves, as the trans partner begins to feel more comfortable and in touch with their body. For some, sex does not continue, because either the trans partner's sexuality has changed away from being attracted to their cis partner, or the cis partner's sexuality is no longer attracted to the trans partner's changing body, but this is not in any way inevitable.

Sometimes, partners develop sexual relationships elsewhere, by mutual agreement. For some, sex was never that important a part of the relationship and they continue in a monogamous, non-sexual relationship. Sometimes social prejudices about 'sexless' relationships are the biggest barrier to happiness. Being told that sex is important for bonding is a myth quickly dispelled by all the non-sexual bonds we have with people throughout life. Many relationships go through challenges and ups and downs in closeness and attraction. Many relationships go through shifts in sexuality and periods of little or no sex, and yet are still comfortable and happy. What people want from a primary partner, or even if they want a primary partner, is highly variable.

But for many couples, sex is important, and learning to negotiate changes in sexuality can be both daunting and exciting. 'Our sex life shifted to being more "lesbian"...I actually preferred this', says one partner, while another marks the loss of penetrative sex and lower libido from hormones (Green 2017, pp.88–89). Partners of trans men talk about negotiating increased sex drive but also lower libido from gender incongruence, while some expressed a sense of loss towards their partners' bodies (Green 2017, pp.89–91). Trying new ways to be with each other can reinvigorate a relationship. Learning to avoid triggering incongruence through touch and by changing language away from gendered terms for body parts might make sex easier. Surgical healing can also create a barrier to sex, and relearning partners' bodies after surgery, particularly the many stages of phalloplasty, can be a challenge some will view with excitement and others with fear.

Sexual awakenings

There is an abiding myth about trans women, rooted in the now debunked theory of *autogynephilia*. This theory by Blanchard (1989) proposed that trans women who are not attracted to men are 'aroused by the thought or image of themselves as women'. In other words, there was in his view a dichotomy between heterosexual trans women (what Blanchard erroneously called homosexual) and lesbian or bi trans women. Blanchard's study delegitimised those who were not transitioning to be straight, reducing their gender incongruence to a sexual desire. Sadly, this idea persists to this day, long after it has been debunked.

The most important counter to Blanchard's theory was by Moser (2009) who used Blanchard's own criteria to diagnose most of their cis women subjects with autogynephilia. In other words, both cis and trans women can *feel sexy* when they wear certain clothes that make them feel good, and the feelings of trans women and cis women are indistinguishable. For trans women who have been trapped in male attire that entirely suppresses them, it is unsurprising that sexuality is awakened by wearing clothes that make them feel good about themselves. The idea that this is some sort of self-objectification or perversion says more about Blanchard's attitude to women and sexuality than it does about trans people.

It is difficult for us to separate these narratives of sexual deviance that are pinned onto trans women, and it can be hard for some emerging trans women or non-binary people, who may be crossdressing in secret, not to pin these narratives onto themselves. 'Transvestic fetishism' is a term used to diagnose those 'crossdressers' (that may or may not be trans) who experience clinically significant distress around a sexual need to cross-dress. As Lev (2004, p.171) states, distress may be associated with stigmatisation, or fear of social impact on reputation or marriage. She also points out the sexism in the notion that 'males who want to emulate females – the inferior and more despised sex – are exhibiting a mental disorder, but females who desire to emulate male power in their dress are mentally healthy' (Lev 2004, p.170).

It is not uncommon for trans people to find their sexuality is intimately linked to being able to express a stifled part of their identity, in other words freeing their gender identity can awaken their sexuality, and if this is pathologised that can be harmful to the emerging self. It should be okay for trans women to feel sexy, but they may be receiving a very different, twisted message about their sexuality from society.

It also is not uncommon for trans people (of any assignment) pre-transition to atypically focus their sexuality in the form of what some call a 'fetish', and this might sometimes be a way to avoid feelings of physical incongruence.

The sexual changes and awakenings that come with transition can sometimes be complicated and difficult to manage. 'Some of us felt good at sex before and then transitioning makes us feel like we are just starting over again, clumsy and scared' as Taylor puts it (Roche 2018, p.124). It is not uncommon for a trans person to want to explore these changes on their own, rather than with a partner, just as most people in puberty discover their sexuality through solo experimentation and exploring erotica or pornography. A temporary withdrawal within a long-term relationship is not unusual, but partners can become confused as to why their partner is watching porn alone, but not wanting to be sexual with them, for example.

Assigned female trans people can become confused and worried as their increased libido from testosterone prompts them to consume kinds of pornography or erotica they have not previously (or recently) been interested in. They can also withdraw from relationship because their sex drive feels 'too much'. This can lead to conflict about the emerging sexuality, especially if they have negative feelings towards men and sex. Myths about testosterone can also exacerbate this problem, so it is helpful if clients have information about testosterone myths. Fine's *Testosterone Rex* (2017) is a good place to start. The belief that testosterone causes a particular kind of sexuality or makes people more aggressive is a reductive notion, but testosterone may change the sensations associated with sex, including intensity of orgasm, an observation that has been made by people travelling in both directions, towards and away from a testosterone-dominated hormonal profile.

It can be helpful to remind trans men that they do not have an adult male sexuality, but a pubertal one. Trans women may need similar reminders, but for different reasons, as will transitioning non-binary folk. It is not unusual for all adolescents to be absorbed with pornography or erotica during sexual puberty. It is not unusual to be constantly masturbating. Discovering a new sexuality for the first time can be absorbing. Wanting to read about or watch types of sex that are new or different is understandable. For the conflicted feminist trans person, it is better to remind them that feminist pornography exists than to assist them feeling shameful about their watching habits. Let us dismantle the shame around consuming pornography when it is a habit of most people (Molloy 2014).

Sexual abuse and trans people

As mentioned previously, sexual abuse is a high risk for all gender divergent children (Cook-Daniels 2015; Scottish Trans 2010), whether assigned female or male, most likely due to the ease with which such children are marginalised, isolated and disbelieved.

Contrary to the misjudged opinions that people become trans *because* they were abused, abuse can stand in the way of a trans person connecting to their gender identity. Dissociation due to trauma can make it hard for trans people to connect to their bodies. A trans man who had a male abuser or a trans woman who had a female abuser might fear becoming more like their abuser by transitioning, particularly if the abuser was a parent. If the abuser was the same as their assigned gender, they might tell themselves their feelings about their gender are connected to the abuse. The ubiquitous narratives around any divergent gender or sexuality being 'caused' by sexual abuse will also play in their heads, making them doubt the authenticity of their feelings.

Trans people will often ask their counsellor 'could abuse have caused these feelings?' A responsible counsellor can help a client understand that being trans is not a kind of damage that happens to people, but an authentic part of human diversity. When we start to understand that child sexual abuse happens to particularly vulnerable groups such as LGBT+ people, physically disabled or autistic children and not just to girls, perhaps we will be able to change the narrative that 'trauma causes difference' to 'difference causes trauma'.

Unfortunately, sexual assault is also a feature of the lives of adult trans people. Because of vulnerability, marginalisation, loneliness, poverty and homelessness, trans people are more likely to be sexually exploited, lured or groomed into unsafe or exploitive relationships. The rape and sexual assault statistics are high for all genders of trans people (Scottish Trans 2010), but the misogynistic objectification and sexualisation of trans women makes them particular targets. Counselling for sexual abuse of trans people of all genders is a vital component of any survivor's service, but sadly many women-only services are still inaccessible to all trans people.

Sex work and trans people

It may be that some of the readers of this book are harbouring prejudice and ignorance about sex work, as I was before I read up on feminist sex-positive approaches to the subject. It is not surprising, given what passes for portrayals of sex work in the media, that we harbour such prejudices. It is not that sex work is always amazing, feminist, empowering, but it can be, and even when it is not, it should always be entirely safe and set up in a way that ensures the people who do it are not put in extra danger because of bad laws and social prejudices (Bell 2009). Most importantly, we need to understand the difference between sex work, and sexual exploitation, pimping and trafficking (Bell 2009). Sex trafficking is one aspect of a vast upsurge in modern-day slavery of farm workers, cleaners and other labour (End Slavery Now 2018). The legal and economic conditions (including our treatment of immigrants) that enable this are a separate issue to sex work in the same way they are separate from legal farm work or cleaning work.

> My experience with sex work is not that of the trafficked young girl or the fierce sex-positive woman who proudly chooses sex work as her occupation. My experience mirrors that of the vulnerable girl with few resources who was groomed from childhood, who was told that this was the only way… I knew, even at sixteen, that I did what I had to because no one was going to do it for me. (Mock 2014, p.148)

Many of us who work with and are friends and colleagues with sex workers would like to see social and legal change that would increase safety. Sex workers need to feel safe to report rapes without being arrested, investigated or having their immigration status checked; just because some of them are having sex for money does not mean they cannot withdraw consent. Sex workers also need to be able to organise with other sex workers for safety, which is currently illegal, even though sex work is not. They need to be able to get support for any drug addiction or for any traumatic histories, to be free of exploitation and pimps, to earn a fair wage, and to have other options available if they want them.

In a world where so many trans people are barred from many types of employment, sex work is a readily available form of employment for them, as it is for other marginalised people, including disabled people. For some sex work is a pleasant lifeline, for others an unpleasant necessity. More than usual numbers of trans people are in sex work, although this is still a tiny portion of the trans population. Some high profile trans people have been sex workers including UK writer Juno Roche (2018), US TV presenter Janet Mock (2014) and UK journalist Paris Lees (2017), who said 'If I hadn't had sex for money to support myself through university and a year or so of unpaid internships, you wouldn't be reading my words now.' Some sex work is exploitive and dangerous, and while not all of it is, the argument goes if there was less stigma and criminalisation attached to sex work, it would be much safer for the people doing it. This is especially an issue for BAME people:

> The line between culturally permissible work and 'deviant' labor is often blurred for women of color, depending on their treatment in the socioeconomic system, whether as second-class citizens, colonial subjects, or undocumented immigrants. Since the 1970s, feminist debates have excluded prostitution from women's labor possibilities in ways that do not recognize the increased globalization and deployment of a female work force—often outside middle-class parameters of 'decent' employment. (Vidal-Ortiz 2009, p.100)

It is not ideal that trans people are objectified, sexualised and fetishised in a way that can be dehumanising. It is troubling that in a world where most people would not consider trans people as legitimate partners (Blair and Hoskin 2018), many people are also consuming pornography featuring trans people. However, many trans people feel a sense of acceptance, validation and closeness they cannot otherwise find through sex work, and many sex workers whether trans or not thoroughly enjoy their work.

Trans people may also want to use sex workers, for many different reasons. Sexological bodywork and somatic sex education, for example, support people to become more erotically embodied. This can be through talk, somatic awareness, breath and movement practices as well as using touch and bodywork. A trans aware practitioner can offer trans people educational and therapeutic work around body image, confidence, body incongruence/dysphoria, trauma, sexual expression and regaining and experiencing pleasure and arousal, whether they transition socially or with hormones and/or surgery (Body Curious 2017). Sexual surrogates can help trans people overcome dysfunction and learn to enjoy sex. Many sex workers do similar work, albeit unqualified, and work sensitively with trans people who are just learning to explore sex in a changing body. Despite the enormous crossover between sex work and counselling, and the many comparisons drawn, sex work is still stigmatised, and sex workers who train as counsellors are often discriminated against (Glyde 2018).

Trans people as valid sexual partners

A recent study made depressing reading. Eighty-seven-and-a-half per cent of those polled stated that they would not date a trans person (Blair and Hoskin 2018). The poll also showed a greater bias against dating trans women, leading the researchers to conclude transmisogyny plays a role in dating preferences. More depressing still, participants expressed a greater interest in sleeping with trans people than dating them, which indicates the way trans people are objectified and sexualised (Blair and Hoskin 2018). This echoes other research about people being more willing to sleep with bisexuals than date them (Feinstein *et al.* 2014). Also, lesbians expressed more interest in sleeping with trans men than trans women, although overall gay and lesbian people were more likely to date trans people than straight people were (Blair and Hoskin 2018).

What legitimises prejudice against trans partners is what people consider 'biological facts', particularly if they have not had lower surgery. But the reality is that when people do fall in love with trans people, they tend to find a person's genitals (or chromosomes) are not, after all, the most important thing about them, and that if they like a certain kind of sex, there are work-arounds. 'My genitals are the dicks that I purchase, which are more a part of me than any other' (Roche 2018, p.146). While there will be people who, for whatever reason, are triggered by certain body parts, attraction to men and women is about far more than just what is between a person's legs.

Perhaps it is worth emphasising, men who date trans women and find them attractive are not gay, even though this is often implied by others. Just as playing with a cis girlfriend's dildo or liking anal penetration do not make a man gay, liking his trans girlfriend's penis, is she has one, does not make a man gay. Sexual acts are not what make an identity. Likewise, cis lesbians can legitimately date trans women, cis gay men and straight women can date trans men. Being lesbian or gay is, like everything else, a multi-determined, expansive and diverse category, and ultimately what makes someone fit the label is an identification with it.

Because of the stigma around dating trans people, many do so in secret, which is difficult for the trans person. Being viewed as a shameful person to be attracted to can be difficult for someone's self-esteem, particularly in the social context of a world that constantly seeks to delegitimise you by using the wrong pronouns, questioning your identity or calling you deluded. Unfortunately, such relationship inequality and messages about undesirability make trans people very vulnerable to abusive relationships (Scottish Trans 2010).

When trans people, particularly trans women, wish to discuss the pain they feel at not being viewed as legitimate partners, this can be interpreted by some as acting 'entitled' to sex. This is another way in which trans women are sexualised and viewed as sexually predatory. The idea that someone is lonely and feeling unloved and allowed to talk about the experience of being stigmatised as a sexual partner is overlooked in favour of more salacious and troubling narratives. To be clear, nobody should date anyone who they do not want to date, but that does not mean we cannot look at how social narratives stigmatise and exclude trans people from legitimate love and affection.

Safer sex

There are some great safer sex guides out there for trans people, particularly trans people who have sex with men, who are at greater risk of HIV. Globally, trans people are 49 times more likely to have HIV (Mullin 2016). We need to understand the complex and diverse reasons trans people might be particularly vulnerable. Writer Juno Roche says 'You're terribly vulnerable because, if you try to affirm your gender by sex – which I certainly have done – you become less keen to create boundaries like asking people to use condoms' (Mullin 2016).

We need to remember that things have changed a lot for people living with HIV. Treatments are so good now, most people with access to them will be able to have their viral load lowered to the point they cannot transmit HIV to a partner. Things are very different for people with no access to treatment or untreated HIV, and health campaigns frequently miss out women and trans people (Mullin 2016). PrEP, a drug to reduce HIV infection, is aimed at cis gay men, leaving trans people out of the equation (Mullin 2016). For many of us who learned about HIV in the 1980s, things have changed a lot, and we need to catch up with our reading and challenge our ongoing misconceptions. Of course, things are very different for HIV positive people who do not have access to appropriate healthcare.

CASE STUDY

Gail came out as a lesbian at the age of 45 and is now at 48 exploring their gender identity and toying with the word *genderqueer* as an identifier. They cite the sexual abuse they experienced as a teenager as the reason for the delay in realising their sexuality and gender. They feel they were groomed into cisgender heterosexuality, and unthinkingly went on to get married and have children. Lesbian and gendered feelings they had in the past were easily explained away as being a product of the abuse and dismissed. The narrative that sexual abuse causes lesbianism in women is a well-known trope that they had internalised, and this made it easy for them to reject these feelings. It was only when Gail had counselling over their sexual abuse that they were more able to get in touch with their true feelings and come out.

Because Gail uses a wheelchair, they find themself disregarded as a sexual being or potential date. At times when they have tried to talk in queer kinky spaces about the ableism that stops people from looking past the chair and seeing a human being, they have been told that they should not act 'entitled to sex'. Ideally, Gail wants to be done with monogamy and is drawn to 'relationship anarchy' as a way of doing relationships going forward.

The first thing Gail needs of us is a full mind-cleanse from the idea that sexual abuse causes divergent identities. In Gail's case, the abuse was *clouding* Gail's identity, leaving them to simply follow the path that was written for them. In some ways, we could say that abuse made them cis-het, but that's simplistic. They adopted the default identity because the abuse prevented them from deeper reflection. It is not unusual for more organismic identity aspects to surface when trauma issues have been dealt with. That should make sense – trauma can get in the way of a lot of full functioning. But the patterns counsellors see when they work in trauma services can be misinterpreted – LGBT+ identities do not *come* from exploring trauma, they just can come to the surface. People rarely suddenly realise they are straight in these situations, because straight is the identity we are more likely to default to when something is obscuring our organismic identity.

Gail needs that stillness from the counsellor that can only come from a lot of work having been done previously. The counsellor needs to be at a point where no gender identity or sexuality is better than another, where trans identities are affirmed, but not preferred. Where Gail can try things out in therapy – new names, pronouns, ways of thinking of things, without our influence. Gail needs to be *seen*; as a valid human being, as a sexual being, a legitimate sexual partner for someone.

We need to be fully aware of the pictures that pop into our head when we hear the words *kinky, genderqueer, relationship anarchist*. They are likely to be negative – call for another mind-cleanse. And a bit of research – perhaps relationship anarchy, a surprisingly careful approach to relationships, is new to us (Nordgren 2006).

Those of us from a humanistic stable may well be cheering for Gail to shake off their conditions of worth and find a more authentic self. But we may not realise how many of our own conditions of worth are getting in the way of us fully meeting Gail. Do we really think it is okay for a person nearing fifty, who uses a wheelchair, to be all the things Gail identifies with? If not, why not?

CONCLUSION

Sexualities may tend to get put into a very narrow selection of boxes, but they are as diverse as anything else in human nature. How or whether people have sex, when, with whom and for what reason are purely individual choices, as long as nobody is being harmed and everyone is consenting. 'Is there any good reason for thinking some kinds of sex are "more proper" than others?' ask Barker and Hancock (2017, p.5). We have long ago separated sexuality from reproduction, probably as part of our earliest evolution as humans (Fine 2017, pp.46–79), so why and how we do sex are entirely socially constructed, in combination with our various natural inclinations. Certainly, we can go beyond simplistic ideas of male and female sexuality; 'all erotic tissue is simply the same Jell-O poured into different moulds' (Carrellas 2017, p.xxi).

Sexuality is such a difficult thing for many of us to talk about, even though we live in a highly sexualised society. An absence of interest in sex, or an unusual interest in sex, remain suspect in many people's minds. Counsellors must learn to work not only with our own shame and stigma response around some aspects of sex, but with the shame and stigma responses of our clients as well. When clients are trans, the sexualisation of trans people in common narrative adds another layer of complication. Trans bodies are sexualised, and their genitals are obsessed over, when in fact what is between a trans person's legs may be irrelevant to that person's self-experience, and when on average trans people are less likely than the average person to be interested in sex.

We have all got a lot of work to do. We must discard much of the pathologising that the ICD and DSM have inflicted on the world around sexual diversity, and realise often the bad, unhappy feelings that go with some sex acts, or attractions and lack thereof, are associated with stigmatisation, not the acts themselves. There are some unsafe, non-consensual practices we need to have hard boundaries around, but even if what our clients are doing is unusual, if nobody is being harmed we can be free to say, with conviction, 'there is nothing wrong with you'.

PERSONAL REFLECTION

1. Make a note of the personal issues, queries and thoughts that came up for you whilst reading this chapter.
2. Which issues do you feel confident about within this chapter, and which do you feel you need to do further reading about? For instance: sex work, asexuality, bisexuality and queerness, BDSM/kink, polyamory/non-monogamy/relationship anarchy.

3. Reflect on your own sexuality, and how it does, or does not, fit into the boxes available.
4. Reflect on whether, hypothetically, you would date a trans man, a trans woman, or a non-binary person. Note any barriers or reservations that come up, and whether you are seeing trans people fully as their identified gender, and if not, why not?
5. Re-read the case study above. Take a pause and a breath, maybe close your eyes, and notice any sensations or awareness (or lack of) in your body about aspects of what you have read. Write down what you noticed. If this process is helpful to you, you could try it with other passages that spoke to you or you had difficulty with.

Chapter 9

DO'S AND DON'TS FOR COUNSELLORS

This is the final chapter of the book and I am aware what I have written so far might confuse and unsettle readers as much as make them feel competent to work with trans people. I cannot apologise for this, as my purpose when training people around trans issues and diversity in general is always as much to help people unlearn as it is to learn. As I have said, it is often our unconscious assumptions that get in the way when we are working across difference. We cannot connect to a person if our understanding of them is unconsciously overlaid by myths we have introjected as truth.

If counsellors go into a relationship with trans clients feeling that they are sailing into uncharted territory where the clients' own self-knowledge is the best navigation tool, this can only be a good thing. If we rely on what we think we already know, our client's excellent internal compass may well seem faulty and be disregarded. They will never arrive where they need to be.

I also hope we can hold onto the sense of wonder that it is possible to feel in these strange waters, both as counsellor and client. There is more to be found here than fear – being trans is not a tragedy, though the current status quo does make it unnecessarily challenging. The excitement and awe of uncovering something unique and curious about oneself or another person cannot be underestimated. Trans lives are all the more beautiful, wondrous, spectacular for being somewhat rare. I hope that, when the initial frustration some of the words in this book will cause wears off, readers may share my excitement at embarking into new areas and thoroughly exploring with maps held lightly and eyes and ears prepared for wonder.

However, I understand the need for guides and maps and anchors, even though I would caution against the false sense of security they can give us. Something solid to hold onto for the journey can feel reassuring, so this last chapter offers some concrete(ish) advice about working alongside trans people as clients, colleagues and supervisees.

Trans people are people, so once we clear away our assumptions and biases, the skills we already have should be enough in most cases. But there are some specifics worth noting. I have consulted many trans people on and offline on their therapy experiences as part of refining my training for counsellors. Here, I will distill what I have learned from my own experiences and those of other trans people.

COUNSELLOR COMPETENCE

If a trans person goes to a counsellor and hears the words 'transgendered' or 'sex change' or other such out-of-date language, it is not going to help them feel confident that they are up to date and well prepared to work with trans people.

The incompetent counsellor will ask lots of questions and will not know whether those questions are appropriate or necessary. They will either resist learning at all or will learn some very basic and quite possibly out-of-date information and rigidly apply it, forgetting their person-centredness. It is essential to have learned from a variety of sources, and those more than a few years out of date will be missing the development of the non-binary movement, the emergence of the first notable healthcare academics who are trans themselves, and some important language changes.

It is fine to not know everything about a client's situation. Once we have done all that reading, we need to hold it lightly, because each trans client will tell us something new about being trans. Knowing to own up to lack of knowledge and asking clients to correct as and when necessary is fine, but it is important to reassure them that we are not expecting them to be our educators. Knowing when it is okay to ask and when we need to do research after the session is vital.

'Transgender people have a right to access practitioners with the skills, awareness, and knowledge necessary to support them in the development of...psychophysical integrity' (Riley *et al.* 2011, p.406).

We should never need to reassure our clients of our competence; it will be apparent that we are (or are not) a safe enough pair of hands for a trans person. We should all be humble in the face of such a complex area and realise there is always a lot to learn.

It is common for people trying to learn to use one trans person as their knowledge base in a very tokenistic way; either a book, a friend, a colleague or a client. We see this in work places and organisations that do not check out whether the trans colleague they ask to 'train' them has any awareness of the rest of the community or any experience in training on trans competencies. When I work as a trainer I am not bringing the perspective of just one trans person, I am bringing the accumulated knowledge of somebody who has worked with and organised with many trans people over the course of the last 15 years and has also continued to update my knowledge via research. No one trans person can be an expert on transness and I do not speak for all trans people. I have tried my very best, however, to diversify my knowledge to the greatest extent possible, and I would expect this of any trans trainer.

Making space for people to talk about gender

Both my partner and I had excellent, long-term counselling with counsellors who were also LGB, back in our younger days. He brought up the issue of his gender, but the counsellor asked him if he could really see himself as one of the guys in a regular pub, and when he said no, the matter was dropped. It was an obvious, albeit possibly unconscious on the part of the counsellor, attempt to put him off the idea that he was trans. My own counsellor, as far as I can remember, was able to seamlessly absorb my gender divergence into the word 'lesbian' and never said to me what I needed to hear: 'you have never once talked about desire for women, everything you are saying to me is about gender, not sexuality'.

I do not want to diminish the worth of these two excellent counsellors. Who knows if either of us were ready to come out as trans, had we been with more trans aware counsellors. Nevertheless, being trans-affirmative needs to be something that happens not just with trans people but with all our clients. We do not know which clients will come out as trans and which will have trans children, trans partners, parents or friends.

Becoming trans-affirmative takes a lot more work than turning on the core conditions. Until we know and understand a diversity of trans experiences, and have learned to fully believe, accept and equalise trans people onto our level of humanity, how can we possibly create and hold space for trans people to emerge into?

If we are unable, when around cis people, to begin to question the gendered structures that are such an imposition to trans people, how will we have developed the kind of psychic muscle to hold what trans clients bring? If we sit with a transprejudiced cis client or a reluctant family member and are congruently able to be comfortable with all their ignorance, how can we then congruently sit with a trans client and say, 'I accept you'?

Gender stereotyping

'The need for counselors to be reflexive and insightful of their subjectivities when working with transgender clients is imperative, for there is the potential to invoke preconceived ideas about sexuality and gender' (Riley *et al.* 2011, p.403). Our clients will be required to buy into socially constructed 'rules' about gender to be viewed as acceptable, or simply to move through the world more easily. Accepting that need, whilst affirming that there is no one way to be a man or woman or non-binary person is essential. 'I can see why you might need to not wear pink even when you like it but remember you're still as much of a man when you wear pink,' is the kind of affirmative message our clients need. 'Women don't do x' is the sort of statement that gets in the way of our clients finding their authentic place within womanhood. Trans women may be super-femme, but they also might be motorbike-riding butch women who work in engineering and love pints of beer.

As we saw in the case of my partner's counsellor, ideas about cis manhood or womanhood might also be very narrow. Counsellors need to examine their beliefs and biases about manly men, femme men, femininity and butchness, as well as about the relationship between gender presentation and sexuality, which is not as linear as people would like to believe. What are the requirements of masculinity? Of femininity? Where do they come from? Counsellors must have 'the ability to examine their values, assumptions, and motivations regarding gender and sex' (Riley *et al.* 2011).

Crucially, counsellors also need to be aware of the 'constraints imposed on transgender people' around gender and understand the ways in which trans people are constantly forced to adapt (Riley *et al.* 2011, pp.405, 401). There is no blank slate, no free space, no inner or outer region that is free from the shackles of gender. Trans people may be working to dismantle these constraints, but it is hard to dismantle a trap that has you in its grip.

Gatekeeping and infantilising

It is our job as counsellors to dismantle hierarchy within the therapy room. We need to watch out for power imbalances, especially with trans and other minority clients. The imbalance between trans people and cis people is so invisible we may not notice it.

If I notice myself drawn towards advice giving or suspecting I might know better than my client, that is a clue to me that there is a power differential at work. We saw this before in misgendering, where our own understanding of the client trumps their self-understanding. It is not hard for cis people, even trained counsellors, to believe that trans people are deluded, mistaken, unbalanced or damaged rather than genuine in their experiences.

Our clients do not need advice about how quickly or slowly to transition, what to wear, what name to use or how to pass. When I had my first gender clinic appointment the friend who accompanied me quickly said to me before I went in, 'sit with your legs further apart if you want to be taken seriously!' I hope that nobody reading this book will think that it was a counsellor's place to say such things but sadly some do. I would like to add at this point that manspreading is not a thing that I have added to my repertoire.

Gatekeeping is an enormous problem in trans people's lives, whenever they see a professional. Hopefully counsellors will not add to this, but we can also help prevent it by writing to a reluctant-to-refer GP or mental health service, for instance, to encourage a referral to a gender clinic. Trans people do not need to be totally sure of everything before they get referred to a clinic. Clinic waits are so long (two years plus) that they will have plenty of time to reflect. Often far too much time in fact, to the detriment of some people's mental health. If a client is considering transition, it is okay to encourage them to get on the waiting list now, in case they need it later. No clinic is going to rush an uncertain person through transition, due to funding constraints they tend to be looking hard for excuses not to treat.

What if the trans person is making a mistake? Well what if it would be a mistake for them to delay or be delayed? People should be permitted to make their own mistakes, even trans people. Trans regrets are astonishingly low (Wiepjes *et al.* 2018). The fear of a cis person mistakenly transitioning alongside society's lack of concern for all the trans people still miserably trying to be cis demonstrates the disparity between how these two identities are valued.

At its worst, the infantilising and gatekeeping of trans people can leave the counsellor feeling responsible for knowing whether their client should or should not transition, and trying to block the client if they are unsure, particularly if the client has mental health problems or other unresolved issues, is autistic, or is someone who is never going to blend in and may continue to have a hard time being visibly trans. These are the clients' conflicts to resolve, though, not ours, and we can trust our trans clients and their process just as we trust all our clients.

If a counsellor's belief that transition will 'resolve' things does not come from the client, perhaps they are overlooking the possibility of a bias against non-transitioning, non-binary identities. Livingstone suggests 'though social and physical transition may be necessary for some trans-identified people, such treatment should not be regarded as a predetermined destination, or a criterion for success' (2011, p.142). We need to accept client's uncertain, fluid or in-between identities as equally worthy to those of transitioning trans men and women. If we expect a client's complex, non-binary identity to resolve into a more neat, binary one, we have some work to do on our weddedness to the gender binary.

Telling trans people to 'make lemonade'

One of the other things that some cis people can be guilty of is a process of denying, minimising and blaming in response to trans distress or protest at discrimination, oppression or abuse. This is a process that frequently happens when someone with power does not want to acknowledge the imbalance. The phrase 'denying, minimising and blaming' comes from models of domestic violence, but it is useful in any situation where one group or person has power over another.

There are many ways that counsellors can miss the extent of transprejudice and the seriousness of it. Trans people need to be heard about how difficult their lives are and not be dismissed. But sometimes, seeing the extent of a problem like this can be uncomfortable. Counsellors may not, for instance, understand the impact of misgendering. Or we might dismiss a client's fears that family will not accept them. We might see the trans person as bringing something on themself through the way they dress or act or through their activism. Or refuse to take seriously the impact of anti-trans campaigners and tell the client to 'just ignore it'. We might suggest they come offline when many trans people require an online presence for connecting to other trans people.

A word about the internet might be useful here. Many counsellors are quite computer-averse, and suspicious of things like social media. Let us be clear, the internet has liberated trans people (Cavalcante 2016). It enabled a tiny population to connect with each other and start to organise. When trans people 'hide behind' avatars on profiles, we can conversely be ourselves, free of the mislabelled body we have to carry around with us that confuses more than clarifies who we are. There are some trans people who live and work online and are happy. It particularly suits some autistic people, as online interaction lessens sensory input while still allowing for connection. It is important that counsellors check out the prejudices we have, particularly those of us who are not 'net natives', around social media, and around what are normal ways to work and socialise. We may see the internet world as void of real connection, but this is far from the reality for many people.

Counsellors can sometimes also side with the cis people surrounding a trans person. Trans people are very aware of cis attitudes and concerns and will often want to mentally minimise these to reach a point of self-acceptance. Instead of helping trans people lift the weight of those around them from their shoulders, some counsellors invite the trans person to imagine how difficult it is for others or to put themself in other people's shoes. For the trans person who has spent their entire life in other people's shoes this can be a cruel request.

The counsellor is sometimes unable to see the psychic distress trans people experience as a part of the social marginalisation and bullying they experience rather than a symptom of them being trans itself. 'It is the experience of being socially rejected, due to the refusal to conform to society's dichotomy of femininity and masculinity, which creates problems for transgender individuals, and not the nonconforming behavior itself' (Riley *et al.* 2011, p.399). We cannot assume that things are going to be bad for the client. Our fears on the client's behalf are unhelpful. There are many happy, well adjusted, well supported people living in a good bubble and never having to deal with hate. But we cannot assume that things will be okay or safe for our clients. It is foolhardy for us to tell a client that it is safe for them to do the things that they are afraid of. In some areas trans people can move about the world quite safely but in others they are at high risk of assault and hate crime. Some workplaces will be tremendously supportive, and others will find ways of forcing the trans person out. We must trust the client's judgement and let them talk through their fears. The client is more qualified than anyone else to then weigh their fears and make sense of whether these are realistic.

The necessity of hope

As toxic as the 'make lemonade' approach is a position that being trans is necessarily tragic, that suffering is a given. The acceptance of trans suffering is unacceptable; we need to want better for our clients and believe in better. If our client is getting street harassment in her small town, telling her it will be the same everywhere is tantamount to telling her she must get used to it. Many trans people have relocated to big cities like Leeds, Nottingham, Manchester and Brighton and found a thriving trans community and much more accepting environment. Equally, though, she should not have to move – one trans friend who was getting stones chucked at her windows by kids took the brave decision of doing a talk at the local school.

> Another of the 'common factors' that needs to be emphasized is the ability to instill hope in the clients that therapy will be of benefit. Expressing hope and showing belief in the client in the first few sessions helps to establish a client's sense of esteem in his or her own abilities. (Riley *et al.* 2011, p.405)

Hope in the counselling room is more about trusting the client and having faith in *them* to know what is right. Sometimes, we need to be able to hold seemingly conflicting entities. If a client is struggling repeatedly with the question of whether they are male or female with no apparent resolution, offering the possibility to be both can be a relief. Remembering that our ideas of gender and sex being *opposites* does not fit the overlapping complexity of gender or sex. Is a beach part of the land or sea? It has aspects of both, and tides that flow between two states. Some genderfluid people experience something very similar and can only say with certainty where they are *right now*, knowing tomorrow they may feel very differently. Gendered feelings can also be situational, with the overall sum of self being constant, but with different themes coming forth at different times.

We cannot say with confidence that transition is right for our client, but we can have confidence in the reality that transition is right for those who undertake it, that mental health tends to improve when trans people are permitted and supported to live as close to their organismic identity as possible, and that medical transition has highly successful outcomes in terms of better mental health and low regrets (Bauer *et al.* 2015; Cornell University 2017; Wiepjes *et al.* 2018). We can confidently be affirmative of our clients doing what they need to do and embody a positive attitude towards all the various transition options, including doing nothing.

Burnes *et al.* (2010) 'advocate using a strength-based approach to highlight the strengths and resilience transgender individuals may have despite the significant experiences of multiple oppressions transgender people may have experience' (p.136). I would add to this, that this should not be an individualised process. Often effective support from other people – trans groups, online spaces, services – are a vital component to building resilience. But that support needs to be competent or it is worthless. Sheerin (2009, p.54) found that the competencies of counsellors were strongly associated with client satisfaction and working alliance.

Problematic attitudes towards trans sexuality

Trans people can struggle not only to find a counsellor that is trans friendly but also one that understands about different sexualities and relationship types. While some trans people are happily and heterosexually monogamous they are not the majority. Trans people need to know that if they are talking about being bi or asexual, or about an issue that is happening in their relationship, they do not have to worry that their counsellor is going to pathologise, disrespect or simply not understand. Asexual, bisexual and/or polyamorous, non-monogamous, kinky or otherwise people may find themselves self-censoring in the presence of a lot of counsellors, or simply misunderstood.

Even for monogamous, heterosexual, vanilla trans people there can still be misunderstandings about trans sexuality. For instance, confusing gender and sexuality, assuming all trans people will be transitioning to straight respectability or believing that transness is a sign of unresolved sexuality issues.

Trans people who are sex workers might find it very hard to find a counsellor who is supportive of their work and non-judgemental, and even harder to find anybody who understands much about sex work. If a sex worker has had a difficult time they do not need a counsellor who blames sex work for the difficulty or assumes 'better' options are available to them.

Trans women's sexuality can especially be judged and misunderstood. Because of harmful media clichés, any expression of sexuality in trans women is often associated with something deviant. Or the assumption is that because female stereotypes have women as less sexual than men, sexuality in trans women is held up as 'proof' of maleness. Trans women should not have to be entirely chaste to be respected as women, because naturally there are plenty of hypersexual, polyamorous, kinky cis women out there, and as Fine (2017, pp.46–79) demonstrates, male sexuality is not, after all, fundamentally different from female sexuality.

Trans enough

There is a concept within trans discourse called 'trans enough' by which we mean that trans people are under constant scrutiny to prove their transness or their right to require support as a trans person. Counsellors can collude with this issue by placing expectations on a client around what constitutes a legitimate trans person.

Some counsellors will have a measure in their minds that trans people are constantly being compared to, particularly if they have a narrow experience of what trans means or have had one single experience of a trans person previously. Trans people themselves will be constantly questioning whether they are trans enough, whether they have the right to transition, whether they really match up to other trans people in terms of their experience or needs. I frequently hear trans people saying they 'don't really experience dysphoria the way others do' only minutes after relating to me their distressing gender incongruence. This is reminiscent of how the worst trauma victims say, 'others have it worse', perhaps to distance themselves from the enormity of what they are dealing with.

Being trans is such a diverse experience that it is impossible to compare two trans people. Besides, trans people are expected to project certain narratives and assuredness, however they feel inside. If a trans person wavers or expresses doubt, someone might judge them or even block the path. Many trans people therefore compare their backstage mess with other people's front of house and naturally find themselves wanting. What is vital is that counsellors do not collude with this.

Trans people do not have to have certain surgeries to be trans. Non-binary people do not have to wear certain clothes to be trans. Trans people can use the toilet that makes them comfortable and whichever they choose does not make them more or less trans. Trans women do not have to wear make-up, trans men are allowed to wear pink. This may seem obvious, but these are the sorts of things we do hear counsellors getting wrong. There is still a problematic tendency for trans people to be validated more if they blend or 'pass' (Carroll, Gilroy and Ryan 2002, p.133).

There is sometimes an assumption that people will further transition from a non-binary to a more binary identity. If this happens, it is entirely valid, as transition is a process and different people need to do it in different stages. However, it is just as likely that a non-binary person will stay non-binary or that a more binary-aligned person will later discover that they are non-binary. These course corrections in transition are nothing to be afraid of. Each step our clients take, even steps backward to detransition, are important parts of self-discovery. We should not assume what trajectories our clients will take or that the current identities are simply staging posts rather than valid in their own right.

Another way that counsellors can judge clients is around whether they are 'out' or performing their gender in all aspects of their life prior to accessing transition support. There will be some trans people who are out at work but not at home, or out at home but not at work. There are people who require some transition before they face the world as themselves, and people who transition in all aspects of their life the second they figure themselves out. There are so many factors that play into this, and again we can trust our clients that they are making the right decisions for themselves.

More than just trans

Many trans people feed back in utter frustration that whenever they go to therapy, a lot of the time is taken up talking about trans issues when that was not the reason they went to therapy. Sometimes, it is taken up with educating, but often it is about the counsellor connecting everything back to them being trans.

> Some trans survivors...have spent hours of their time and hundreds of dollars trying to educate their therapist on trans issues before they could get to a point where they can discuss sexual assault and its implications in their lives. Some trans survivors have also discovered that some...therapists may attribute causality to being trans or being assaulted – linking gender identity/expression and the violence that occurred. (Munson and Cook-Daniels, 2015, p.35)

In the physical healthcare field, the term for this is 'trans broken arm syndrome', where any ailment, even a broken arm, is traced back to someone's trans status. In the genuine case of the broken arm, the question from a health insurer was 'could your hormones have affected your bone density, making your arm more likely to break?' If so, the broken arm would have counted as a 'pre-existing condition'.

Trans people experience this particularly in therapy. Relationship issues? Because we're trans. Job dissatisfaction? Because we're trans. Bereavement? The inexperienced counsellor will somehow link it back to us being trans. Physical health problems? Psychosomatic stress of being trans, of course.

I know if we are person-centred and non-directive this should not happen, but if our brain takes us down a road then it will influence the session, so we need to try and remember, they are not a TRANS person they are a trans PERSON. We need to hold their transness lightly. This will be much easier when we are more familiar with trans issues.

It is also important to remember that we need certain additional skills if we are working with a lot of trans people. In trans populations we will come across higher levels of complex post-traumatic stress, autism, abuse survival, hate crime survival. We need to be prepared to manage suicidality, trauma and a constantly changing and re-traumatising field for our clients. Our ability to be flexible, steady and meet client's exact needs moment to moment is vital.

Holding trans people's anger

The problem with a social hierarchy is that people lower in it are not allowed to be angry. Various pieces of research show that, for example, black people and women are misperceived as angrier than they are, meaning they can be judged or censured for behaviour that would be acceptable in white men (Adams 2015; Halberstadt and Shipman 2018; Walley-Jean 2009). Terms like 'stroppy teenager' or 'aggressive feminist' are also (often) code for people lower in the social hierarchy standing up for themselves.

The 'aggressive' trans activist is now a well-known social trope. Trans people are going to be angry about having weak civil rights, constantly being maligned in the media and high levels of hate crime, to name just a few things. But it is very hard to express that anger safely. If a trans person cannot bring all that stifled anger into a therapy room, then where can they take it?

MISGENDERING AND OTHER LANGUAGE ISSUES

The following is a scenario based on multiple experiences: I am training a group of counsellors on a private CPD day. One of the attendees, a lovely woman who seems very respectful of her trans client, says 'my client says he finds things very difficult at work'. I *think* her client might actually be a trans woman, so I ask if 'he' is the pronoun this trans person has asked you to use?' The answer is invariably no, or 'I don't know' or 'I find it really difficult'.

Misgendering is no trivial thing. It undermines a deeply held part of a trans person's identity. It signals what the person really thinks their gender is. Generally, we gender people based on their appearance and the sound of their voice. In most cases we do not know their genitals, their chromosomes or their reproductive capability. Gendering people with words like ladies, gentlemen, miss, mister, he, she, etc. is a social process, not a biological one. But it is deeply ingrained in us. Here is an uncomfortable truth: We are not fully accepting of our client's gender if we are misgendering them, we cannot be. If we see the client as a woman, we will call them she. Sometimes, people find it easier to use 'they' for trans women and men, and at the same time struggle to use 'they' for non-binary people. 'They' is not a compromise between calling your client he or she; it is a gender-neutral pronoun for those who require it, those whose pronouns we do not know and those who have not yet decided on pronouns.

Person-centred counsellors hold that our clients are experts on themselves, so why is it we find their correct pronouns so hard to use? There are several reasons, but they all boil down to a judgement of our clients or unconscious bias against our clients.

One possible reason is that we believe the client is currently a man and will 'become' a woman by medical transitioning (or vice versa). Although some older trans people may put it that way, because that is the parlance that was imposed upon them, it does not reflect what is really happening. The trans woman has likely been experiencing gender incongruence that makes her lived experience very different from that of a man. She may well have been feeling this her whole life, and even when she could not put it into words, it is possible the feelings that are causing her now to say 'I identify as a woman' were always there, at least partially. If she is uneducated or old-fashioned she may say 'I want to be a woman', but the underlying feelings will often be the same. If she tells us she wants to be 'he' until she transitions, fine, but otherwise, use 'she'.

The rule here – and it is a rule – is to *always* ask what pronouns your client uses if it is unclear. If he/she is a well-into-transition self-declared trans man or woman, he/she might be offended because the answer should be obvious. A trans man is *he*; a trans woman is *she*. If the trans person has not visibly transitioned, is non-binary, or is not 'out' then we ask, 'what pronouns would you like me to use for you, just in this room, in my notes, and when I talk about you confidentially with my supervisor?' If they are unsure, we should offer to talk about them gender-neutrally, using they/them/their/themself pronouns, and stick to that.

Importantly, when talking about the client prior to coming out, or in their childhood, we need to talk about them gender-neutrally or gender-affirmatively unless they have expressed a different preference for how we talk about them. There is a reason we call old names 'deadnames' – because most trans people want them to be fully buried. Not everyone – I quite like my old name. But for many an old name is a trigger for a life lived behind a mask, and in pain, and it does not represent who they ever were. Therefore, we do not say 'when you were a girl' to a trans man, we say 'when you were little', or 'in your teens' or whatever applies. And we do not say 'when Tim was Sally', or 'when you were Sally' we say, 'before Tim/you chose his/your current name'.

Correct gendering is not something trans people need to 'earn' by transitioning into a correct standard of cisgender appearance or embodiment. Correct pronouns are mandatory if we truly respect trans identities. If we are unable to manage correct pronouns, some self-reflection is required about just how valid we see our client's identity. When I started tripping over gender-neutral pronouns at the support group I help run, I realised I needed to reflect on how valid I saw my own non-binary identity. I had internalised a lot of invalidating ideas.

We cannot be in person-centred relationship while misgendering a client, because we are judging them, putting our understanding of them above their own. This includes when we are talking to our supervisor about them, and supervisors and supervisees must learn to correct each other's slipups. Mistakes happen, but need to be owned, reflected on, and apologised for.

This brings me to another reason that counsellors get pronouns wrong, particularly in supervision. They are looking for permission from another cis person to use the trans person's pronouns. Our desire to socially conform is strongly challenged by the prospect of being supportive of a trans person when we do not know how this will be received by others. Supporting trans people and validating their identities still feels socially risky to many people, and the only way this will change is when cis people take the risk to be confident in their support.

Misgendering a trans person is psychologically damaging, because it is at the very core of the trauma trans people experience: being told their identities are not legitimate and being on the receiving end of violence and inequality based on the marginalising effect of this invalidation. If we cannot fully believe and accept trans people's identities, we should not be working with them or anyone associated with them. 'Nobody should feel that they need to fit somebody else's model of being in order to be accepted as a valid person' (Livingstone 2011, p.142).

Often the cis person in this scenario is hung up on how difficult it is for them to get it right and can lose contact with the client entirely. It is vital to notice feelings of frustration and anger associated with this process. If properly understood, it can give us real insight into how difficult life is for our clients. If saying a different pronoun is that difficult for us due to the cultural programming we've had around gender, we can start to get a picture of the power of the structures trapping our clients.

Using the client's words

There are other language issues that counsellors need to be aware of. The most important of these is to learn to track the client's language so long as it is not problematic. For example, if a client uses the word 'tranny', we need to not repeat the word if we are cis or transmasculine, as it is a reclaimed slur that it is best to leave trans women alone to use.

The client is likely to have names for body parts that are different than the biological ones we are familiar with. These words are designed to avoid feelings of incongruence, so it is important that we check before naming body parts in traditional ways. I particularly like the word *strapless* (CATIE 2013) if we need to refer to that part of a trans woman's anatomy. A trans guy might call his parts *manhole*, *click*, or *dick*, while a period is usually *shark week*. Euphemisms and references like *lower area* are just fine. This is not shyness or prudery that can be blasted away be a counsellor confidently saying, 'you mean your vagina'. It is gender incongruence, and the word vagina might have a triggering effect on your assigned female client.

Language constantly *changes*. We should give ourselves a language refresher every few years because this is a new and evolving community, in terms of organising. I try to update my terms and definitions sheet on my website yearly. Naturally, while this book is UK and US-centric, we need to be aware that across the globe there are many ways of conceptualising and describing gender divergence. Tuning into our client's personal and cultural language around their gendered experiences is essential. Their words will not always neatly translate into our words.

POOR THEORISING

As person-centred counsellors we are taught not to theorise about, or diagnose, our clients, but we still do it. We read theory, we absorb it through our social world even if we do not intend to.

Unfortunately, there is an inverse correlation between *accurate* theories about trans people and *popular* theories about trans people, in just the same way that climate change denial is far more known about and consumed than legitimate climate science. Here I list some of the pits counsellors fall into over theory:

Outdated research

Using old, discredited or antagonistic theories/theorists that are popular at the wrong end of the internet, e.g. Autogynephilia, Ray Blanchard, Ken Zucker, Anne Lawrence, Desistence, Gender Critical, Harry Benjamin Syndrome, Sheila Jeffreys, Janice Raymond. If you must appraise these theories, make sure you equally consume the literature critiquing them, and follow up any citations and references, which are often misrepresented. Often these ideas *sound* plausible because they connect to pre-existing prejudices that we do not know we have. Look at what up-to-date literature has to say and read current trans voices and researchers.

Mistaking gender dysphoria and body dysmorphia

Dysmorphia is a *false perception* of the body. Trans people are not misperceiving their body, or their biology. Dysphoria is the opposite of euphoria, it means clinically significant distress, for instance in relation to the body as they know it is configured.

It is a mistake to assume that all trans people 'hate their body' or experience physical incongruence, or do not associate with anything to do with their biological sex attributes.

Our lives are not theory

Assuming being trans is a political or theoretical interest rather than a lived experience and that therefore an opposing political theory can argue against trans existence. Believing that 'gender is socially constructed' and 'trans people exist' are at odds, for instance, rather than exploring the ways of incorporating trans existence into gender theory, by deepening it. Trans people may themselves theorise (well or poorly) about why they are trans, but we need to separate out what is theoretical (*why* they are trans) from what is fact (*that* they are trans).

Gender divergent people existed before 'trans'

There are two ways we erase the rich gender diversity that has existed throughout global history. One is to think of trans identities being a 'western, medical' phenomenon, related to 'big pharma', the 'medicalisation of distress' (Sanders 2005) and other negative things many person-centred counsellors associate with western medicine. It is important to remember that people like trans people existed, and modified their bodies, long before western medicine existed. Where there is a critique of medical intervention to be made, it is around those critics who believe trans people must have a medical intervention to change their social gender. Such medical intervention *is* unnecessary, or at least would be in a world that accepted trans identities.

The second erasure is when we only see white western trans identities and do not understand them as existing on continuums of global and historic gender *and* sexuality divergence. b. binaohan, someone who describes themself as *bakla* from the Philippines, describes the issues with the standard 'trans 101' guide:

> How can we talk about transgender without locating the identity in a larger global context? Or without mentioning the way that these guides, intended and whose purpose is explicitly to simplify complex issues, erase experiences of many people, while normalizing others? (2014, p.3)

They go on to analyse the way binary cis heterosexuality was used as a tool of oppression across the colonised world (binaohan 2014). Thus, *this* trans community at *this* moment is struggling within a particular context, and the communities of other cultures might see their identities, and their liberations, differently, even though we still have a lot in common.

ATTITUDES TO TRANS COUNSELLORS AND TRAINEES

Once a supervisor asked, in response to me saying I was getting a referral to the gender clinic, if I was going to 'get a willy'. They claimed, when challenged, that they had a duty of care to make sure that I was fit to counsel, and surgery might affect that. Not only was it infantilising of them to believe that they would be more aware of how transition would impact my work than I, but they were worrying about a potential set of surgeries that I would not be able to have for years even if I was intending to have them at all. They knew I had been considering a gender clinic referral for some time. Nonetheless we spent the entire supervision session unpacking what was mostly their ignorance around trans issues and I never got a chance to bring my client material.

I would like to say that this is an isolated incident but sometime later I was asked at a job interview how my gender identity affected my clients. I am sure some readers are gasping in horror and saying, 'They're not allowed to ask that!' This was discriminatory behaviour. We established later that this was not a question they asked all interviewees. I am sure that they did not usually feel it is necessary, but somehow, they did with a trans counsellor. In an explanation afterwards, they again talked about their duty of care to clients. Once again it was considered that I as a trans person would not have spent an inordinate amount of time reflecting on how my transness will impact my work for both myself and my clients.

This is a mere snippet of a larger problem – the infantilising of trans people, the concern counselling colleagues and trainers and supervisors have that we simply cannot be up to the job. From the trans trainees squeezed out of training courses all over the country, the under-representation of us in the professional field, to the limited effort put in by professional bodies to up their game on trans issues, things within counselling and related professions have a very long way to go. Until trans people have an equal footing within the profession, they will never have an equal footing in the therapy room.

I hope those reading this are aware we need to reflect on the issues that do not affect us, more than the ones that do. It is my white, English-speaking, middle-class raised self that needs to be under scrutiny. I have spent a lot more time reflecting on my gender and sexuality because in a transprejudiced, gay prejudiced world I have no choice. As a white person I have not had such need to reflect on my whiteness or what that means to others or myself. When we feel the urge to ask our supervisees, students or interviewees how their differences impact their work I suggest we learn to ask them to talk about how their whiteness or their cisness or their straightness etc., impacts their BAME, gay or trans clients. We see white, male, straight, cis, able people as 'default', a sort of universal remote that can connect to everything. We do not consider enough how people in these more advantaged categories have never had to think about so many things more marginalised people face every day, and therefore how difficult it is to connect to narratives from outside of their range.

Davies (1996, pp.29-30) talks about how training courses continue to work from a heteronormative model, and that we will therefore need to put our existing therapeutic models aside when we work with minorities, prioritising an affirmative approach. If we do not do this, the biases woven into our cis-heteronormative models will be invisible to us. When difference is added into the curriculum, it is generally done in one afternoon workshop with an imported tutor, rather than woven through the syllabus.

We question what a trans counsellor can offer people who are not trans, but rarely ask ourselves what we can offer trans clients if we are cis. I have repeatedly observed trans students and counsellors treated with suspicion or belittled or even pushed out of their courses and their workplaces. Told they have 'too much going on' to be a counsellor. Told they might make clients uncomfortable. Therapy is not always about comfort. We can learn a lot from discomfort and from difference.

I believe that my transness has been a benefit for cis clients. Most, to be fair, are too involved with their problems to notice I am trans. Even in my student counsellor role I rarely received comments though I am visibly genderqueer and wear a badge saying, 'they pronouns please'. We go about the session as if nothing untoward is happening, and they come back the next session almost as if they can accept a counsellor who is trans without any drama. When it is mentioned, it is useful. The client is trans; the client is from another culture and excited to know about me and tells me it helps her be her real self too; the client is curious and, in that curiosity, learns something interesting.

TIPS FOR A TRANS FRIENDLY WORKPLACE

If you go to my website, you will find 'top tips' guides for trans inclusion in various settings. They are free to download, and I adapt them here.[1] There are a few simple steps you can make so that your course, office, department, etc. is accessible to trans people:

1 www.hopecat.co.uk

Cultural competence takes work

Trans people are different and have different needs, which require learning. Go to credible trans-led sources: not the media, not just the trans person you happen to know, and not just generic LGBT+ organisations.

Language matters

Treat a trans person as if they've just revealed their secret identity, and that's who they always were. Even when you talk about them in the past, they were that person, you just didn't know. Stick to the right names, pronouns and gendered words, and avoid inaccurate terms like 'sex change'.

Does everything really need to be gendered?

Review all the ways you record gender and all the gendered practices of your organisation (e.g. clothing; toilets; forms with M/F, Mr/Mrs; greeting customers with sir/madam; gendering callers by sound of voice on the phone; using he/she instead of *they* in reports). But it is legal and important to monitor gender and gender identity for equality purposes. Notts Trans Hub (2017) has a great booklet on getting sex/gender questions on forms right.

Misgendering matters

Take misgendering of all kinds seriously and realise the pain it causes. If you do it accidentally, apologise and move on. If it happens deliberately or maliciously, treat it as the transprejudice it is. Pronoun badges, 'pronounarounds'[2] at the starts of groups and meetings, help create a culture that supports considerate use of gendered words.

Don't assume it's going to be a problem

Don't anticipate problems, and set an accepting, congratulatory (rather than worried/shamed) tone to model a positive response. If a client or

2 We say our pronouns as we introduce ourselves, e.g. 'I'm Sam, I use they/them pronouns.'

colleague does have a problem, don't centre their needs and prejudices, centre the person who is most vulnerable.

Work can be a sanctuary

Commit to being supportive, kind and understanding. Regular meet-ups to check in and an open-door policy work wonders. Appreciate the mental health impact of being trans. Understand the employee/student may be openly trans in work/education but not at home, or vice versa.

We are not all about surgery

Treat all medical leave as the life-saving treatment it is. Do not assume what treatment, if any, a trans person will have, and do not wait for treatment to happen to consider them fully as who they say they are. Also private parts are private, don't ask about them.

There are trans people here already, you just don't know it

So, make the environment trans-positive through good policy, and know your legal duties under the Equality Act 2010. Mention trans people in equality and diversity policies. Have a protocol for staff/students transitioning (e.g. support; legal duties; changing name consistently throughout documents and IT systems; communicating the change). Also have a best practice policy for trans clients.

Understand the challenges trans people face

Surveys show trans people face discrimination at every stage of employment. Be aware of the kinds of discrimination, including subtle micro-aggressions, trans employees might face that can easily be dismissed or overlooked.

Celebrate diversity

Stonewall says 'We know that people perform better when they can be themselves' (2017b). What better way to signal that a workplace allows people to be themselves than one that is trans-positive? Be celebratory of difference; let everyone know you see it as an asset that will make your organisation stronger.

CASE STUDY

Elesha is a student on a counselling diploma course. She is 40, black and a trans woman. At first, the group bonded well with Elesha, admiring her wealth of experience and wisdom, and her generosity in educating the group about her experiences. She was patient with misgendering and spent a lot of her time explaining trans issues to people, including the tutors, when they made mistakes.

At the start of the second year, something seemed to change. Elesha was less patient when colleagues continued to call her 'he', and when asked questions, started to reply, 'Why don't you try Google?' She also tried to instruct her colleagues about gender and colonialism, but increasingly she was complained about as 'aggressive' and 'having an agenda' and some, including one tutor, felt her issues were taking up too much space on the course. There was discussion of whether she was suitable, or whether she had 'too much going on'. When it came to light that Elesha made money from sex work, she was called to a meeting with staff to decide whether it was suitable for her to continue on the course.

Elesha lives at the intersection of black, trans and women's experiences of oppression. Her life is suddenly taking up 'too much' space on her course, purely because space has not been made for her. If there was a culture of respecting and correcting her pronouns, we would not have got to the second year with people still slipping up. If there was a culture of doing the work to learn about difference and not always expecting minorities to devote their uncosted labour, people would not be shocked to find that labour a finite resource. If the course offered training on minorities, and more importantly, weaved difference into every aspect of their work, Elesha would be a *part* of the course and not find herself an awkward outsider having to challenge the lack of space made for her. Is she being aggressive? Well, studies suggest black women are *perceived* as aggressive when this is far from the case (Walley-Jean 2009). It may be, if people see Elesha as 'lesser', that without realising it, they also expect her to be more polite, grateful and submissive than they would expect, say a white cis man, to be.

Racism, without anyone realising they are racist or meaning to be racist, could be playing a big part in the dynamic here. There is already a culture in many predominantly white countries of seeing black women as too 'masculine' even when they are cis, so Elesha has a double-strength barrier between her and perceptions of appropriate femininity: 'Just as trans women are stereotypically caricatured as faking femininity, black women are caricatured as innately non-feminine—as pretending, and failing, to be women' (Berlatsky 2014). And Elesha is a sex worker. White people do not always want to look at the consequences of racism, one of which is the fact that unemployment is more than double for black people than white people (McGuiness 2018). We tend to celebrate conventionally successful black people and ignore poverty and the consequences of poverty. Add in that appalling income gap between trans and cis people, and we can begin to realise why sex work may have been a positive career move for Elesha. Or maybe she just likes the work. Chances are she could teach us a lot about psychological contact, about embodiment, about boundaries. But respectable, middle class counsellors often fail to see the parallels between sex work and counselling or are even horrified at the thought (Glyde 2018). I hope the faculty make room for Elesha on the course, and do some work on diversity. There is a richness of experience that we squander when we are unable to make space for diverse people to bring all that they are into the room. Sadly, I am hearing too many trans people, sex workers and black people, among others, reporting systemic barriers to them qualifying as counsellors. As a profession, we must do better, and I very much include myself in that statement – I still have a lot to learn.

CONCLUSION

'It feels well past time that the trans-identified population was deemed well worth understanding and met with the genuineness, empathy and unconditional positive regard of a facilitative phenomenological approach', so says Tina Livingstone in her paper on person-centred work with trans people (2011, p.138). But understanding takes work, and cultural competence. Much of that work is clearing away the things that come too easily to us – the wrong pronouns, a desire to mock certain gender presentations, a need to keep gender minorities in a place we did not even know had been made for them. Livingstone goes on to remind us it is not enough just to hold back judgement, we need to *actively affirm* our gender divergent clients, so they can connect to their organismic identity, whatever form it takes (2011, p.139). And we cannot affirm what we do not understand.

It is true that in a world where there is so little understanding, small acts can make a huge difference. Please do not underestimate your impact in doing a small, kind thing for a trans person. But the world changes quickly. From my grandmother's to my mother's generation we went from not accepting to accepting left-handedness. Since I was born, we have gone from gay people being treated as mentally ill and still partially criminalised, to same-sex marriage and openly gay politicians in many places. Therefore, I hope many of the people reading this book will join the push for full civil rights and acceptance for trans people everywhere. Rather than being timidly grateful for things being a little better than they used to be, I invite the reader to be bold in imagining a world where there are no systemic barriers placed in the way of trans people. Where the full rich diversity of being trans is understood, like left-handedness, as just a natural part of human diversity.

Our job, as counsellors, supervisors, colleagues, is surely then to make sure, above all, that we do not get in the way of trans people fully living their potential and bringing all that they can be into the world.

I will leave Carl Rogers with the last word, to remind us why he developed person-centred practice to begin with:

> ...in my early professional years I was asking the question, How can I treat, or cure, or change this person? Now I would phrase the question in this way: How can I provide a relationship which this person may use for his own personal growth? (1961, p.32)

PERSONAL REFLECTION

1. Now the book is finished, what thoughts and feelings are you left with?

2. Do you still have questions? Write them down and think about how you can go about resolving them.
3. What came up for you reading this chapter? What issues are you wrestling with right now? Note the bits you don't understand, resist or need to come back to.
4. Think about the spaces you work in, teach in, learn in. What could be done to better bring trans and gender diverse people into those spaces and make them feel safe and welcome? Go down the 'top tips' section and think about what can be improved. Pick three practical things that you will work to improve on in the next year.
5. Write down some misconceptions you used to have about trans people and note the moment that shifted.
6. What three things can you do next to deepen this work?

Glossary

Please note: terminology shifts and evolves; some trans people will use words now seen as incorrect or even offensive. Words mean different things to different individuals – there is no one, unified trans story.

AFAB/AMAB (assigned female/male at birth) – the gender category a person was given when they were born. Avoids problematic terms like 'biological male' or 'female bodied'. Note: this is not an identity, so avoid saying things like 'they are an AFAB trans person'. For preference, I shorten this to assigned female/assigned male, as intersex people often do not get assigned into a binary gender at birth, but rather after some deliberation and possibly surgery.

Aromantic/biromantic/heteroromantic – just as we can have sexual orientations, so too can we have romantic orientations. Some people's sexual and romantic orientations do not match each other, e.g. they are romantically interested in women, but sexually interested in men.

Asexual (also known as Ace) – a person who experiences no sexual attraction to others. May still experience romantic love, may enjoy sex with others for bonding or relational reasons. Can have sexual feelings, just not sexual attraction. Not the same as celibate, ace is a genuine orientation as much as gay or bi.

BDSM (Bondage, Discipline, Domination, Submission, Sadism, and Masochism) (not necessarily LGBT+, but there are crossovers between communities) – a physical, psychological and usually sexual power role-play with consensual participants.

Bisexual – an umbrella term used to describe people who are sexually and/or romantically attracted to people of more than one gender. The bisexual community has long recognised the existence of more than two genders and the definition long ago evolved from a simplistic 'bi means two' definition. A bisexual person does not necessarily experience equal or constant levels of attraction to all genders.

Butch/femme – used within the LGB community to describe people who present in typically masculine or feminine ways. Can also be an aspect of gender identity. Not necessarily the same as being trans. For example, woman can be typically masculine (butch) in presentation, while identifying 100 per cent as a woman.

Cisgender/cis – the opposite of transgender, someone who does not experience significant incongruence with the binary gender they were assigned into. Using this term avoids problematic ways of describing non-trans people.

Crossdresser/freedresser – somebody who wears clothing that falls outside of what is expected for their gender. Some are trans, some are not. 'Transvestite' is also used but decreasing in popularity. Note: if someone identifies as a woman and dresses as a woman, they are not crossdressing.

Drag queen/king – currently, someone who dresses as the opposite sex for performance purposes. Historically, these terms were used for identity, so there was crossover between drag queen and trans woman.

Gay – generally used by men; sexually and/or romantically attracted only to people of the same sex.

Gender divergent/gender variant/gender non-conforming – someone who diverges from the norms of their assigned gender but may or may not consider themself or be considered trans. Useful terms for children, but also as umbrella terms to include those who do not identify with the word trans. 'Trans and gender divergent/diverse' is better than 'trans and non-binary' because non-binary is not a separate identity from trans. We use diverse more broadly, and divergent more narrowly, depending on context.

Gender dysphoria – former medical diagnosis for the 'clinically significant distress' trans people experience from the misalignment of their gender from that assigned to them. Many trans people prefer 'gender incongruence', and this is now in the ICD-11. Not all trans people experience dysphoria.

Gender identity – a person's experience of themself in relation to sex/gender. Note: not all trans people relate to this term.

Gender incongruence – the core experience of trans people in relation to physical, social or internal aspects of the binary gender they were assigned into.

Gender recognition certificate – a trans man or women's gender can be legally recognised if they are over 18, have lived as their gender for two years and been diagnosed with gender dysphoria. Legal name change and change of title can take place at any time by deed poll; many do not have GRC.

GSRD (gender, sexual and romantic diversity) – a term particularly useful for training that includes the whole spectrum of gender, relationships and sex, including monogamous, straight, cisgender and normative. Some suggest this term can replace LGBT+. However, it includes everyone, and the broadness of the term is not always helpful if you are, for instance, applying for funding for a centre to support specifically LGBT+ people. Also note the difference between diversity, which covers everyone, and divergent, which specifies those who diverge from normative expectations.

Homosexual – a term only used in scientific circles for same-sex attraction, it is now offensive to use informally. Use lesbian or gay instead.

Homosocial/heterosocial/bisocial – we also can have social orientations. Although most people have friends of different genders (bisocial), some people will only have friends of their own gender (homosocial), or not of their own gender (heterosocial).

Intersex – a person whose reproductive biology deviates from standard ideas of male and female (this can be hormonal, chromosomal or anatomical – e.g. ambiguous genitalia, XXY or XO chromosomes, androgen insensitivity). Some intersex children are still subject to controversial 'normalising' medical and surgical interventions. As intersex people in the UK are often assigned 'sex indeterminate' at birth, the terms cis/trans do not neatly map onto intersex experiences. Some intersex people, however, also identify as trans and transition away from the binary gender they were assigned into, often coercively, as children.

Kink/kinky – anything that turns you on is your 'kink', but usually unusual sexual interests fall into the 'kinky' category, and there is overlap with BDSM.

Lesbian – women who are sexually and/or romantically attracted only to other women. Some also use it to mean gender non-conforming women, although this is being replaced by 'genderqueer' in younger spaces.

LGBT+ (also LGBTIQA, QUILTBAG) – umbrella terms that seek to describe a diverse community, but often fall short of representing its complexity. Nevertheless, I use LGBT+ in this book. Where I say LGBT+, I am including everyone under the bi and trans umbrellas, plus intersex people who want to be included, queer and asexual identities. I use LGB or LGB+ where trans identities are not included, and LGBT when speaking of research or organisations that only had LGBT in their remit. Note: Often the acronym is more inclusive than the project it is attached to. Many 'LGBT+' projects, for instance, are almost exclusively focussed on cisgender gay men. It is therefore inadvisable to add letters, or a + sign, without true representation.

Non-binary or genderqueer – someone who identifies outside of the 'gender binary'. Other terms are agender (having no gender), bigender (having two or more genders or encompassing both binary genders), genderfluid (gender that changes over time), third gender (used in some countries for registry purposes, generally not used as an identity), neutrois (neutral gender), androgyne (a blend of gender characteristics), enby (or nb, short for non-binary – enby is favoured because nb is also short for non-black), non-binary butch, non-binary femme, non-binary trans man, non-binary trans woman. (Non-binary people are not always 'in the middle', they can lean towards male or female, masculinity or femininity, and still be non-binary.) For some, genderqueer has a political association, for others it is a preferable term to non-binary, as a) gender is not a binary so technically everybody is non-binary and b) non-binary defines people in terms of what they are not rather than what they are. Nevertheless, non-binary has won the race of being the main term used.

Non-monogamy – forms of relationship that include sexual or romantic relationships with more than one person. Open relationships allow sex outside of the primary relationship. Polyamory allows more than one intimate relationship.

Pansexual – under the bisexual umbrella, someone who is sexually and/or romantically attracted to people regardless of gender.

Personal pronouns – the pronouns we want people to use for us (generally, he, she or they). If in doubt, ask; not everyone's appearance conforms to their gender. Many people use gender-neutral pronouns, such as singular they/them/their, or others. It is okay to use 'they' if you are unsure, but do not use it if you know someone prefers he or she or identifies as a man or woman.

Queer – once this was a slur, but it has been reclaimed within the LGBT+ community (although some still find it offensive, and it should be used with care). Used as an umbrella term for LGBT+ but also by people who find their gender and/or sexuality hard to clearly define. Politically and academically, queer signals a postmodern approach that insists that all experience is subjective and there is no single, knowable truth about anything, therefore all categories are unstable.

Singular they/them/their/themself – pronouns we use when we do not wish to gender someone, or they identify outside the binary. Example: 'I saw Sam today. They look tired. I hope they are looking after themself. I've asked if I can help them with their workload.' Note: there are other possible gender-neutral pronouns, such as zie/hir or ey/em. Ask a client what pronouns they use.

Trans slurs – shim, trap, tranny, he/she, it, ladyboy; even though some trans people use these for themselves, we should never apply these words to other people.

Trans* – some people self-identify as trans*, however it has become unpopular as an umbrella term due to the fact it made non-binary people feel like a footnote.

Transgender/trans (never 'transgendered') – someone who experiences incongruence, wholly or partially, with the gender they were assigned into (not everyone will use this term). Note this is an adjective, so say 'a transgender person' not 'a transgender' or 'a trans'. Trans people may jokingly say things like 'no tran is an island' but this is in-community, idiosyncratic usage intended to be humorous, not to be copied.

Transition – the process of developing congruence with your gender. May or may not involve surgery, hormone replacement therapy and changes to assist being correctly identified through clothes, speech, etc. Note: 'sex change' is an inappropriate term, as is 'used to be a man' or other inferences that someone's gender was 'created' by their transition, rather than revealed by it.

Transsexual – someone who has medically transitioned or is going to (but many prefer the term transgender).

Two Spirit – only Indigenous Americans may use this identity, which is not directly synonymous with trans or gay. Many other cultures have their own words and ways of conceptualising gender, which do not neatly map onto our ways of speaking about it; some have been erased/stigmatised by colonisation.

Vanilla – the opposite of kinky, a normative sexual practice.

WSW/MSM – (women who have sex with women/men who have sex with men) – a term used within certain services, e.g. medical environments, that describes a behaviour without using labels people may not identify with.

References

Adams, R. (2015) 'People reward angry men but punish angry women, study suggests.' Accessed on 9/9/18 at www.huffingtonpost.co.uk/entry/people-reward-angry-men-but-punish-angry-women-study-suggests_us_561fb57be4b050c6c4a47743.

Ahmed, I. (2017) 'Debating the British Empire's "legacy" is pointless – this is still an imperial world.' Accessed on 14/7/18 at www.theconversation.com/debating-the-british-empires-legacy-is-pointless-this-is-still-an-imperial-world-74222.

Andrews, J. (2015) 'Autism and diversity: sex, gender and sexuality.' Accessed on 21/7/18 at www.vercida.com/uk/articles/autism-and-diversity-sex-gender-and-sexuality.

Anything Left-handed (2017) 'Famous left-handers – professions.' Accessed on 11/12/18 at www.anythinglefthanded.co.uk/being-lh/famous/professions.html.

Arain, M., Haque, M., Johal, L., Mathur, P. *et al.* (2013) 'Maturation of the adolescent brain.' *Neuropsychiatric Disease and Treatment 9*, 449–461.

Aron, E.N., Aron, A. and Jagiellowicz, J. (2012) 'Sensory processing sensitivity: A review in the light of the evolution of biological responsivity.' *Personality and Social Psychology Review*. Accessed on 21/7/18 at https://journals.sagepub.com/doi/10.1177/1088868311434213.

Ashenden, A. and Braidwood, E. (2018) 'What was Section 28? The history of the homophobic legislation 30 years on.' Accessed on 22/8/18 at https://www.pinknews.co.uk/2018/05/24/what-was-section-28-homophobic-legislation-30-years-thatcher.

Baba, T., Endo, T., Honnma, H., Kitajima, Y. *et al.* (2006) 'Association between polycystic ovary syndrome and female-to-male transsexuality.' *Human Reproduction 22*, 4, 1011–1016.

Baeza-Velasco, C. Hamonet, C., Baghdadlic, A. and Brissot, R. (2016) 'Autism Spectrum Disorders and Ehlers-Danlos Syndrome Hypermobility-Type: Similarities in clinical presentation.' *Medicina Psicosomática y Psiquiatría de Enlace Revista Iberoamericana de Psicosomática 118*, 49–58. Accessed on 7/7/18 at https://www.researchgate.net/publication/290436400_Autism_Spectrum_Disorders_and_Ehlers-Danlos_Syndrome_Hypermobility-Type_Similarities_in_clinical_presentation.

Barker, M.J. and Hancock, J. (2017) *Enjoy Sex: How, When and IF You Want to.* London: Icon Books.

Bauer, G., Scheim, A., Pyne, J., Travers, R. and Hammond, R. (2015) 'Intervenable factors associated with suicide risk in transgender persons: A respondent driven sampling study in Ontario, Canada.' *BMC Public Health 15*, 525.

BBC (2013) 'EDL leader Tommy Robinson takes on rapper Akala.' BBC via Youtube. Accessed on 29/6/18 at www.youtube.com/watch?v=FtA21eiSmT8.

BBC News (2014) 'Stag gore victim Dr Kate Stone says press "trampled on private life".' London: BBC News. Accessed on 10/8/18 at www.bbc.co.uk/news/uk-england-27405267.

BBC News (2018) 'How many transgender inmates are there?' London: BBC News. Accessed on 10/8/18 at www.bbc.co.uk/news/uk-42221629.

Beardon, L. (2017) 'Why do autistics need to be compared to the predominant neurotype all the time?' Sheffield: Perspectives on Autism. Accessed on 21/7/18 at https://blogs.shu.ac.uk/autism/?doing_wp_cron=1535375106.33295488357543945312 50.

Beattie, H.J. (2003) 'The repression and the return of bad objects: W.R.D. Fairbairn and the historical roots of theory.' *The International Journal of Psychoanalysis 84*, 5, 1171–1187. Accessed on 18/3/18 at www.tandfonline.com/doi/abs/10.1516/WR94-57GH-BVXH-LEPT.

Begeer, S., El Bouk, S., Boussaid, W., Meerum Terwogt, M. and Koot, H.M. (2009) 'Underdiagnosis and referral bias of autism in ethnic minorities.' *Journal of Autism and Developmental Disorders 39*, 142. Accessed on 20/7/18 at https://link.springer.com/article/10.1007/s10803-008-0611-5.

Belcher, B. (2018) 'Better Press and TV.' In Burns, C. (ed.) *Trans Britain: Our Journey from the Shadows.* London: Unbound.

Bell, K.J. (2009) 'A feminist's argument on how sex work can benefit women.' *Inquiries Journal, 1*, 11. Accessed on 10/8/18 at www.inquiriesjournal.com/articles/28/a-feminists-argument-on-how-sex-work-can-benefit-women.

Bellot, G. (2016) 'On noise, Richard O'Brien and transphobia.' Accessed on 31/12/18 at www.autostraddle.com/on-noise-richard-obrien-and-transphobia-330749.

Bennet, H. (2015) 'Kids and kindness: Can you teach compassion?' Accessed on 17/7/18 at www.todaysparent.com/family/parenting/kids-kindness-compassion.

Berlatsky, N. (2014) 'Michelle Obama trans-truthers reveal persisting prejudices: Black and trans women are still stereotyped as unfeminine.' US: *Pacific Standard*. Accessed on 9/9/18 at https://psmag.com/social-justice/michelle-obama-trans-truthers-reveal-persisting-prejudices-92320.

binaohan, b. (2014) 'decolonizing trans/gender 101.' Toronto: biyuti publishing.

Bisexual Resource Centre (2018) 'What is bisexuality.' Accessed on 8/8/18 at https://biresource.org/resources/youth/what-is-bisexuality.

Blair, K.L. and Hoskin, R.A. (2018) 'Transgender exclusion from the world of dating: Patterns of acceptance and rejection of hypothetical trans dating partners as a function of sexual and gender identity.' *Journal of Social and Personal Relationships: Research Article*. Accessed on 7/7/18 at www.journals.sagepub.com/doi/10.1177/0265407518779139.

Blanchard, R. (1989) 'The concept of autogynephilia and the typology of male gender dysphoria.' *Journal of Nervous and Mental Disease 177*, 10, 616–623.

Body Curious (2017) '11 ways Sexological Bodywork is useful for trans people.' Accessed on 10/8/18 at www.body-curious-sexcoach.co.uk/trans-people-sexological-bodywork.

Bornstein, K. (1994) *Gender Outlaw: On Men, Women and the Rest of Us*. New York: Routledge.

Braidwood, E. (2018) 'The Sunday Times comes under fire for "scaremongering" and 'anti-trans' article on women's toilets.' London: Pink News. Accessed on 31/12/18 at www.pinknews.co.uk/2018/07/29/the-sunday-times-comes-under-fire-for-scaremongering-and-anti-trans-article-on-womens-toilets.

Broadhead, W.E., Kaplan, B.H., James, S.A., Wagner, E.H. *et al.* (1983) 'The epidemiologic evidence for a relationship between social support and health.' *American Journal of Epidemiology 117*, 5, 521–537.

Broomfield, M. (2016) 'GCHQ apologises for "horrifying" treatment of Alan Turing and discrimination against other LGBT people.' *The Independent*, 16 April. Accessed on 12/7/18 at www.independent.co.uk/news/uk/gchq-apology-horrifying-treatment-alan-turing-lgbt-people-a6987021.html.

Brown University (2018) 'Brown statement, community letter on gender dysphoria study.' Accessed on 29/8/18 at https://news.brown.edu/articles/2018/08/gender.

Bullock, A. (1953) *Hitler: A Study in Tyranny*. New York: Harper and Brothers.

Burnes, T.R., Singh, A.A., Harper, A.J., Harper, B. *et al.* (2010) 'American Counseling Association competencies for counseling with transgender clients.' *Journal of LGBT Issues in Counseling 4*, 135–159.

Burns, K. (2018) 'The dire realities of being a trans woman in a men's prison.' Accessed on 22/8/18 at www.them.us/story/the-dire-realities-of-being-a-trans-woman-in-a-mens-prison.

Butler, J. (1988) 'Performative acts and gender constitution: An essay in phenomenology and feminist theory.' *Theatre Journal 40*, 4, 519–531. Accessed on 15/6/18 at http://facweb.northseattle.edu/mjacobson/SPECIAL%20TOPICS%20IN%20PSYCHOLOGY/Subjectivity/PerformativeActs.pdf.

Cage, E., Monaco, J.D. and Newell, V. (2018) 'Experiences of autism acceptance and mental health in autistic adults.' *Journal of Autism and Developmental Disorders 48*, 2, 473–484.

Carrellas, B. (2017) *Urban Tantra: Sacred Sex for the Twenty-First Century*, 2nd edition. New York: Ten Speed Press.

Carroll, L., Gilroy, P.J. and Ryan, J. (2002) 'Counseling transgendered, transsexual, and gender-variant clients.' *Journal of Counseling and Development 80*, 131–139.

CATIE (2013) 'Brazen: Trans women's safer sex guide.' Accessed on 10/9/18 at http://librarypdf.catie.ca/PDF/ATI-20000s/26424.pdf.

Cavalcante, A. (2016) '"I did it all online": Transgender identity and the management of everyday life.' *Critical Studies in Media Communication 33*, 1, 109–122.

Choudrey, S. (2016) 'Inclusivity: Supporting BAME trans people.' Accessed on 4/2/18 at www.gires.org.uk/wp-content/uploads/2016/02/BAME_Inclusivity.pdf.

Choudrey, S. (2018) 'My queer Ramadan.' Accessed on 7/7/18 at https://sabahchoudrey.com/2018/06/01/my-queer-ramadan.

Chown, N., Robinson, J., Beardon, L., Downing, J. *et al.* (2017) 'Improving research about us, with us: A draft framework for inclusive autism research.' *Disability and Society 32*, 5, 720–734.

Cook-Daniels, L. (2015) 'Trans men experience far more violence than most people assume.' Accessed on 7/11/17 at www.advocate.com/commentary/2015/07/23/op-ed-trans-men-experience-far-more-violence-most-people-assume.

Cornell University (2017) 'What does the scholarly research say about the effect of gender transition on transgender well-being?' Accessed on 25/2/18 at https://whatweknow.inequality.cornell.edu/topics/lgbt-equality/%20what-does-the-scholarly-research-say-about-the-well-being-of-transgender-people%20.

COSRT (2017) 'Memorandum of understanding on conversion therapy in the UK version 2.' Accessed on 20/8/18 at www.cosrt.org.uk/wp-content/uploads/2017/10/MoU2_FINAL.pdf.

Crenshaw, K. (1991) 'Mapping the margins: Intersectionality, identity politics, and violence against women of color.' *Stanford Law Review 43*, 6, 1241–1299.

Crenshaw, K. (2016) 'The urgency of intersectionality.' Accessed on 4/1/18 at www.ted.com/talks/kimberle_crenshaw_the_urgency_of_intersectionality?language=en.

Crespi, B. (2016) 'Autism as a disorder of high intelligence.' *Frontiers in Neuroscience 10*, 300. Accessed on 7/7/18 at www.ncbi.nlm.nih.gov/pmc/articles/PMC4927579.

Cukor, G. (dir.) (1944) *Gaslight.*

Davies, D. (1996) 'Towards a Model of Gay Affirmative Therapy.' In Davies, D. and Neal, C. (eds) *Pink Therapy*. Bristol: Open University Press.

Davis, S.R. and Tran, J. (2001) 'Testosterone influences libido and wellbeing in women.' *TRENDS in Endocrinology and Metabolism 12,* 1, 33–37.

Dawson, J. (2017) *The Gender Games.* London: Two Roads Books.

De Beauvoir, S. (1949) *The Second Sex,* book 2, part 4. France: Gallimard.

De Gallier (2016) 'I got kicked off a Mumsnet forum after asking people about transphobia.' Accessed on 10/8/18 at www.vice.com/en_uk/article/nnkjak/mumsnet-transphobia-north-carolina-bathroom-bill.

De Simone, D. (2016) 'The killer the police missed.' Accessed on 11/12/18 at www.bbc.co.uk/news/resources/idt-d32c5bc9-aa42-49b8-b77c-b258ea2a9205.

De Vries, A.L.C., McGuipacere, J.K., Steensma, T.D., Wagenaar, E.C.F., Doreleijers, T.A.H. and Cohen-Kettenis, P.T. (2014) 'Young adult psychological outcome after puberty suppression and gender reassignment.' *Pediatrics*. Accessed on 17/9/17 at www.gendersurgeryamsterdam.nl/wp-content/uploads/2014/09/de-Vries-2014-Young-Adult-Psychological-Outcome_Pediatrics.pdf.

Dexter, J. (dir.) (1972) *I want what I want.* Accessed on 12/7/18 at www.youtube.com/watch?v=TPoePTH_X3M.

Diamond, M. and Sigmundson, H. K. (1997) 'Sex reassignment at birth: Long-term review and clinical implications.' *Archives of Pediatrics and Adolescent Medicine 151*, 3, 298–304.

Dickerson, J. (2016) 'Child psychiatry consult: Autism spectrum disorders in gender-nonconforming youth.' Accessed on 7/7/18 at www.mdedge.com/pediatricnews/article/109815/mental-health/autism-spectrum-disorders-gender-nonconforming-youth.

Duffy, N. (2017) 'The UK has rejected thousands of gay asylum seekers.' Accessed on 1/12/17 at www.pinknews.co.uk/2017/11/30/the-uk-has-rejected-thousands-of-gay-asylum-seekers.

Edelson, M.G. (2010) 'Sexual abuse of children with autism: Factors that increase risk and interfere with recognition of abuse.' *Disability Studies Quarterly 30*, 1. Accessed on 10/8/18 at http://dsq-sds.org/article/view/1058/1228.

Endocrine Society (2017) 'Transgender health: An endocrine society position statement.' Accessed on 2/1/18 at www.endocrine.org/advocacy/priorities-and-positions/transgender-health.

Equality Act (2010) *Chapter 15, Section 7.* London: The Stationery Office. Accessed on 15/11/17 at www.legislation.gov.uk/ukpga/2010/15/pdfs/ukpga_20100015_en.pdf.

Equality Archive (2015) *Transgender women of color at Stonewall.* US: Equality Archive. Accessed on 10/6/18 https://equalityarchive.com/history/transgender-women-of-color-at-stonewall..

Erickson-Schroth, L. (2013) 'Update on the biology of transgender identity.' *Journal of Gay and Lesbian Mental Health 17,* 2, 150–174.

Fairbairn, W.R.D. (1952) 'The Repression and Return of Bad Objects (with Special References to the "War Neuroses").' In *Psychoanalytic Studies of the Personality.* London: Routledge & Kegan Paul.

Fair Play for Women (2017) 'Half of all transgender prisoners are sex offenders or dangerous category A inmates.' Accessed on 10/8/18 at www.fairplayforwomen.com/transgender-prisoners.

Falk, L. (2015) 'The 8 genders of the Talmud.' Accessed on 22/8/18 at www.thejewniverse.com/2015/the-6-genders-of-the-talmud.

Farndale, N. (2006) 'I'm all boy.' *The Telegraph*, 30 July. Accessed on 8/8/18 at www.telegraph.co.uk/culture/3654174/Im-all-boy.html.

Fausto-Sterling, A. (2000) 'The five sexes, revisited.' *The Sciences 40*, 4, 18–23.

Feinberg, L. (1996) *Transgender Warriors: Making History from Joan of Arc to Dennis Rodman.* Boston: Beacon Press.

Feinstein, B.A., Dyar, C., Bhatia, V., Latack, J. and Davila, J. (2014) 'Willingness to engage in romantic and sexual activities with bisexual partners: Gender and sexual orientation differences.' *Psychology of Sexual Orientation and Gender Diversity 1*, 3, 255–262.

Fine, C. (2010) *Delusions of Gender: How Our Minds, Society, and Neurosexism Create Difference.* New York: W.W. Norton and Co.

Fine, C. (2017) *Testosterone Rex: Unmaking the Myths of Our Gendered Minds.* New York: W.W. Norton and Co.

Furfaro, H. (2017) 'Race, class contribute to disparities in autism diagnoses.' Accessed on 15/7/18 at www.spectrumnews.org/news/race-class-contribute-disparities-autism-diagnoses.

Fury (2016) 'Trans mission: How to tell our stories on stage and screen.' *The Guardian*, 17 May. Accessed on 10/8/18 at www.theguardian.com/society/2016/may/17/how-to-tell-trans-stories-on-stage-and-screen.

Gadsby, H. (2018) *Nannette.* UK: Netflix.

Gannon, S.P. (2009) *Translating the Hijra: The Symbolic Reconstruction of the British Empire in India.* Alberta: University of Alberta.

Garkawe, S. (1997) 'Book Reviews: Hidden Holocaust? Gay and lesbian persecution in Germany 1933–1945.' Accessed on 22/8/18 at http://classic.austlii.edu.au/au/journals/MelbULawRw/1997/29.pdf.

Gavrilets, S. (2014) 'Collective action and the collaborative brain.' *Journal of the Royal Society Interface 12*, 102. Accessed on 10/8/18 at http://rsif.royalsocietypublishing.org/content/12/102/20141067.

Gender Recognition Act (2004) *Chapter 7.* London: The Stationery Office. Accessed on 15/6/18 at https://www.legislation.gov.uk/ukpga/2004/7/pdfs/ukpga_20040007_en.pdf.

General Medical Council (2018) *Trans healthcare.* UK: General Medical Council. Accessed on 7/7/18 at https://www.gmc-uk.org/ethical-guidance/ethical-hub/trans-healthcare---advice-based-on-gmc-guidance.

George, R. and Stokes, M.A. (2018) 'Sexual orientation in autism spectrum disorder.' *Autism Research 11*, 1, 133–141.

Giovanniello, S. (2013) 'NCAVP report: 2012 hate violence disproportionately target transgender women of color.' Accessed on 5/1/18 at www.glaad.org/blog/ncavp-report-2012-hate-violence-disproportionately-target-transgender-women-color.

Glidden, D., Bouman, W.P., Jones, B.A. and Arcelus, J. (2015) 'Gender dysphoria and autism spectrum disorder: A systematic review of the literature.' *Sexual Medicine Reviews 4*, 3, 14.

Glyde, T. (2018) 'Pink Therapy's Sex Work and Psychotherapy Conference – history in the making.' Accessed on 10/8/18 at https://londoncentralcounselling.com/2018/03/25/pink-therapys-sex-work-and-psychotherapy-conference-history-in-the-making.

Government Equalities Office (2018) 'National LGBT Survey: Summary report.' Accessed on 10/8/18 at www.gov.uk/government/publications/national-lgbt-survey-summary-report/national-lgbt-survey-summary-report.

Grant, J.M., Mottet, L.A., Tanis, J., Harrison, J., Herman, J.L. and Keisling, M. (2011) *Injustice at every turn: A Report of the National Transgender Discrimination Survey*. Accessed on 31/12/18 at www.ncgs.org/wp-content/uploads/2017/11/Injustice-at-Every-Turn-A-Report-of-the-National-Transgender-Discrimination-Survey.pdf.

Green, J. (2017) *The Trans Partner Handbook: A Guide for When Your Partner Transitions*. London: Jessica Kingsley Publishers.

Guarino, N., Scommegna, S., Majore, S., Rapone, A.M., Ungaro, L., Morrone, A., Grammatico, P. and Marrocco, G.A. (2013) 'Vaginoplasty for disorders of sex development.' *Frontiers in Endocrinology 4*, 29. Accessed on 21/8/18 at www.ncbi.nlm.nih.gov/pmc/articles/PMC3593621.

Gust, O. (2014) 'Hyperbole and horror: hijras and the British imperial state in India.' Notches: (re)marks on the history of sexuality. Accessed on 15/6/18 at www.notchesblog.com/2014/01/06/hyperbole-and-horror-hijras-and-the-british-imperial-state-in-india.

Halberstadt, A. and Shipman, S. (2018) 'Prospective teachers more likely to view black faces than white faces as angry.' Accessed on 9/9/18 at https://news.ncsu.edu/2018/07/prospective-teachers-bias.

Herman, J.L. (1997) *Trauma and Recovery: From Domestic Abuse to Political Terror*. London: Pandora.

Hickling, A. (2016) 'Breaking the Code review – telling autistic Turing's fateful truth.' *The Guardian*, November 6. Accessed on 15/7/18 at www.theguardian.com/stage/2016/nov/06/breaking-the-code-review-autism-alan-turing-enigma.

Hill, P. (2013) 'Busting the Margaret Thatcher voice coaching myth.' Accessed on 20/8/18 at www.workingvoices.com/busting-margaret-thatcher-voice-coaching-myth.

Hope, S. (2017a) 'Setting the record straight on trans issues.' Accessed on 10/8/18 at https://hopecounsellingandtraining.wordpress.com/2017/01/02/setting-the-record-straight-on-trans-issues.

Hope, S. (2017b) 'Navigating age and ageism within trans communities.' Accessed on 7/8/18 at www.thequeerness.com/2017/11/08/navigating-age-and-ageism-within-trans-communities.

Huke, V., Turk, J., Saeidi, S., Kent, A and Morgan, J.F. (2013) 'Autism spectrum disorders in eating disorder populations: A systematic review.' *European Eating Disorders Review 21*, 5, 345–351.

Human Rights Campaign (2012) [video] *Lana Wachowski receives the HRC Visibility Award*. Accessed on 5/5/17 at www.youtube.com/watch?v=crHHycz7T_c.

Human Rights Watch (2008) 'Coercion and intimidation of child soldiers to participate in violence.' Accessed on 10/9/18 at www.hrw.org/news/2008/04/16/coercion-and-intimidation-child-soldiers-participate-violence.

Hunt, J. (2014) 'An initial study of transgender people's experiences of seeking and receiving counselling or psychotherapy in the UK.' *Counselling and Psychotherapy Research 14*, 4, 288–296.

Intersex Society of North America (2018) 'Frequently asked questions.' Accessed on 8/8/18 at www.isna.org/faq/printable.

Ira (2017) 'Chest binding 101.' Accessed on 22/8/18 at https://transguys.com/features/chest-binding.

Jackson, J. (2017) 'Four signs that you might subscribe to the politics of respectability.' Accessed on 10/9/18 at www.watercoolerconvos.com/2017/03/08/four-signs-that-you-might-subscribe-to-the-politics-of-respectability.

Janoff-Bulman, R. (1992) *Shattered Assumptions: Towards a New Psychology of Trauma*. New York: Free Press.

Jaswal, V.K. and Akhtar, M. (2018) 'Being vs. appearing socially uninterested: Challenging assumptions about social motivation in autism.' *Behavioral and Brain Sciences*, June, 1–84. Accessed on 2/9/18 at www.cambridge.org/core/journals/behavioral-and-brain-sciences/article/being-vs-appearing-socially-uninterested-challenging-assumptions-about-social-motivation-in-autism/4E75B5E49CC0061E65A4D78552482AF9.

Joel, D. (2012) 'Genetic-gonadal-genitals sex (3G-sex) and the misconception of brain and gender, or, why 3G-males and 3G-females have intersex brain and intersex gender.' *Biology of Sex Differences 3*, 27. Accessed on 21/12/17 at https://bsd.biomedcentral.com/articles/10.1186/2042-6410-3-27.

Kacala (2018) 'Toxic masculinity and femmephobia were front and center during this gay couple's reality show date.' Accessed on 7/8/18 at https://hornet.com/stories/femmephobia-first-dates-straight-acting.

Kanner, R. (2018) 'I detransitioned. But not because I wasn't trans.' Accessed on 20/8/18 at www.theatlantic.com/family/archive/2018/06/i-detransitioned-but-not-because-i-wasnt-trans/563396.

Karin (2009) 'Lili Elbe's autobiography, *Man into Woman*.' Accessed on 22/8/18 at https://ihra.org.au/789/book-review-man-woman.

Kelly, L. and Karsna, K. (2017) 'Measuring the scale and changing nature of child sexual abuse and child sexual exploitation: Scoping report'. Accessed on 11/4/19 at https://www.csacentre.org.uk/csa-centre-prod/assets/File/CSA%20Scale%20and%20Nature%20full%20report%202018.pdf.

Kirkland, F. (2017) 'Great Ormond Street Hospital failing intersex children.' Accessed on 13/10/17 at www.bbc.co.uk/news/uk-41593914.

Koch, C. and Wisdom, T. (2017) 'Surgery to make intersex children "normal" should be banned.' *The Sydney Morning Herald*, 5 July. Accessed on 8/8/18 at www.smh.com.au/lifestyle/surgery-to-make-intersex-children-normal-should-be-banned-20170705-gx4txg.html.

Kort, J. (2017) 'The misleading "sexual addiction" label: Wrong labels make for poor therapy.' Accessed on 10/9/18 at www.psychologytoday.com/us/blog/understanding-the-erotic-code/201701/the-misleading-sexual-addiction-label.

Kray, K. (2015) '10 things trans activists and allies need to remember that have nothing to do with Caitlyn Jenner.' Accessed on 10/9/18 at https://everydayfeminism.com/2015/06/trans-activists-need-to-remember-indp-of-jenner.

Lago, C (2013) 'Counselling across Difference and Diversity.' In Cooper, M. O'Hara, M. Schmid, P.F. and Bohart, A. (eds) *The Handbook of Person-Centred Psychotherapy and Counselling*. London: Palgrave MacMillan.

Lambert, M.J. and Barley, D.E. (2001) 'Research summary on the therapeutic relationship and psychotherapy outcome.' *Psychotherapy: Theory, Research, Practice, Training* 38, 4, 357–361.

Lander, M. (2018) 'An event hosted in Parliament reportedly compared trans people to parasites.' Accessed on 25/8/18 at www.indy100.com/article/event-house-of-commons-trans-people-parasites-david-davies-mp-sheila-jeffreys-8258041.

Latarche, J. (2018) 'Get TERFs out of feminism.' Accessed on 10/8/18 at https://freedomnews.org.uk/get-terfs-out-of-feminism.

Lawson, W.B. (2017) 'Women and girls on the autism spectrum: A profile.' *Journal of Intellectual Disability – Diagnosis and Treatment* 5, 90–95. Accessed on 21/7/18 at http://lifescienceglobal.com/pms/index.php/jiddt/article/view/4971/2813.

Lees, P. (2017) 'I sold sex to fund my unpaid internships. Poor kids are still battling the class gap.' *The Guardian*, 25 October. Accessed on 10/8/18 at www.theguardian.com/commentisfree/2017/oct/25/sold-sex-fund-unpaid-internships-poor-kids-battling-class-gap.

Lester, CN (2017) *Trans like Me: A Journey for All of Us*. London: Virago Press.

Lev, A. (2004) *Transgender Emergence: Therapeutic guidelines for working with gender-variant people and their families*. New York: Routledge.

Levesley, D. (2017) 'The media needs to stop weaponising children in their crusade against trans people.' Accessed on 11/8/18 at www.inews.co.uk/opinion/comment/media-needs-stop-weaponising-young-children-crusade-trans-people.

Liss, M., Mailloux, J. and Erchull, M.J. (2008) 'The relationships between sensory processing sensitivity, alexithymia, autism, depression, and anxiety.' *Personality and Individual Differences 45*, 3, 255–259.

Liss, M., Timmel, L., Baxley, K. and Killingsworth, P. (2005) 'Sensory processing sensitivity and its relation to parental bonding, anxiety, and depression.' *Personality and Individual Differences 39*, 8, 1429–1439.

Littman, L. (2018) 'Rapid-onset gender dysphoria in adolescents and young adults: A study of parental reports.' *Plos One 13*, 8, e0202330.

Livingstone, T. (2011) 'The relevance of a person-centered approach to therapy with transgendered or transsexual clients.' *Person-Centred and Experiential Psychotherapies 7*, 2, 135–144.

Loch, C.H., Galunic, C.D. and Schneider, S. (2006) 'Balancing cooperation and competition in human groups: The role of emotional algorithms and evolution.' *Managerial and Decision Economics 27*, 2–3, 217–233.

Lussenhop, J. (2016) 'Why did Prince change his name to a symbol?' Accessed on 20/8/18 at www.bbc.co.uk/news/magazine-36107590.

Marhoefer, L. (2008) 'Among abnormals: The queer sexual politics of Germany's Weimar Republic, 1918–1933.' New Jersey: Rutgers University. Accessed on 22/8/18 at https://rucore.libraries.rutgers.edu/rutgers-lib/24724/PDF/1/play.

Marks, L.E. and Mulvenna, C.M. (2013) 'Synesthesia, at and near its borders.' *Frontiers in Psychology*. Accessed on 21/7/18 at www.frontiersin.org/articles/10.3389/fpsyg.2013.00651/full.

McConnell, E.A., Birkett, M. and Mustanski, B. (2016) 'Families matter: Social support and mental health trajectories among lesbian, gay, bisexual, and transgender youth.' *Journal of Adolescent Health 59*, 6, 674–680. Accessed on 10/10/17 at www.ncbi.nlm.nih.gov/pmc/articles/PMC5217458.

McGuiness, F. (2018) 'Unemployment by ethnic background.' London: House of Commons Library. Accessed on 9/9/18 at http://researchbriefings.files.parliament.uk/documents/SN06385/SN06385.pdf.

McNeil, J., Bailey, L., Ellis, S., Morton, J. and Regan, M. (2012) 'Trans mental health and emotional wellbeing study 2012.' Accessed on 1/2/18 at www.scottishtrans.org/wp-content/uploads/2013/03/trans_mh_study.pdf.

Merry, T. (1995) *Invitation to Person Centred Psychology*. London: Whurr Publishers Ltd.

Mey (2013) 'Who's afraid of the big, bad trans woman? On horror and transfemininity.' Accessed on 10/8/18 at www.autostraddle.com/whos-afraid-of-the-big-bad-trans-woman-on-horror-and-transfemininity-198212.

Meyer, I.H. (2003) 'Prejudice, social stress, and mental health in lesbian, gay, and bisexual populations: Conceptual issues and research evidence.' *Psychological Bulletin 129*, 5, 674–697.

Michaelson, J. (2015) 'What it was like to transition 50 years ago.' Accessed on 9/9/17 at www.thedailybeast.com/what-it-was-like-to-transition-50-years-ago.

Michelraj, M. (2015) 'Historical evolution of transgender community in India.' *Asian Review of Social Sciences 4*, 1, 17–19.

Milton, D.E.M. (2014) 'Autistic expertise: A critical reflection on the production of knowledge in autism studies.' *Autism 18*, 7, 794–802.

Miltona, D. and Sims, T. (2016) 'How is a sense of well-being and belonging constructed in the accounts of autistic adults?' *Disability and Society 31*, 4, 520–534.

Minou, C.L. (2010) 'Julie Bindel's dangerous transphobia.' Accessed on 10/8/18 at www.theguardian.com/commentisfree/2010/feb/01/julie-bindel-transphobia.

Minto, C.L., Liao, L. Woodhouse, C.R.J., Ransley, P.G., Creighton, S.M. (2003) 'The effect of clitoral surgery on sexual outcome in individuals who have intersex conditions with ambiguous genitalia: A cross-sectional study.' *The Lancet 361*,1252–1257.

Mock, J. (2014) *Redefining Realness: My Path to Womanhood, Identity, Love and So Much More.* New York: Atria Books.

Molloy, A. (2014) 'British sex survey 2014: Over three-quarters of men watch porn, but women prefer erotica.' Accessed on 8/10/18 at www.independent.co.uk/life-style/british-sex-survey-2014-over-three-quarters-of-men-watch-porn-but-women-prefer-erotica-9762906.html.

Money, J. and Ehrhardt, A.A. (1972) *Man and Woman, Boy and Girl: Differentiation and Dimorphism of Gender Identity from Conception to Maturity.* Oxford: John Hopkins University Press.

Money, J., Hampson, J.G. and Hampson, J.L. (1955) 'An examination of some basic sexual concepts: The evidence of human hermaphroditism.' *Bulletin of the Johns Hopkins Hospital 97*, 4, 301–319.

Morgan, C. (2018) 'How not to erase trans history.' Accessed on 22/8/18 at www.historymatters.group.shef.ac.uk/erase-trans-history.

Morgan, J. (2018) 'Trans woman stabbed to death in London hotel: RIP Naomi.' Accessed on 7/7/18 at www.gaystarnews.com/article/trans-woman-stabbed-death-london/#gs.dfBI38o.

Morgensen, S.L. (2012) 'Theorising gender, sexuality and settler colonialism: An introduction.' *Settler Colonial Studies 2*, 2, 2–22.

Mosbergen, D. (2017) 'Battling asexual discrimination, sexual violence and "corrective" rape.' Accessed on 10/8/18 at www.huffingtonpost.co.uk/entry/asexual-discrimination_n_3380551.

Moser, C. (2009) 'Autogynephilia in women.' *Journal of Homosexuality 56*, 5, 539–547.

Mullin, F. (2016) 'The dangerous silence around HIV prevention for women and trans people.' Accessed on 18/8/18 at www.vice.com/en_uk/article/yvxa4b/frankie-mullin-women-trans-excluded-from-hiv-aids-help.

Munson, M. and Cook-Daniels, L. (2015) 'Let's talk about it! A transgender survivor's guide to accessing therapy.' Accessed on 10/8/18 at https://forge-forward.org/2015/05/07/lets-talk-about-it-a-transgender-survivors-guide-to-accessing-therapy.

National Centre for Transgender Equality (2015) 'US transgender survey.' Accessed on 10/9/18 at www.transequality.org/sites/default/files/docs/usts/USTS%20Full%20Report%20-%20FINAL%201.6.17.pdf.

National Centre for Transgender Equality (2018) 'The discrimination administration: Trump's record of action against transgender people.' Accessed on 20/8/18 at www.transequality.org/the-discrimination-administration.

Nordgren, A. (2006) 'The short instructional manifesto for relationship anarchy.' Accessed on 10/8/18 at www.theanarchistlibrary.org/library/andie-nordgren-the-short-instructional-manifesto-for-relationship-anarchy.

Nottinghamshire Healthcare NHS Foundation Trust (2017) 'Mental health survey report for LGBT+ people in Nottinghamshire.' Accessed on 28/7/18 at https://nottstranshub.files.wordpress.com/2018/07/2017-mental-health-survey-report-for-lgbt-people-in-nottinghamshire.pdf.

Notts Trans Hub (2017) 'Asking about Gender on Forms.' Accessed on 10/7/18 at https://nottstranshub.files.wordpress.com/2017/11/asking-about-gender-on-forms.pdf.

NSPCC (2018) 'Sexual abuse facts and statistics.' Accessed on 20/8/18 at www.nspcc.org.uk/preventing-abuse/child-abuse-and-neglect/child-sexual-abuse/sexual-abuse-facts-statistics.

Oliver, M. (2013) 'The social model of disability: Thirty years on.' *Disability and Society 28*, 7, 1024–1026.

Olson, K.R., Key, A.C. and Eaton, N.R (2015) 'Gender cognition in transgender children.' *Psychological Science 26*, 4, 467–474.

Ottoman, E. (2015) 'Dr. James Barry and the specter of trans and queer history.' Accessed on 22/8/18 at https://acosmistmachine.com/2015/11/24/dr-james-barry-and-the-specter-of-trans-and-queer-history.

PACE (2015) 'The RaRE research report: LGB&T mental health – risk and resilience explored.' Accessed on 21/8/18 at www.queerfutures.co.uk/wp-content/uploads/2015/04/RARE_Research_Report_PACE_2015.pdf.

Papisova, V. and Kheraj, E. (2017) 'Why intersex genital mutilation needs to stop.' Accessed on 21/8/18 at www.teenvogue.com/story/intersex-genital-mutilation.

Pearce, R. (2018) *Understanding Transgender Health: Discourse, Power and Possibility*. Bristol: Policy Press.

Pflum, S., Testa, R., Balsam, K., Goldblum, P. and Bongar, B. (2015) 'Social support, trans community connectedness, and mental health symptoms among transgender and gender nonconforming adults.' *Psychology of Sexual Orientation and Gender Diversity 2*, 3, 281–286.

Polderman, T.J.C., Hoekstra, R.A., Posthuma, D. and Larsson, H. (2014) 'The co-occurrence of autistic and ADHD dimensions in adults: An etiological study in 17 770 twins.' *Translational Psychiatry 4*, 435. Accessed on 7/7/18 at www.nature.com/articles/tp201484.

Posserud, M., Hysing, M., Hellande, W., Gillberg, C. and Lundervold, A.J. (2018) 'Autism traits: The importance of "co-morbid" problems for impairment and contact with services. Data from the Bergen Child Study.' *Research in Developmental Disabilities 72*, 275–283. Accessed on 7/7/18 at www.sciencedirect.com/science/article/pii/S0891422216300026.

Reiner, W.G. (2005) 'Gender identity and sex-of-rearing in children with disorders of sexual differentiation.' *Journal of Pediatric Endocrinology and Metabolism 18*, 6, 549–553.

Richards, C. and Barker, M. (2013) *Sexuality and Gender for Mental Health Professionals*. London: Sage.

Riedel, S. (2016) 'The trans people who are detransitioning to stay safe in Trump's America.' Accessed on 24/8/18 at: https://www.huffingtonpost.com/entry/the-trans-people-who-are-detransitioning-to-stay-safe_us_5840bb7ce4b04587de5de897.

Riley, E.A., Wong, W.K.T and Sitharthan, G. (2011) 'Counseling support for the forgotten transgender community.' *Journal of Gay and Lesbian Social Services 23*, 395–410.

Robinson, K. (2016) 'Look beyond the binary.' *Therapy Today 27*, 9, 16–19.

Robles, A., Hamid, V., Cruz-Islas, J., Rodríguez-Pérez, V. *et al.* (2016) 'Removing transgender identity from the classification of mental disorders: A Mexican field study for ICD-11.' *The Lancet Psychiatry 3*, 9, 850–859.

Roche, J. (2018) *Queer Sex: A Trans and Non-Binary Guide to Intimacy, Pleasure and Relationships.* London: Jessica Kingsley Publishers.

Rocks, C. (2016) 'Being Bi – Borderline Personality Disorder.' Accessed on 21/7/18 at www.thisisbiscuit.co.uk/borderline-personality-disorder.

Rogers, C. (1957) 'The necessary and sufficient conditions of therapeutic personality change.' *Journal of Consulting Psychology 21*, 95–103. Accessed on 22/10/17 at: http://shoreline.edu/dchris/psych236/Documents/Rogers.pdf.

Rogers, C.R. (1961) *On Becoming a Person*. New York: Houghton Mifflin.

Roman, A. (2018) 'Trans-doubt.' Transubstantiation [blog] on Medium. Accessed on 30/7/18 at https://transsubstantiation.com/trans-doubt-373bfe4af92c.

Rosenberg, S. (2018) 'The complex reality of trans womens sexuality.' Accessed on 31/12/18 at www.sbs.com.au/topics/sexuality/agenda/article/2018/04/24/complex-reality-trans-womens-sexuality.

Rothschild, B. (2000) *The Body Remembers: The Psychophysiology of Trauma and Trauma Treatment.* London: W.W. Norton and Company, Ltd.

Roughgarden, J. (2004) *Evolution's Rainbow: Diversity, Gender, and Sexuality in Nature and People.* Berkeley, CA: University of California Press.

Russell, H. (2015) 'Gerda Wegener: "The Lady Gaga of the 1920s".' *The Guardian*, 28 September. Accessed on 22/8/18 at www.theguardian.com/lifeandstyle/2015/sep/28/gerda-einar-wergener-danish-girl-trans-painter.

Rutter, M., Andersen-Wood, L., Beckett, C., Bredenkamp, D. *et al.* (1999) 'Quasi-autistic patterns following severe early global privation.' *The Journal of Child Psychology and Psychiatry and Allied Disciplines 40*, 4, 537–549.

Sanders, P. (2005) 'Principled and Strategic Opposition to the Medicalisation of Distress and All of Its Apparatus.' In Joseph, S. and Worsley, R. (eds) *Person -Centred Psychopathology: A Positive Psychology of Mental Health*. Ross-on-Wye: PCCS Books Ltd.

Sasson, N.J., Faso, D.J., Nugent, J., Love, S.D., Kennedy, D.P. and Grossman, R.B. (2017) 'Neurotypical peers are less willing to interact with those with autism based on thin slice judgments.' *Nature: Scientific Reports 7*, 40700.

Scottish Trans (2010) 'Out of sight, out of mind? Transgender people's experiences of domestic abuse.' Accessed on 7/11/17 at www.scottishtrans.org/wp-content/uploads/2013/03/trans_domestic_abuse.pdf.

Serano, J. (2007) *Whipping Girl: A Transsexual Woman on Sexism and the Scapegoating of Femininity.* Berkeley, CA: Seal Press.

Serano, J. (2013) *Excluded: Making Feminist and Queer Movements More Inclusive.* Berkeley, CA: Seal Press.

Serano, J. (2018) 'Everything you need to know about Rapid Onset Gender Dysphoria.' Accessed on 29/8/18 at https://medium.com/@juliaserano/everything-you-need-to-know-about-rapid-onset-gender-dysphoria-1940b8afdeba.

Sheerin, J. (2009) 'Transgender individuals' experiences in therapy and perception of the treatment experience.' Smith College School for Social Work Northampton, Massachussetts 01063. [Unpublished Master's Thesis].

Skills for Action (2018) 'Autism spectrum disorders and motor skills.' Accessed on 7/7/18 at https://skillsforaction.com/autism-spectrum-disorders.

Southern Poverty Law Centre (2017) 'Christian Right tips to fight transgender rights: Separate the T from the LGB.' Accessed on 3/1/19 at www.splcenter.org/hatewatch/2017/10/23/christian-right-tips-fight-transgender-rights-separate-t-lgb

Spencer, S. J., Steele, C.M. and Quinn, D. (1999) 'Stereotype threat and women's math performance.' *Journal of Experimental Social Psychology 35*, 4–28.

Stonewall (2015) 'Trans people and Stonewall.' Accessed on 10/8/18 at www.stonewall.org.uk/resources/trans-people-and-stonewall-2015.

Stonewall (2017a) 'LGBT in Britain: Hate crime and discrimination. London: Stonewall.' Accessed on 20/8/18 at https://www.stonewall.org.uk/sites/default/files/lgbt_in_britain_hate_crime.pdf.

Stonewall (2017b) 'Workplace.' Accessed on 10/10/17 at www.stonewall.org.uk/get-involved/workplace.

Stonewall (2018a) 'LGBT in Britain: Trans report.' Accessed on 20/8/18 at www.stonewall.org.uk/sites/default/files/lgbt-in-britain-trans.pdf.

Stonewall (2018b) 'Supporting trans women in domestic and sexual violence services: Interviews with professionals in the sector.' Accessed on 22/8/18 at www.stonewall.org.uk/sites/default/files/stonewall_and_nfpsynergy_report.pdf.

Stonewall (2018c) 'Media coverage of Naomi Hersi's death is a disgrace.' Accessed on 10/8/18 at www.stonewall.org.uk/our-work/blog-naomi-hersi.

Subbaraman, N. (2014) 'Study on "extreme male brain" theory of autism draws critics.' Accessed on 15/7/18 at www.spectrumnews.org/news/study-on-extreme-male-brain-theory-of-autism-draws-critics.

Taylor, D. (2013) 'Birth of a transsexual separatist and then born again.' Accessed on 7/7/18 at www.transadvocate.com/birth-of-a-transsexual-separatist_n_9417.htm.

TDoR (2007) 'About TDoR.' Accessed on 7/7/18 at https://tdor.info//about-2.

Temple Newhook, J., Pyne, J., Winters, K., Feder, S. *et al.* (2018) 'A critical commentary on follow-up studies and "desistance" theories about transgender and gender-nonconforming children.' *International Journal of Transgenderism 19*, 2, 212–224.

The LGBT Bar (2017) 'Gay and trans panic defense.' Accessed on 7/7/18 at www.lgbtbar.org/what-we-do/programs/gay-and-trans-panic-defense.

Tomasello, M., Melis, A.P., Tennie, C., Wyman, E. and Herrmann, E. (2012) 'Two key steps in the evolution of human cooperation: The interdependence hypothesis.' *Current Anthropology 53*, 6, 673–692.

Tomchek, S.D. and Dunn, W. (2007) 'Sensory processing in children with and without autism: A comparative study using the Short Sensory Profile.' *American Journal of Occupational Therapy 61*, 2, 190–200.

Totaljobs (2016) 'Totaljobs trans employee survey report 2016.' Accessed 12/1/18 at www.totaljobs.com/insidejob/trans-employee-survey-report-2016.

Townsend, M. (2016) 'Homophobic attacks in UK rose 147% in three months after Brexit vote.' *The Guardian*, 8 October. Accessed on 10/8/18 at www.theguardian.com/society/2016/oct/08/homophobic-attacks-double-after-brexit-vote.

Trans Media Watch (2017) 'Charity condemns BBC misinformation about trans children.' Accessed on 20/8/18 at www.transmediawatch.org/Documents/Press%20Release%2020170112.pdf.

Trans Student Educational Resources (2014) 'The Gender Unicorn.' Accessed on 6/9/17 at www.transstudent.org/gender.

Transgender Foundation of America (2008) 'Transgenders and Nazi Germany.' Accessed on 5/10/17 at http://tgdor.org/holocaust.shtml.

Uchino, B.N., Cacioppo, J.T. and Kiecolt-Glaser, J.K. (1996) 'The relationship between social support and physiological processes: A review with emphasis on underlying mechanisms and implications for health.' *Psychological Bulletin 119*, 3, 488–531.

Van Der Miesen, A.I.R., Hurley, H. and De Vries, A.L.C. (2016) 'Gender dysphoria and autism spectrum disorder: A narrative review.' *International Review of Psychiatry, 28*, 70–80.

Vanderburgh, R. (2009) 'Appropriate therapeutic care for families with pre-pubescent transgender/gender dissonant children.' *Child and Adolescent Social Work Journal 26*, 2, 135–154.

Veale, J.F., Watson, R.J., Peter, T. and Saewyc E.M. (2017) 'The mental health of Canadian transgender youth compared with the Canadian population.' *Journal of Adolescent Health 60*, 1, 44–49.

Vedantum, S. (2006) 'Male scientist writes of life as female scientist.' *Washington Post*, July 13. Accessed on 3/11/17 at www.washingtonpost.com/wp-dyn/content/article/2006/07/12/AR2006071201883.html.

Vidal-Ortiz, S. (2009) 'The figure of the transwoman of color through the lens of "doing gender".' *Gender and Society 23*, 1, 99–103.

Vincent, B. (2018) *Transgender Health: A Practitioner's Guide to Binary and Non-Binary Trans Health Care*. London: Jessica Kingsley Publishers.

Virupaksha, H.D., Muralidhar, D. and Ramakrishna, J. (2016) 'Suicide and suicidal behavior among transgender persons.' *Indian Journal of Psychological Medicine 38*, 6, 505–509.

Wallace, A. (2018) 'Film and Television.' In Burns, C. (ed.) *Trans Britain: Our Journey from the Shadows*. London: Unbound.

Walley-Jean, J.C. (2009) 'Debunking the myth of the "angry black woman": An exploration of anger in young African American women.' *Black Women, Gender and Families 3*, 2, 68–86.

Webber, B. (2014) 'Leslie Feinberg, writer and transgender activist, dies at 65.' *New York Times*, November 24. Accessed 5/8/18 at www.nytimes.com/2014/11/25/nyregion/leslie-feinberg-writer-and-transgender-activist-dies-at-65.html.

Welz Geselowitz, S. (2016) 'Rationalizing sex: The hermaphrodite in eighteenth century medical writing.' Accessed 22/7/18 at https://pdfs.semanticscholar.org/8ad1/274571767151563e320c7a537e378d682ee8.pdf.

Weslynn, E. (2016) '12 mainstream movies you forgot were transphobic.' Accessed on 10/8/18 at www.advocate.com/film/2016/1/22/11-mainstream-movies-you-forgot-were-transphobic.

Westwood, H. (2017) 'Slipping through the cracks: Do some women with anorexia nervosa have unrecognised autism spectrum disorder?' *Psychology Postgraduate Affairs Group Quarterly 104*, 11–14.

Wheeler, M. (2011) 'Syndrome or difference: A critical review of medical conceptualisations of Asperger's syndrome.' *Disability and Society 26*, 7, 839–851.

Whittaker, F. (2018a) 'Schools urged to ignore "dangerous" gender guidance.' Accessed on 20/8/18 at https://schoolsweek.co.uk/schools-urged-to-ignore-dangerous-gender-guidance.

Whittaker, F. (2018b) 'Teachers are responsible for a tenth of serious LGBT bullying incidents in schools.' Accessed on 20/8/18 at https://schoolsweek.co.uk/teachers-are-responsible-for-a-tenth-of-serious-lgbt-bullying-incidents-in-schools.

Wiepjes, C.M., Nota, N.M., de Blok, C.J.M., Klaver, M. *et al.* (2018) 'The Amsterdam cohort of gender dysphoria study (1972–2015): Trends in prevalence, treatment, and regrets.' *The Journal of Sexual Medicine 15*, 4, 582–590.

Wilder, M. (2015) 'Meet the Guevedoces: the "girls" who grow a penis during puberty.' Accessed on 20/7/18 at www.vice.com/sv/article/9bg8wa/guevedoces-boys-dont-grow-a-penis-until-age-12-interview-dr-michael-mosley-876.

Williams, S. (2013) 'Greece is waging a horrifying war on transgender women.' Accessed on 5/11/17 at https://www.care2.com/causes/greece-is-waging-a-horrifying-war-on-transgender-women.html.

Witten, T.M. and Whittle, S. (2004) 'Transpanthers: The greying of transgender and the law.' *Deakin Law Review 9*, 2, 403. Accessed 2/11/18 at https://ojs.deakin.edu.au/index.php/dlr/article/view/253-522.

World Health Organisation (2018) *International Classification of Diseases (ICD-11).* Geneva: World Health Organisation. Accessed on 2/8/18 at www.who.int/health-topics/international-classification-of-diseases.

WPATH (2018) *WPATH position statement on 'RAPID Onset Gender Dysphoria'.* World Professional Association for Transgender Health (WPATH).

Yaeger, L. (2015) 'Happy birthday, Iggy Pop!' Accessed on 10/3/18 at www.vogue.com/article/happy-birthday-iggy-pop.

Subject Index

Page numbers in *italics* refer to figures. Footnotes are indicated with the letter 'n'.

Author Index

Footnotes are indicated with the letter 'n'.